THE FOOTPRINT OF THE BUDDHA

1. The Footprint of the Buddha.
Fresco from Lankatilaka near Kadugannawa, showing the sacred footprint with its markings on the mountain with animals paying homage to it

THE FOOTPRINT
OF THE
BUDDHA

E. F. C. LUDOWYK

Ruskin House

GEORGE ALLEN & UNWIN LTD

MUSEUM STREET LONDON

294.31
L946f
126356

PRINTED IN GREAT BRITAIN
in 12 point Centaur type
BY ROBERT MACLEHOSE AND CO. LTD
THE UNIVERSITY PRESS, GLASGOW

PREFACE

This book seeks to bring before the common reader the Buddhist monuments of old Ceylon—a distinctive and valuable portion of the art of the ancient and medieval world. It will not be necessary to indicate that this is no learned treatise for the specialist in archaeology and religion, who will neither need the instruction provided here, nor seek what he may need at such a source. If this book will have provided the general reader with some intimations of the development of an artistic achievement not as well known as it deserves to be, it will have served its purpose.

T. S. Eliot writing many years ago remarked that he did not think that it was possible for a Christian fully to appreciate Buddhist art, or vice versa. With this opinion it is difficult to agree, since the common experience of many generations of people who have lived in Ceylon, or visited it, tends to disprove the validity of the statement. Although understanding or appreciation may be of various kinds, no esoteric lore or traditional belief would seem to be a necessary prerequisite for the ability to recognise the beauty and the appeal of the objects appraised here. The language they speak is comprehensible to the generality of mankind.

I have throughout these pages which follow acknowledged my indebtedness to the researches of eminent workers in the fields of archaeology and history. I owe, in addition, a special debt to Mr C. W. Nicholas and Bhikkhu W. Rabula, who, reading through the manuscript, made a number of important suggestions and criticisms. Naturally theirs is not the responsibility for the sins of omission and commission of this study. I am grateful, too, to Mademoiselle Suzanne Karpeles for her helpful references and advice and I wish to thank the Government of Ceylon for permission to quote extensively from Dr S. Paranavitane's *Sigiri Graffiti*, and the Pali Text Society for allowing me to make generous use of its translations.

Menikdiwela, Ceylon. June 1956

TO EDITH AND C.W.N.
who taught me how to see and understand
Ceylon

CONTENTS

ILLUSTRATIONS

*All the illustrations are taken from photographs made
by Ina Bandy during her visit to Ceylon November
1955–February 1956*

THE MOUNTAIN

The most ancient map of the island known today as Ceylon is Ptolemy's in the first century after Christ. In its asteroid outlines it bears only a faint resemblance to that pendent drop which in present-day maps seems to tremble on the edge of the Indian peninsula and into the vastness of the ocean. But in its major details Ptolemy is not far from wrong. He sets down correctly the island's mountain mass— then known as Malaya—somewhere in the central south; further north he marks another group of mountains he calls the Gatiba, from which two rivers flow to the east. He was in error here, although the course of the largest river in Ceylon, which he called the Ganges (from Ganga the Sanskrit for river) is fairly recognizable as plotted by him. This river, now known as the Mahaveli-ganga, rises in the central mountain mass, its springs flowing from a peak so closely connected with the legends of Ceylon, that to think of the island is to remember the peak.

The myths and legends which accompany every stage of a people's history need not be accepted as anything but the mode in which a people has attempted to satisfy its unconscious needs. Not only the poet who has given the legend artistic form, but all those who have handed down the tradition of some mythical event, like the descent of the founder of the race from the sun-god, receive gratification for the deepest unknown longings through their fantasies. And if for man there exists something that is supernatural, then he may be able to raise himself from his insignificance through participation in this supernatural. The garb in which these fantasies appear says more perhaps of the cultural and social circumstances of a people than its recorded history. To discard legend, and myth, and fairy tale would just as much rob one of one's most valuable sources of information about a people as to reject its art and literature as unimportant.

Some of the legends which deck a people's history still survive because the need that brought them into being still exists. Sometimes the most memorable portions of history are reflected in legendary events which never took place. An event as recent as the Battle of Waterloo has its own legends, and they vary with the nations concerned—the French, the English and the Prussians. A number of the legends which belong to the history of Ceylon correspond to no actual fact—for instance, the Buddha, so far as is known, never visited Ceylon; the story of the landing of Vijaya on the coast of Ceylon is the provision of a gratifying ancestry necessary for a nation; the signs and wonders which mark the poet's account of the *thera* Mahinda's visit to Ceylon are projected by the fervour of his need to accept what his account enunciated, the special destiny of Ceylon. In fact whatever record there is of Ceylon's ancient history is intertwined with legend. It is the historian's arduous task to disentangle truth from imagination. But if one wants—as is the object of this study—to give some picture of the island and its spirit, then reality and dreams unseparated will bring them closer to one's understanding.

Many legends cluster round the peak—the Sumanakuta of the ancient Pali poet of the fifth century A.D. It was on this peak, according to them, that the Buddha set the print of his foot for all to see. Here is the poet's account: 'In the eighth year after he had attained the Buddhahood, when the Vanquisher was dwelling in Jetavana, the Master set forth surrounded by five hundred bhikkhus, on the second day of the beautiful month of Vesakha, at the full moon, and when the hour of the meal was announced, the Vanquisher, prince of the wise, forthwith putting on his robe and taking his alms-bowl went to the Kalyani country, the habitation of Maniakkhika. Under a canopy decked with gems, raised upon the spot where (afterwards) the Kalyani-cetiya was built, he took his place, together with the brotherhood of bhikkhus, upon a precious throne-seat. And rejoicing, the naga-king with his following served celestial food, both hard and soft, to the king of truth, the Conqueror, with his followers. When the Teacher, compassionate to the whole world, had preached the doctrine there, he rose, the Master, and left the trace of his footsteps plain to sight on Sumanakuta. And after he had spent the day as it pleased him at the foot of this mountain, with the brotherhood, he set forth for Dighavapi.'[1]

Here, whether it is in legend or in history, whether one accepts it as sober fact, or regards it as poetic fancy, is celebrated, as one can regard it today, the most significant event in Ceylon's history—the imprint on it of enlightenment and civilization from India. The footprint which symbolizes the mark left by India's greatest son on the island of Ceylon, is the sign of the impression made upon the small southern island by the culture of its great continental neighbour. For it was India which imprinted a new way of life upon Ceylon. So that if the stories of the Buddha's three visits to Ceylon were the invention of a later age, then the poet of that age fabled wisely, and in his recounting of how the Buddha placed the print of his foot on the mountain-top, is to be

[1] *Mbv*, I, 72 ff.

seen in emblematic fashion the picture of Ceylon's history. In his poetic narrative of the Buddha's visits to Ceylon is to be marked the chronicler's genius and not his credulousness.

Ceylon, Lanka as it was in Sanskritic literature, was in pre-Buddhistic times described as being the abode of *yakkhas, nagas,* and *devas.* These legendary beings were, according to the popular tradition, demons whose king Ravana abducted the princess Sita from her husband. Her face, if it did not launch a thousand ships, yet raised a war resembling the Trojan, waged by her husband Rama, his brother Lakshmana, and the monkey-god Hanuman. The most interesting passages of the Sanskritic epic, the *Ramayana,* tell of Hanuman's marvellous passage to Lanka, and his finding of Sita in the magnificent palace of the demon king Ravana. The hero Hanuman, who united in himself several traits of the demi-gods of Greek fable, was thus the first visitor to Ceylon—if the Lanka of the epic was indeed Ceylon—of whose wanderings in the island we have record. It is significant that he too should have come from India, and that he should have come on what may be termed an errand of salvation.

In the same way the story of the Buddha's first visit to Ceylon is a parable of the banishment of fear and ignorance by the superior power of wisdom and truth. Once again the legend repeats the pattern of what historically took place—the subjugation of the island by North Indian peoples of a more highly developed civilization: 'And when he had eaten his meal near the Lake Anotatta, the Conqueror, in the ninth month of his Buddhahood, at the full moon of Phussa at evening time, himself set forth for the isle of Lanka, to win Lanka for the faith. For Lanka was known to the Conqueror as a place where his doctrine should (thereafter) shine in glory; and (he knew that) from Lanka, filled with yakkhas, the yakkhas must (first) be driven forth. And he knew that in the midst of Lanka, on the fair river bank, in the delightful Mahanaga garden, three yojanas long and a yojana wide, the (customary) meeting place for the yakkhas, there was a great gathering of (all) the yakkhas living in the island. To this great gathering of yakkhas went the Blessed One, and there, in the midst of that assembly, hovering in the air over their heads, at the place of the (future) Mahiyanganathupa, he struck terror into their hearts by rain, storm, darkness and so forth. The yakkhas, overwhelmed by fear, besought the fearless Vanquisher to release them from terrors, and the Vanquisher, destroyer of fear, spoke thus to the terrified yakkhas: "I will banish this your fear and your distress, O yakkhas, give ye here to me with one accord a place where I may sit down." The yakkhas thus answered the Blessed One: "We all, give you even the whole of our island. Give us release from our fear." Then, when he had destroyed their terror, cold and darkness, and had spread his rug of skin on the ground that they bestowed on him, the Conqueror, sitting there, made the rug to spread wide, while the burning flame surrounded it. Daunted by the burning heat thereof and terrified they stood around on the border. Then did the Master cause the pleasant Giridipa to come here near to them, and when they had settled there, he made it return to its former place.'[1]

In his note on Giridipa, the translator states that it would be 'a mistake to look for a clear geographical statement. The underlying notion here expressed is simply that the yakkhas were driven back to the highlands (giri) in the interior of the island.'

The pattern persists in the legend of how the island was settled shortly afterwards by a prince who came from India. Of the pre-Buddhistic civilization of Ceylon very little is known. That there was a civilization which had reached a fair level of attainment in the cultivation of the fields is not to be doubted. If few traces of it remain, it is on account of that long and successful period of acculturation Ceylon went through after it was developed by these Indian settlers. The ancient legend may be composed of a tissue of fables and old wives' tales, but what runs through its inextricable mass of fancy is the single gold thread twisted out of India's rich civilization and its coming to Ceylon.

The legend, as it was set down centuries later, ran as follows. The daughter of a powerful king of the Gangetic plain was loved by a lion (sinha in the Sanskritic form of the word). She was abducted by the royal beast, and bore him two children, a boy and a girl. When the boy, Sinhabahu, was sixteen, he rescued his mother and sister from his father the lion, and escaped with them. In his grief and rage the lion laid waste the country, until his son slew him and won the reward offered by the king of the country for freeing the land from the terror of the lion. Sinhabahu succeeded the king and took his own sister to wife. Of their union was born the prince Vijaya who, as he came of the race of the lion, was a Sinhala. His descendants were the Sinhalese—people of the lion race—and the country he colonised Sinhala, which by later process of change became Ceylon.

So far the ancient tale has familiar markings: the tribe with the eponymous ancestor, the son who slays the primal father, frees his country from the ravening beast, and then marrying his sister lays the foundation of the race to which he gives his name. But as the story develops, it shows how definitely local tradition and legend linked together the coming of Vijaya to Ceylon with the life of the Buddha.

The prince of Sinhapura, whose grandfather was a lion, grew up into a wild and lawless young man whom his father at his peoples' request had to exile. 'Then did the king cause Vijaya and his followers, seven hundred men, to be

---

[1] *Ibid.*, 18 ff. I am indebted to Bhikkhu W. Rahula for pointing out to me that 'at evening time' was wrongly placed by Geiger after 'he had eaten his meal'. The Buddha did not partake of an evening meal.

shaven over half the head and put them on a ship and sent them forth upon the sea, and their wives and children also. The men, women, and children sent forth separately landed separately, each (company) upon an island, and they dwelt even there. The island where the children landed was called Naga-dipa and the island where the women landed Mahiladipaka. But Vijaya landed at a haven called Supparaka, but being there in danger by reason of the violence of his followers he embarked again. The prince named Vijaya, the valiant, landed in Lanka, in the region called Tambapanni on the day that the Tathagata lay down between the two twin-like Salatrees to pass into nib-bana. . . . When the Guide of the World, having accomplished the salvation of the whole world and having reached the utmost stage of blissful rest, was lying on the bed of his nibbana, in the midst of the great assembly of gods, he, the great sage, the greatest of those who have speech, spoke to Sakka who stood there near him: "Vijaya, son of King Sinhabahu, is come to Lanka from the country of Lala, together with seven hundred followers. In Lanka, O Lord of gods, will my religion be established, therefore carefully protect him with his followers and Lanka." When the lord of gods heard the words of the Tathagata he from respect handed over the guardianship of Lanka to the god who is in colour like the lotus.'[1]

We shall hear more of this god to whom Sakka handed over the 'guardian-ship of Lanka', but what is to be noted immediately is how the waves of colonization from the North West of India, which in pre-Buddhistic times changed the character of Lanka, were themselves given a Buddhist colouring. No wonder that it should have been so. What the legend crystallizes is what successive generations of Sinhalese had felt. The island of Lanka was the island on which the Buddha had left his mark, it was Buddhism from India which brought both civilization and enlightenment to the country. The original inhabitants were banished into the interior of the island, although in order to get possession of the country the Aryan invader had first to take an aboriginal princess as his mistress. Her descendants, when she was disowned, 'fleeing with speed . . . went from thence to the Sumanakuta. The brother, the elder of the two (children) when he grew up took his sister, the younger, for his wife, and multiplying with sons and daughters, they dwelt, with the King's leave there in Malaya.'[2]

So the peak which bore the impress of the Buddha's foot was also the sanctuary of those who once were the rulers of Lanka. It has been doubly bound up with the story of the island.

Travellers from antique lands who went about their lawful occasions in the

[1] *Mbv*, VI, 42 ff.

[2] *Mbv*, VII, 67. See also A. L. Basham, 'Prince Vijaya and the Aryanization of Ceylon', CHJ, Vol. I, No. 3, 1952.

Indian ocean, traders and pilgrims from Eastern kingdoms gave to the island the many names by which it has been known. Greeks who traded along the western coasts of India, Ethiopians, Persians, Arabs, and Chinese knew the island by one or other of its various names. Taprobane of the Greeks, Serendib of the Arabs, Hsia-lan-shan of the Chinese, are only some of those which occur in the folklore of travellers. But whether the island was known as Taprobane or Sinhala-dipa, or by any of its names earlier or later, those who lived in it or travelled to it, knew it as the island of the peak which rose out of its central highlands, the peak which, in seasons of calm weather seen some twelve miles out at sea, seems to assert itself with magnificent serenity over the land it dominates. In the south the plains and the wooded slopes of the smaller hills, in the west fields, woods and slopes crowd up to the plateau which makes the bastion of the hill country, out of which the peak stands out. From earliest times, from times of which there is no record now, it must have been specially venerated. The inhabitants of ancient Ceylon before the waves of Aryan immigrants settled there, all those whom legend depicts as a kind of devil, must have known the peak as an object of primitive worship. Indeed it would be strange if they did not, for there is hardly a headland, or rock, or mountain, distinguished by some natural peculiarity of structure which has not compelled the admiration and reverence of men in ancient times.[1]

The peak celebrated in ancient legend came to be honoured as a place of pilgrimage early in the history of Ceylon. It even drew travellers from countries far away and remote. There is that intrepid and curious traveller Fa-hsien who with his companions journeyed across the wilds of Tartary, across desert, high plateau and mountain range to the kingdoms of Buddhist India and Ceylon. He sets down what he knew of the mountain in his account of the Land of the Lion, where he spent two years early in the fifth century A.D. 'This country,' he writes, 'was not originally inhabited by human beings, but only by devils and dragons. . . . When the Buddha came to this country, he wished to convert the wicked dragons; and by his divine power he placed one foot to the north of the royal city and the other on the top of Sumanakuta, the two points being fifteen yojanas apart. Over the footprint to the north of the city a great pagoda has been built, four hundred feet in height and decorated with gold and silver and with all kinds of precious substances combined. By the side of the pagoda a monastery has also been built, called No-Fear-Mountain, where there are now five thousand priests. There is a Hall of Buddha of gold and silver carved work with all kinds of precious substances, in which stands his image in green jade, over twenty feet in height, the whole

---

[1] 'Every hill or mountain had some degree of sanctity, especially in the Himalayas, which were the foothills of Mount Meru, the centre of the world. . . .' A. L. Basham, *The Wonder that was India*, London, 1954, p. 320.

of which glitters with the seven preciosities, the countenance being grave and dignified beyond expression in words. On the palm of the right hand lies a priceless pearl.'[1] This was the Abhayagiri, which Fa-Hsien literally renders as No-Fear-Mountain, and by its green jade image in Anuradhapura he wept when he saw a merchant make an offering of a white silk fan which came from his own country, because he was sick for home in an alien land.

Islam stretched out a hand towards the peak in its hey-day. It would have been surprising if the fame of the shrine had not interested the adherents of a religion which ran spectacularly through all Eastern Lands. Besides, the known tolerance of the Buddhist rulers of Ceylon must have aided a process which would ultimately have been inevitable. By the end of the tenth century A.D. the mountain was connected in the imagination of Arab traders with Adam. Serendib, as they called Ceylon, was the mountain on which Adam took his last lingering look at the Paradise he had forfeited. Soleyman, an Arab trader who is supposed to have visited Ceylon in the ninth century, refers to 'Al-rohoun . . . to the top of which it is thought that Adam ascended, and there left the print of his foot, in a rock which is seventy cubits in length; and they say, that Adam at the same time stood with his other foot in the sea. About this mountain are mines of rubies, of opals and amethysts.'[2]

Marco Polo, when he touched Ceylon in the thirteenth century in the splendid convoy which conducted a princess of Cathay to her future husband in Persia, takes over something of this conglomerate of tales of Sinbad the sailor and Islamic legend. The first person he mentions in connection with the peak is Adam: 'Furthermore you must know that in the island of Seilan there is an exceeding high mountain; it rises right up so steep and precipitous that no one could ascend it, were it not that they have taken up and fixed to it several great and massive iron chains, so disposed that by the help of these men are able to mount to the top. And I tell you they say that on this mountain is the sepulchre of Adam our first parent; at least that is what the Saracens say.'[3]

The first record we have of a pilgrim's journey up the peak is that of the fourteenth-century Muslim traveller Ibn Batuta, a man of prodigious energies and a great exponent of Islamic law. He visited Ceylon in 1344 with the sole object of 'visiting' the footprint. He had heard of its reputation, and also of the benevolence of the inhabitants of the island, whom he called with the orthodoxy of the Mussulman, 'idolators': 'I visited this island of Ceylon,' he writes, 'its people still live in idolatry, yet they show respect for Muslim darwishes, lodge them in their houses amidst their wives and children. This

[1] H. A. Giles. *The Travels of Fa-Hsien*, Cambridge, 1923, p. 67

[2] W. Skeen, *Adam's Peak*, London, 1870, refers to this on p. 40. He took it from Philalethes, *History of Ceylon*, London, 1817.

[3] Yule, *The Book of Ser Marco Polo*. (Third Ed.), London, 1926, Vol. II, p. 307.

is contrary to the usage of other Indian idolators, who never make friends with Muslims, and never give them to eat or drink out of their vessels, although at the same time they neither act nor speak offensively to them.'[1]

When the 'idolator Sultan' of the north of Ceylon offered him the choice of the handsomest pearls of the island, and told him, 'Do not blush; ask of me anything you desire,' the old traveller, who had seen from far out at sea the mountain of Serendib raised in the air like a column of smoke, replied: 'I have no other desire, since I arrived in this island, but to visit the foot of Adam.' 'That is easy enough,' the Sultan answered, 'We shall send someone to conduct you.'

So Ibn Batuta set out borne in a palanquin. Of the peak which he climbed he writes: 'It is one of the highest mountains in the world: we saw it from the open sea, when we were distant from it upwards of nine days' march. While we were making the ascent, we saw clouds above us, hiding from view the lower parts of it. There are upon this mountain many trees of kinds which do not cast their leaves, flowers of diverse colours, and a red rose as large as the palm of the hand. It is alleged that on this rose is an inscription in which one may read the name of God Most High and that of his Prophet. On the mountain are two paths leading to the Foot of Adam. The one is known by the name of "the Father's path" and the other by that of "the Mother's path." By these terms are Adam and Eve designated. The Mother's route is an easy one, and by it the pilgrims return; but any one who took it for the ascent would be regarded as not having done the pilgrimage. The Father's path is rough and difficult of ascent. At the foot of the mountain, at the place of the gateway, is a grotto bearing the name of Iskander, and a spring of water. . . . The impression of the noble Foot, that of our father Adam, is observed in a black and lofty rock, in an open space. The Foot is sunk in the stone, in such wise that its site is quite depressed; its length is eleven spans.'[2]

As years went on traders of the West succeeded those of the East in Indian waters, the caravels of the Portuguese replaced the Arab dhows. The first impulsive driving force of Islam declined, and the missionaries of a new religion, every whit as fanatical as their predecessors, set out to conquer Ceylon for a new faith. Ancient kingdoms of India toppled in the dust before the soldiers and mercenaries of European trading companies, and in the East, which was always changing, a stronger movement of change became noticeable. In the records of these times there is nothing more revealing in Western man's reaction to the peak than that passage where the Portuguese historiographer Diogo do Couto, suggested that the peak might really be a Christian

---

[1] Gibb, *Selections from the Travels of Ibn Batuta*, London, 1929, p. 95.

[2] Gray, 'Ibn Batuta in the Maldives and Ceylon', translated from the French of Defremery and Sanguinetti, JRAS (CB), 1882.

site. Couto spent a lifetime in the colony of Goa—forty-five years in the service of the king, first as soldier, then as chronicler. He never set foot in Ceylon, but continuing the chronicles of a predecessor, wrote mainly of the Portuguese campaigns and their uneasy rule over maritime Ceylon, in his estimation and theirs a priceless possession.

He had conversed with many Sinhalese whom he had met in Portuguese India, and impressed by what he had learned from them about their island home, he sets down what he had been told of the peak: 'Almost at the edge of this mountain range, a matter of twenty leagues from the sea-coast, is a mountain so high and steep that it rises to the height of seven leagues; and on the summit of it is a flat surface of such small extent in circumference, that it will be little more than thirty paces in diameter. In the middle of which is a stone of two cubits higher than the other flat surface in the manner of a table, and in the middle of it is figured a man's footprint, which will have a length of two spans, the which footprint is held in great reverence, on account of the opinion which prevails among the natives; for they assert it to be that of a holy man, a native of the kingdom of Delij . . . and from this heathen opinion our people came to call this mountain the Peak of Adam, who they call by the proper name of Budo.'[1]

Couto never forgot what he had been told. He kept returning to the peak again and again in his historical record; and then indulged the desperate supposition that it might be regarded as an ancient Christian monument, with the footprint on it as that of 'the blessed St Thomas' who first preached the gospel in India. Although, Couto states, 'his legend does not state that he visited that island, it is a thing that might have been, since a record has not been made of all the places that he visited.'[2] It was the spiritual conquest of Ceylon which was dangled in front of the Portuguese soldiers and administrators by their zealous missionaries, so Couto's suppositions were in keeping with these aspirations.

Quite other, and equally characteristic, was the reaction of the English soldier, the first Englishman who made his way to the summit, and saw the footprint venerated by Buddhists and Hindus who went thither on pilgrimage. On the 27th April 1815, Lieutenant Malcolm of the 1st Ceylon Rifle Regiment reached the top of the peak 'after great exertions . . . between eight and nine a.m.'. His great regret was that there was no Union Jack provided on the summit which he could have flown, to signify that a British armed party had, in spite of the awful warnings of a native priest, reached the top of the mountain. The best he could do, in the circumstances, to express his opinion

[1] D. W. Ferguson, 'The History of Ceylon from the earliest times to 1600', translation of Barros & Couto, JRAS (CB), Vol. XX, No. 60, Colombo, 1908, p. 36.

[2] *Ibid.*, p. 114 ff.

of these superstitions, was to fire 'three vollies',[1] to the great astonishment of the Buddhists, and not unnaturally to that of all those who read the brief account of his expedition now.

The British soldier was refusing, in the best way he knew, through the *ultima ratio* of the bullet which resolves all conflicts, to credit everything he had heard or had been told. That is surely one way of reacting to the peak. We have considered others in the course of this chapter. The peak stands for something which symbolizes the imprint of Indian civilization on the island. It stands for something else too, something which is older than civilization, something anterior to the Buddha, which still is a living force. It belongs to the old gods who are not dead yet. It is not a high mountain, nor is it a perilous climb, but there is in its associations something which exerts a strong influence on those who in the pilgrim season make their way to its summit. It rises some seven thousand feet, standing out of its accompanying phalanx of mountain and looking in the distance like a slender finger pointing upward. Geologists have noted its difference from the rest of the mountains of Ceylon. Most of the others, even those which rise higher, are gently rounded summits. Few have the conical configuration which distinguishes this. From the north of the island the view of the peak is obscured by the range which interposes itself between it and the northern plain. But from the south and the west, and even from the south east when the monsoon winds which bring the migrant birds to Ceylon are blowing, the peak stands out in fine weather, as if enamelled in a greyish blue against the lighter background of the sky.

Two ancient pilgrim trails lead to the summit, the one from its southern front as it overlooks the lowlands which the Kaluganga irrigates; the other, which attacks it from the rear, and from the north-western saddle of the hills, provides an easier route from Maskeliya. Of the two the first, which is the more arduous, is both the traditional, and on account of its difficulties, the more meritorious route. Along this trail the pilgrim climbs up to Gilimale, and then gathers his energies for the ascent to the peak. He toils on foot, dressed in white and chanting traditional stanzas pilgrim before him have chanted, from one stage to the other, each marked by its little pilgrims' rest, until he reaches the rocky watercourse of Indikatupana (needle gorge). Here according to the story, the Buddha defeated the wiles of a demon, who seeing him engaged in mending his robe with a needle and thread, conjured up an immense rock to halt him. As this proved unavailing, the demon caused the waters to flow over the face of the rock. The Buddha, seeing the flood approaching him drew a semi-circle with his needle, and round this the waters parted, leaving him untouched.

One climbs from one irregularly cut stone step on to the other, over slabs

[1] Skeen, *op. cit.*, p. 339

of rock smoothed by the feet of countless pilgrims in the past, the summit of the peak, as it seems to move with the winding of the trail, appearing less and less a regular cone and more a massy protuberance, faintly pyramidal. Streams and rills flow across the path; the stiffest climb begins when one curves round the neck of the peak to clamber up to the summit.

On the eastern side of the walled enclosure giant rhododendrons once grew, bent by the wind and inclined towards the footprint. Their large red flowers and the angle at which they inclined were held by the faithful to derive their beauty and their position from the sanctity of the object they venerated. The rock on which the footprint is to be seen rises like a broad tuft in a gradual slope towards the south. Over the footprint is a little roofed enclosure sufficient to admit four or five persons at a time. On the slab of rock is the rough indentation of the outline of a foot, somewhat sunk in the stone and regularized by a cemented rim giving it the conventional shape of the mango in Indian design. Its length has been computed at five feet seven inches, and its breadth at two feet seven inches at the ball of the foot. The outlined indentation slopes to the passage outside where worshippers crowd with their offerings of cloth and money.

Having offered their devotions at the shrine, the pilgrims wait on the peak for the first rays of the sun. Before the dawn it grows cold, and when the wind blows from the north-east it seems to search out the innermost being. Those already on the peak huddle together by the fires and flares they have lighted, or press close to each other on the eastward steps of the summit. Down below the line of lights marks the sinuous trail of those yet toiling up, and the wind brings the sound of their chants.

When dawn lights the sky there is a movement of tremulous anticipation, and as the first rays strike the summit of the peak there is an involuntary cry, for not only is the powerful sun-god paying homage to the Master, but in a short while he will perform his miracle and fling on the mountains ranged round the marvellous triangular shadow of the peak. The impressiveness of this natural phenomenon has never failed to move the observor. The shadow seems to float on cloud cover or on the grey-green slopes until the sun climbs higher and it is gone.

Enormous as this depression is, when compared with the normal human foot, it is unquestionably accepted by the Buddhist devotee as the footprint of the Buddha. This is understandable. For to him Gotama is not only the man who wandered about the Gangetic plain two thousand five hundred years ago with his disciples, helping all those who questioned him to the way of truth, he is also the great man, the exceptional being, the *Mahapurisa* of the Pali texts. The eye of faith does not gauge proportions with the same accuracy as the logical eye.

The concept of the *Mahapurisa*, an ancient pre-Buddhistic notion, found its way into early Buddhist thinking. According to tradition, the *Mahapurisa* could be recognized by the presence of thirty-two distinctive bodily marks. The possessor of these marks was destined to become either 'universal monarch' or a Buddha. At the birth of Prince Siddhartha, as the Buddha was then called, one hundred and eight brahmins skilled in the lore were asked to tell his future. The youngest of them all, 'interpreting' these supreme marks, made this one prediction: 'For him there is no remaining in the household life. He will indeed become a Buddha who has cast away all mental and spiritual trappings.'[1]

Of these thirty-two 'supreme signs' the first and the second were as follows: ' . . . feet with level tread. On his soles are wheels with thousand spokes, with fell and hub, and in every way complete.'[2] These marks (which are not found on the footprint on the peak) were emblematic of the teacher who had attained enlightenment. They helped, in the legendary stories, those who knew the signs and could interpret them, to recognize an exceptional being. There is the story of the brahmin Dona, who as he travelled on the high road, saw the footprints of the Buddha and noticed on them the wheels with their spokes and hubs. He knew that they indicated an extraordinary being, and so he followed them. They led him to the Buddha sitting under a tree. When he asked the Buddha in what form he would be reborn in his next birth, the Buddha replied that he would not be reborn at all, as he was already a Buddha and would attain Nirvana.[3]

In the story of the brahmin Magandiya, the footprint as the mark of an exceptional being appears again. According to this story the brahmin Magandiya, impressed with the majestic mien of the Buddha, offered him his daughter in marriage. To this the Buddha made no reply, but as he went away from the house of the brahmin, he left a footprint which Magandiya's wife recognized as that of an exceptional ascetic. In spite of this the brahmin renewed his offer, only to be told by the Buddha that neither Mara nor his daughters could overcome him with temptation, and that nothing would move him to touch Magandiya's daughter even with the sole of his foot.[4]

It is noteworthy that there is only one case in the *Tipitaka* of a man who has some of the marks. The brahmin Bavari has only three of the thirty-two, but these did not include the wheel with the spokes and hub on the sole of his foot. This sign was one of the distinctive iconographical marks used to symbolize the Buddha in early Buddhist sculpture, before under Graeco-Bactrian influence, statues of the Buddha were first made in India. At Bharhut and at Sanchi where the artist was illustrating the life of the Buddha, wherever his

[1] *Jat.* I, p. 55.   [2] *D.* II, p. 17.   [3] *A*, II, p. 37 ff.
[4] *Dha*, III, p. b193 ff.

person would have been represented, one finds either wheel, Bodhi-tree, an empty throne, footprints or umbrella.

But important as the wheel with the spokes, and the other marks of the *Mahapurisa* were, more important and essential was what these legendary marks attempted to express—the real greatness of the Buddha in his wisdom which opened the way to enlightenment. The great man, or superman, however one translates the term *Mahapurisa*, was not just the man on whom three, or seven, or all thirty-two bodily marks were to be espied. Even in the *Tipitaka*, though stress is laid on the marks, according to a truer valuation

> *He who is without craving, who is free from attachment,*
> *Skilled in the mode of expression, Veda-versed and wise,*
> *Who knows the words of the texts, their sequence, their spirit and letter,*
> *It is he who lives in his last body,*
> *He is called the man of great wisdom,*
> *It is he who is called the Great Man.'*[1]

It is in this light that the emblem of the sacred footprint should be considered. It could be taken as the symbol of the imprint of the civilization of the mainland on its island neighbour. It is more, it is the token of the Great Man. Incomprehensible though the devotion shown to it may be, its real value lies in its plain significance too—the veneration Indian civilization has always paid to the great human being, the sage who through his wisdom enables humankind to free itself from ignorance.

[1] *Dh*, V, 352.

CHAPTER ONE

THE LAND AND ITS BACKGROUND

The India of the Buddha, the India of the sixth century B.C., was an extent of country which it would perhaps be better to call Aryavarta than India, lest present-day associations confuse. Restricted geographically to the basin of the two great rivers—the Indus and the Ganges—it was the land peopled by the invading tribes we know as Aryans. Of the people they displaced and conquered, the people who inhabited such cities as Harappa and Mohenjo-daro, recently brought to light, we are beginning to know a little more now. But both conquerors and conquered seem to be wrapped in the vague mists of pre-history, and it seems that we can more readily seize them, these phantom shapes, in legend and literature than elsewhere. To think of India before the Buddha is to remember the timeless region peopled by the characters of impressive poems, and to invoke the memory of sacrificial hymns and an esoteric philosophy.

History presents the Aryavarta the Buddha knew as a country in which larger kingdoms were coming to the fore, and in their rise swallowing up older states and confederacies. It was a time of great spiritual excitements, and these must be traced to the insecurity of a period in which change was so active as to have accelerated its normal rhythm. What social life and man's condition in the community manifested would be the counterpart of that sense of unsettlement which lies at the back of the conflicting claims of rival teachers, the belief in the magic of sacrifice and recommended austerities. To try to plot these social changes, or to render an account of the economic instability of those times is beyond the ability of anyone but the specialist. It is impossible, however, to believe that the strong movements of thought which made themselves felt in Buddhist India (if we must use the term) were the results of pure speculation, and that there was not in the breaking moulds of social life at the time some force which gave an impulse to the systems of rival thinkers.

Politically the time was marked by the rise of new kingdoms, one of which Magadha, the country ruled by King Seniya Bimbisara, showed signs of becoming the first of the great Indian empires known to history. This kingdom, which extended over an area south of the Ganges from its confluence with the Son eastward to the modern Bhagalpur, and southward towards the hill country of the Dekkan, was to continue to expand until it became the dominant power in the Gangetic plain. Its king, during the Buddha's lifetime, was deposed by his son Ajatasattu, who later put his father to death. The same story could be told of another important kingdom in the Buddha's time—Kosala, to the north of the Ganges—ruled by Pasenadi, the uncle of Ajatasattu. Like his brother-in-law Bimbisara, Pasenadi was put to death by his son Vidudabha.

Kingdoms were waxing, older kingdoms had waned, and others, once powerful, no longer existed. Further north of the Ganges lay the old kingdom of Videha, whose legendary king was the scholarly Janaka. In the Buddha's time this kingdom had disappeared, it had been assimilated into a tribal confederacy in which the Licchavis were chief. Older tribes still survived, singly and in groups, but some of them, too, were to face the threat of extinction as independent units. The clansmen of the Buddha, the Sakyans—he himself was often referred to as Sakyamuni, the Sakyan sage—were destroyed by the king of Kosala, the same Vidudabha we have referred to above, and they disappeared as a free people ruled by their chieftains and their tribal assemblies. The Kasis, the clan living near the modern Banarasi, lost their independence too, and were incorporated in the kingdom of Kosala. The Angas, a wealthy clan controlling some of the trade down the Ganges, were swallowed up by the kingdom of Magadha.

In this age of the rise of new powers, whose rulers, related to each other, were frequently at war among themselves, and of the submergence of older tribal units, one can see the reasons for the feelings of insecurity which must have oppressed the minds of many a man. The ancient tribes ruled over by chieftains, who might have been called rajas (kings) without being kings as we understand the term now, were tending to lose in this struggle for power important social institutions which gave them their character. The popular tribal assembly was in decline, and as the threat to these political entities grew, the military autocrat came to the fore. With him came into power too the array of 'janissaries' around him. Wars of political and economic rivalry between kings might not perhaps have disturbed the tenor of life of the tribesman tilling his fields and maintaining the usual routine of village life. But their cumulative effect must have been felt, and the institutions which were supplanted, and the lands laid waste and left untilled, soon lapsed into disuse and oblivion.

To the North West lay the great Achaemenid Empire of the Persians, from which two centuries later Alexander the Great was to issue into Aryavarta. Gandhara, modern Kandahar, the kingdom ruled by king Pukkusati in the Buddha's time, was in the next century to become a satrapy of the rapidly growing Persian empire. So from the North West, too, the threat of imperial expansion is added to the forces redrawing political divisions and changing social forms in the centre. East—in what is now Bengal—and South were regions outside the influence of Aryanization, and therefore almost unknown terrain.

The land where the son of a tribal chieftain of the Sakyan clan preached the new knowledge later called Buddhism was a comparatively small area, made up of a few great cities of the plain, with innumerable hamlets and villages dotting both plain and the slopes of the hills to the north. The spread of Buddhism brought into legends of the Buddha's life countries to which he never journeyed, and of which he could have known hardly anything at all. The India the Buddha knew was the homeland of various tribes, some monarchically ruled, some oligarchically.

In these village communities classes were clearly defined. First of all there were the warriors—the Kshatriyas—the class to which the Buddha himself belonged. They were a noble class, and must have been connected in direct descent with the Aryan tribes who conquered and colonized the regions of the plain and the foothills of the Himalayas. Then there were the Brahmins, the priestly caste, who claimed descent from the Aryan priests and pre-eminence in the hierarchy of caste. The Vaisyas were peasants, and below them were the Sudras, peoples of non-Aryan descent who were the labourers. Yet the lines separating these various classes from each other were not strictly drawn, as Rhys Davids has pointed out.[1] Caste as the fissiparous force which divided and divided again, with its strict taboos and its special privileges, did not exert such pressure on the communities of the Buddha's time as it was to exert in medieval India. It was the foundation of human and social relationships, but the community structure built upon it allowed freedom of intercourse between various groups. The Brahmin did claim to be of the highest class of all, and his monopoly of sacrificial rites tended to give him a certain exclusiveness. But as far as could be judged, the kingdoms and tribal communities of the Buddha's time were definitely not dominated by Brahminical culture. In Buddhist writings the Brahmins are mentioned as a group who had arrogated to themselves the rights of the way through sacrifice. But the Buddha was clear in his teaching of the inferiority of their claims to the way of knowledge and virtue. Buddhism has been represented as the reaction of the times against the social forms taken by Brahminical pretensions. But, it has been pointed out, Buddhism arose in a country geographically remote from the

[1] T. W. Rhys Davids, *Buddhist India*, London, 1903, p. 62: 'It is no more accurate to speak of caste at the Buddha's time in India, than it would be to speak of it as an established institution, at the same time, in Italy and Greece. The caste system, in any proper or exact use of the term, did not exist till long afterwards.'

region where Vedic literature as the expression of the religion of sacrifice and of esoteric lore came into being.[1]

Perhaps the persistence in our minds of this notion of Buddhism as a reaction against the domination of the Brahmin with his way of sacrifice is due to the potency of the poetry with which pre-historic India is associated. If one wanted to try to see and feel the background of the age in which the Buddha lived, then it is to the poetry that one must turn even though some of it is allegedly later than his time. How few, in his time, the clear-cut figures of recorded history are, and how various and convincing the personalities of an earlier age with which the epics are peopled. The materials of peotry, in presenting a record of life as it was lived in ancient times, may be of little value as first-hand evidence. Yet the *Vedas* with the *Mahabharata* do provide the groundwork on which Indian thought was built up; they were the emotional counterpart of what that age and later ages believed; what was known of the world, of time, of man, and of man's function on the earth. It is impossible to know and to feel what India thought and thinks today without reflecting on the significance of the poems which help us to understand the spiritual bases of the India in which the Buddha was born.

The most recent English authority on the history of India denies that its epics tell us anything about its history.[2] This view must command respect.

---

[1] E. J. Thomas, *The History of Buddhist Thought*, London, 1933, believes that Brahminism by the sixth century B.C. had become an 'elaborate sacrificial and sacerdotal system', and that (p. 82) 'the brahmins play a large part in Buddhist polemics'. On p. 89 he writes of Buddhism: 'It was natural that a movement originating in opposition to Brahminism should emphasize its own pretensions and in particular the descent of its founder as a member of the warrior caste.' T. W. Rhys Davids, *op. cit.*, p. 157, quotes Bhandarkar on the language of the inscriptions: 'The period we have been speaking of (that is from the beginning of the second century B.C. to the end of the fourth century after) has left no trace of a building or sculpture devoted to the use of the Brahmin religion. Of course Brahminism existed; and it was probably, during the period, being developed into the form which it assumed in later times. But the religion does not occupy a prominent position, and Buddhism was followed by the large mass of people from princes down to the humble workman.' 'If this position be accepted,' he goes on, 'as accurate for that period (200 B.C. –A.D. 400)—and it certainly seems incontrovertible—then, *a fortiori*, it must be accepted in yet larger measure for the period centuries earlier.'

Basham, *The Wonder that was India*, London, 1954, p. 261: 'Some modern authorities believe that the Buddha had no intention of founding a new religion, and never looked upon his doctrine as distinct from the popular cults of the time, but rather as transcending them—a sort of super-doctrine, which would help his followers further along the road to salvation than Brahmanism or the Upanishadic gnosis. This view is, in our opinion, questionable.' Earlier he points out that 'there were few frontal attacks on Brahmanical pretensions, even in the literature of the Buddhists who came nearest to an anti-brahmanical point of view.' On p. 246 he notes: 'It has been suggested that the development of ascetic and mystical doctrines, especially in the heterodox systems of Buddhism and Jainism, represents a reaction of the warrior class to the pretensions of the Brahman, and to the sterility of the sacrificial cult. This, however, is certainly not the whole truth.'

[2] Basham, *op. cit.*, p. 39.

Agammemnon dead—to take another example—Helen, the daughter of a god, the great Achilles, and Hector, the tamer of horses, what could they tell us about history either? Even if, in the background of the two cultures there is an epical age which never existed, is not the misty period of pre-history clearer to us in the poetry which gave it being than elsewhere? The *Vedas* and the *Mahabharata* call up the significant figures of these times—god, king, warrior, priest and sage.

In the *Vedas* we hear the first notes of one way of thought which distinguished an approach to life which we characteristically associate with the East—the way of sacrifice. These sacrificial hymns are the poet's celebrations of the bright beings to whom sacrifices had to be offered, if the tribe hoped for favours from them. These bright beings, or gods, had helped the Aryan hosts in overwhelming the communities who once ruled the plain. The role of the latter in the Vedic hymns is that of the conquered, sullen, ugly and dark-skinned serf. The old gods, the object of worship in the home, in village, in tree, grove, river and on mountain, continued to exist and to be venerated too, as they always have done in practically every culture where the new has ostensibly supplanted the old. The gods of primitive fertility rites generally revenge themselves on the gods who displace them, and enter the new pantheon suitably transformed by medicine-man or priest.

Out of the *Vedas* and the *Brahmanas*, in spite of their obscurities and difficulties of meaning, one receives a picture of multitudinous gods whom the tribe invoked through an elaborate ritual of sacrifices. The priest, the magical rites, the gods of rain, of fire, of lightning, were a heritage shared with other cultures. The gods and the priests had travelled from afar and were going to travel further. They are still to be met with in various parts of South East Asia, though the rituals they once commanded and performed have been transformed. The *Vedas* speak of a principle of order which it is the duty of gods and men to uphold. What the medieval European believed about the heavenly hierarchy was not so far from the picture, bewildering though it may be, of the Vedic pantheon, and the Vedic conception of the divine regulation of times and seasons, and the necessity for the observance of ritual in a world which, without it, would be disordered and chaotic. Of course, the ethos of the European cosmic order was Christian, but in the invocation of a hierarchy of a Triune god and a multiplicity of saints, and the insistence upon rituals for each event of a carefully regulated year we have in broad outlines much the same pattern. What is important in both is what specifically distinguishes them, but to see some basic similarities in them is to be conscious of the common origins to which both might be traced.

If the *Vedas* reflect the India of the small tribal communities with their prescribed rituals and their priests, the *Mahabharata* allows one to think of the tests to which an individual is subjected, and the choice which is placed before him by gods and by fate. There may be no universally agreed upon scheme of dating the various times at which the poem as we have it now came into being, but it certainly throws light upon the India of the age of the Buddha. One of India's polymaths claimed that it reflected the entire life of ancient India as in a mirror. 'It is a great storehouse which holds within it at least implicitly a large part of ancient Indian culture and history of thought.'[1] It is the expression of a writer, or writers, who felt society to be in conflict with ideals and customs which could threaten the foundations of the traditional and the old. It is not mentioned once in the *Tipitaka*, the canonical Buddhist writings, and it has been concluded, therefore, that in the form in which we have it now, it belongs to a later age than that of the Buddha. Yet to refer to it in speaking of Buddhist India would not be out of place. For that moment of time denoted by the phrase 'Buddhist India' is a moment of time in the unfolding of Indian thought and Indian life which includes much which both precedes and follows upon it. As both a philosophical system and a way of life, Buddhism is too deeply embedded in its Indian antecedents to be torn out of its setting. All the spiritual ferment of those times which produced an Indian appraisal of man's destiny and what he should strive after, is to be seen, as well in the stock of ancient Indian heroic song which makes up the *Mahabharata*, as in that portion of it which celebrated the later cult of devotion to the god Krishna.

Its long and repetitious story tells of the enmity of Duryodhana, the son of king Dhritarashtra, for his cousins, the five sons of the dead king Pandu. Attacked by him, threatened with death, forcibly deprived of their rightful heritage, living in exile and subjected to a multiplicity of tests, the five sons of Pandu ask Duryodhana for even the smallest part of their kingdom back again. But their cousin in his avarice and hatred of the five brothers, of whom the saintly Yudhisthira and the third brother, Arjuna, are the most famous in the story, refuses, and gradually the whole country is involved in the great battle which is the only method of settling the rival claims. This battle is fought on the plain of Kurukshetra, and it ends, after eighteen days of heroic effort, in the death of Duryodhana and the victory of the Pandavas (the five sons of Pandu). But the trials of the brothers are not yet over. Yudhisthira, the eldest of them, reigns thirty-six years, and then makes a pilgrimage with his four brothers and their queen Draupadi to the sacred places of the Himalayas. After the death of his four brothers and Draupadi Yudhisthira reaches heaven, but is told by Indra that he cannot enter with his dog. Faced with this situation Yudhisthira decides that he will stay out of heaven with his dog. The difficulty is overcome after a lengthy argument, and the dog

[1] S. N. Das Gupta and S. K. De, *History of Sanskrit Literature*, Calcutta, 1947, Vol. I, p. li.

stands revealed as *Dharma* (*Dhamma*)—the law, not any legal system in the familiar meaning of the word, but the notion of the divinely appointed order upon which social integrity and social solidarity depend for their very life.

So Yudhisthira enters heaven, but there is yet one test more. His brothers and the queen are not there, but are revealed to him by Indra in the gloomy pit of hell. In heaven are all the enemies of his lifetime, all those who had warred against him and his brothers. Once more, with this new choice before him—between heaven and hell—Yudhisthira does not hesitate. He chooses to remain with his brothers, for where they are it is heaven to him. The god approves his choice, and what before appeared to be both heaven and hell vanishes, and Yudhisthira, his brothers, and their queen enter into that state of being one with god which is true heaven, and not the false appearance which had been conjured up to test the saint.

The most dramatic part of this long poem is that late interpolation which is known as the *Bhagavad Gita*. Arjuna, who has chosen to have Krishna on his side in the battle, even though the latter will take no part in the fighting, is faced with the task of warring against kinsmen and teachers. He cannot make up his mind to advance and to begin the fight. His bow slips uselessly from his hand, and his limbs feel weak. Rather than partake of the kingdom, the power and the glory by slaying them, he would be slain of them.

The *Bhagavad Gita* is, in form, the poet Sanjaya's vision of what takes place between Arjuna and Krishna on this memorable occasion. The poet tells the blind king Dhritarashtra, who asks him what the sons of Pandu and his sons did when they were arrayed in force on the plain of Kurukshetra, of the dialogue between Arjuna and Krishna which preceded the battle.

The world of thought of this poem is perhaps the most characteristic expression of Hindu religious emotion which is known all over the world. The *Upanishads*, which may dispute this claim, belong too much both to an earlier age and to the region of the esoteric to have the same strong popular appeal. The *Gita*, as devotional hymn and philosophical communing, has something of the same feeling which marks the earlier Vedic hymns. Man has arrived at a moment of crisis, on his decision depend not only life and death, but the continuance of the divine process which orders both. The great battle between the Pandavas and the Kurus is, in its epical matter, like that 'last great battle in the West' of the Arthurian legends. The forces assembled to do battle on the plain are the rival armies of two systems, two ways of life. In the dialogue between Arjuna and Krishna, which makes up the substance of the poem, is to be seen the clear understanding of the momentousness of the struggle, in what the god tells the devotee, and in the tragic dilemma of the devotee himself. In the first discourse Arjuna sees the fate which must befall the destruction of family—the perishing of immemorial family traditions, and the lawlessness which follows upon 'class-confusion'.

The social ideal which the *Gita* celebrates is the hierarchy which proceeds from Brahman. It is divinely appointed therefore, and there is no creature, either among men or among the *devas,* who is exempt from the operation of its law. In the eighteenth discourse the god tells the devotee of the various duties cast upon the various degree of men. Brahmin, Kshatriya, Vaishya, Shudra, each has his own duty to perform, and man can reach perfection only by devoting himself to that duty which is his to fulfil. So Arjuna, intent on his duty which is action, but detached from the fruits of action, takes heart again, and the battle is fought. This ideal of acting and being yet detached from the fruits of action is the great paradox of the *Bhagavad Gita,* and it is beautifully moulded by the poet's art in the image of the lotus poised on the waters, yet untouched by them. It belongs to the world's wealth of philosophical aphorisms.

In the *Bhagavad Gita,* it is quite clear that of the three paths which lead to God, treated in it—the path of desireless action, the path of knowledge, and the path of devotion—Krishna prefers the third, which is the way of 'those whose minds are fixed on me in steadfast love, worshipping me with absolute faith'. This was the path characteristic of the later development in Indian religions, but ancient India knew of other paths besides those mentioned here—the way of sacrifice, which has been briefly referred to already, and the way of the ascetic. The latter was the mode of life chosen by numerous contemporaries of the Buddha, and still, both to Westerner and Oriental, it is symbolic of a typically Indian contribution to the history of religious practices. Buddhism itself, according to the most eminent English authority on the subject, 'first appears in history as an ascetic movement.'[1]

In the Buddha's time, as now in India, in the great religious site and all over the country, were known the legion of the mortifiers of the flesh, who sought thereby the release of the spirit from its trammels, and the state of union with the god. Whether they dwelt in forest, or in cemetery where the bodies of the unburied dead were exposed to the ravages of animals and birds, or whether they moved from one place to another in the chosen mode which self-torture dictated, these followers of the ideal of self-mortification were the most frequently met with group of seekers after truth in the India of the Buddha. The Kassapa-Sihanada-Sutta of the *Digha Nikaya,* which Rhys Davids quotes, gives a list of ascetic practices—crouching low on the heels and moving in a series of hops; filth-eating, addiction to the practice of feeding on the four kinds of filth (cow-dung, cows' urine, ashes and clay); non-drinking, or never drinking cold water lest the souls in it should be injured. The Pathika

[1] E. J. Thomas, *op. cit.,* p. 11.

2. Hindagala near Kandy: 19th century fresco with details of Prince Siddhartha's leaving his royal palace on his horse—see p. 42

3. Nillakgama: The entrance to the Bodhi-ghara—see p. 91

Mihintale: The ancient steps, now restored, leading to the sacred sites—see p. 96

4.
Mihintale: Kanthaka-cetiya:
The horse with one of the
stelae—see p. 96

Mihintale: Kanthaka-cetiya:
The frieze of elephants

5. Mihintale: Kanthaka-cetiya: The eastern Vahalkada seen in profile

Suttanta mentions Kora, the Khattiya, who walked on all fours like a dog, and like a dog tore whatever food was offered to him with his mouth, never using his hands for the purpose of feeding himself.

The *Aitraeya Brahmana* shows the high valuation placed on self-mortification: 'Heaven is established on the air, the air on the earth, the earth on the waters, the waters on truth, the truth on the mystic lore (of the sacrifices), and that of *Tapas*.' Rhys Davids points out that '*tapas*' ('Self-mortification or more exactly self-torture') is here 'put in the most important place, higher than sacrifice, which is, in its turn, higher than truth—a most suggestive order'. He notes in this connection that, 'there is no question here of penance for sin, or of an appeal to the mercy of an offended deity. It is the boast of superiority advanced by the man able, through strength of will, to keep his body under, and not only to despise comfort, but to welcome pain.'[1]

This ideal of self-mortification is, strangely enough the obverse of the medal of the meditative ideal of the *yogi*. According to the sixth discourse of the *Bhagavad Gita*, the *yogi* should remain in a secret place by himself, with thought of self subdued, and utterly freed from any hope of desire for the possession of this world. There, sitting on a place of his own, neither too high nor too low, on a cloth-covered antelope skin spread over the sacred grass strewn on the spot, he makes his mind 'one-pointed', concentrated on the single object of his contemplation, with all his thoughts and senses subdued. The very posture in which he should sit is described: 'holding his body, head, and back erect, immovably steady, looking fixedly at the point of the nose, with unseeing gaze.' So the mind of the *yogi* will arrive at the wished-for state described in the familar simile: 'as a lamp in a windless place flickereth not'.[2]

As the *yogi* held his physical self in suspension, so the ascetic, accepting the same disvaluation of the physical, subjected his body to self-mortification. In popular estimate, at the time of the Buddha and later, asceticism and austerities were believed to confer upon their practioner special powers of a magical kind, which were valued for their own sake. The present basis of belief in European countries (and among more sophisticated people in the East) in such things as the famous Indian rope trick (which no reliable witness has ever seen performed), and the mango trick (which is only a conjurer's device), is quite another matter. This seems to be dependent upon that psychological readiness to credit someone markedly different in dress, demeanour and life from the majority of one's fellows, with supernatural powers. The consequence of this, as J. B. S. Haldane has pointed out, is that what is different from what we know, can be readily transformed into what is inferior, even though we may compensate the person so reckoned with the

[1] T. W. Rhys Davids, *op. cit.*, p. 243.
[2] *Mahabharata* VI. 19, trsl. Annie Besant, Madras, 1907.

possession of sensational powers in which we are ready to acquiesce. So the fasting *yogis* and fakirs one notices at fairs, credited though they might be with extraordinary powers, are nonetheless looked down upon. They are non-human even, because they are super-human.

Quite different was the valuation placed upon the special powers claimed by the ascetic in the Buddha's time. Yet he condemned them and advised his followers to abstain from them. There is a charming story in the *Vinaya* which is the occasion for the rule the Buddha gave. It shows that though the Buddha did accept the popular judgement that the ascetic did possess special powers, he regarded any exhibition of them as unworthy of the ideal of the *bhikkhu*. In any case, these powers, to the Buddha, were comparatively of little worth. The story tells of a rich householder of Rajagaha who had a bowl of sandal-wood tied to the top of a number of bamboo poles, and offered it as a prize to the first person who could get it from that height through his supernatural powers. The bowl is claimed, on the strength of their special powers, by numerous ascetics, among whom were various rivals of the Buddha. But the householder observed that if they really had these powers, they should fetch the bowl themselves. Two of the chief disciples of the Buddha pass by at the time, hear of the competition, and with charming modesty one tells the other that since he possessed these powers he should get the bowl. In the end one of them, Pindola Bharadvaja decides to do so. He rises up in the air, takes the bowl from the top of the poles, goes three times round Rajagaha in the air, and finally descends on the residence of the householder who fills the bowl with the choicest food. On his return he is rebuked by the Buddha, who then lays down the rule that such exhibitions are unworthy of a disciple of his.[1]

In the much later commentary, the *Dhammapadatthakatha,* an elaborate and beautiful tissue of stories is woven round this anecdote, the point of which seems to be, that despite his prohibition, the Buddha himself could, if he so wished, perform miracles. What is demonstrated by his performance of them is the utter and total defeat of the rival ascetics who claimed to be superior to him. In the commentary the ascetics, when they hear of the Buddha's prohibition, are pleased that they are free of the competition of a rival who threatened their position. King Seniya Bimbisara who heard the talk of the ascetics, tells the Buddha of it, and the Buddha promises to perform a miracle which would finally demolish all their pretensions.

What follows is the story of the two miracles performed by the Buddha at Savatthi, the first of which was to take place at the foot of Ganda's mango-tree. The rival ascetics hearing of this rooted up every mango-tree within the radius of a league around. On the full-moon day of the month Asalhi, the Buddha receives a mango-seed from Ganda, the king's gardener. He asks the

[1] *Vin,* 11, p. 111.

gardener to plant the seed in the ground. As the Buddha washes his hands over the place where the seed is planted, a fully grown mango-tree fifty cubits high, springs up, sprouts five great branches, four pointing to the four points of the compass and one going straight up. In a second the tree is covered with flowers and fruits, and on one side is a cluster of ripe mangoes. The Buddha has won a notable victory, for the crowd eat the mangoes and pelt his rivals with the mango-seeds, shouting after them in derision.

After this the Buddha performs the great 'miracle' of the *Yamaka Patihariya*, or the 'twin miracle'.[1] Most interesting in the story of this miracle is that a number of the Buddha's followers, women and children included, offer to perform miracles which would sufficiently demonstrate his power and so save him the trouble of exerting himself. For instance, the female disciple Gharani, offers to perform a miracle in which she will convert the great earth to water, dive into it in the shape of a water-bird, and then reappear at the four quarters of the mythical range of mountains encircling the world. The Buddha assures her that he knows that she can do all this, but gently refuses her aid. 'This basket of flowers,' he says, 'is not prepared for you.' The charm of this metaphor seems to have a two-fold value. These displays of power may be impressive, but their attractiveness is only fleeting—they are really a basket of flowers, no more.

In fact the Buddha saw the danger to true understanding in the practice of self-mortification. Spiritual pride and narcissistic self-satisfaction were too often the results of the fanaticism with which the ascetic laid austerities upon himself. He himself—as we shall see—had tried the way of self-mortification, but had rejected it for the way of understanding. In the Udumbarika Sihanada Suttanta he affirmed to the ascetic Nigrodha that where an ascetic, because of his austerities, becomes self-complacent since he has achieved his aim, it is a blemish in the ascetic. He sees, too, the pride of the ascetic in his achievement, his infatuation with himself, and the satisfaction derived from the attention and fame his austerities gain him. Very definitely therefore the Buddha did not reckon the naked ascetic highly.

King, warrior, Brahmin, householder, naked ascetic and wandering sage, pass by in that panorama which literature presents of the land in which the Buddha lived. As one reads Sutta and poem the picture in our minds seems to glow with colours which the life devoted the quest for truth throws upon persons and events of a time so remote from ours as to seem as if it never existed. The scholar working on such a period of time could unconsciously

[1] *Dha*, III, p. 202 ff. The Twin Miracle is one which only a *Tathagata* can perform. The miracle consists of the Buddha's rising in the air, producing a counterpart of himself (hence the name Twin Miracle) with whom he discusses the *Dhamma*. The miracle is accompanied by the emanation of fire and water from the opposite ends of his body in six colours, and his walking on a jewelled promenade in the sky.

be drawn into transferring his idealizations into the past he recreates, and even transforming that past to compensate for the disappointments of the present. So at various times in the history of culture there have been Edens, Utopias, and desert islands which have refreshed the imaginations of men attracted by their own visions of the past into projecting their wishes into times long gone by. Throughout the nineteenth century one notes the symbolic values associated with picturizations of the European medieval community. There is hardly a scholar who has worked intensively on the culture of the past who has not ended by identifying it with the lost heritage of man's primal innocence, succumbing to the powerful nostalgic pull of the golden age of childhood.

In his great work on Buddhist India, T. W. Rhys Davids presents a picture of a country and a time which seem to conform to the pattern of the pastoral paradise. Describing the villages of which the country was made up, he writes: 'The economic conditions in such villages were simple. None of the householders could have been what would now be called rich. On the other hand there was a sufficiency for their simple needs, there was security, there was independence. There were no landlords, and no paupers. There was little if any crime. What crime there was in the country (of which later) was nearly all outside the villages. When the central power was strong enough, as it usually was, to put down dacoity, the people, to quote the quaint words of an old Suttanta, "pleased one with another and happy, dancing their children in their hands, dwelt with open doors." '[1]

But Buddhist India, as has been shown, was a land which knew insecurity and war. Great famines were known. There were the very rich—great merchants and grantees of royal gifts of land—and families so poor that the mendicant was forbidden to beg from them. And as there were people in great need, there was a great deal of crime known too. Dacoity was an ever-present evil, and as well known as crime were the penalties laid down for it, some of them revolting in their sadistic details: 'the skull was first trepanned and then a red-hot ball of iron was dropped in so that the brains boiled over like a porridge; the mouth was fixed open with a skewer and a lighted lamp put inside from the neck downward. . . .'[2]

And as for the quotation from the 'quaint old Suttanta', it describes not what was in fact the objective situation, but suggests what might have been, if a king whose realm was in distress, could depend, not on sacrifices, but on enlightened action. When the Buddha is asked by Kutadanta, the Brahmin, how to perform sacrifices in the right manner, he replies with the story of King Maha Vijita, who, once upon a time, asked his chaplain the very same

[1] Rhys Davids, *op. cit.*, p. 49
[2] Chalmers, *Further Dialogues of the Buddha*, London, 1926–7, Vol. I, p. 61.

question. The chaplain replied in a form which quite obviously conveys the Buddha's approval of his sentiments: 'The king's country, Sire, is harassed and harried. There are dacoits abroad who pillage the villages and the townships, so, to levy a fresh tax, verily his Majesty would be acting wrongly. But perchance His Majesty might think: "I'll soon put a stop to these scoundrels' game by degradation and banishment, and fines and bonds and death!" But their licence cannot be satisfactorily put a stop to so. The remnant left unpunished would still go on harassing the realm. Now, there is one method to adopt to put a thorough end to this disorder. Whosoever there are in the king's realm, who devote themselves to keeping cattle and the farm, to them let His Majesty the King give food and seed-corn. Whosoever there can be in the king's realm who devote themselves to trade, to them let His Majesty give capital. Whosoever there be in the king's realm who devote themselves to government service, to them let His Majesty give wages and food. Then those men, following each his own business, will no longer harass the realm; the king's revenue will go up; the country will be quiet and at peace; and the populace, pleased one with another and happy, dancing their children in their arms, will dwell with open doors.'[1]

Buddhist India was no land of the Golden Age. The old Suttanta tells of what might have been in the community if the king had the virtues of the good monarch of the fairy-tale. If the Suttanta proves anything, it shows that the ideal community, in the eyes of the great teacher of these times, was one in which order and stability ruled, in which each man 'follows his own business'. If the story indicates anything to us at the present time, it may be an early intimation of what might paradoxically be regarded as a monarchical welfare state.

It seems to be clear that the teaching of the Buddha, the essential point of which is the knowledge of suffering and its cause, and the way to end suffering by eliminating its cause, could scarcely have come into being in a country where the extremes of suffering and distress were unknown. If the inhabitant of the India of the Buddha's time had lived in an idyllic age of gold, the teaching of the Buddha would have been meaningless to him. How could he have accepted the idea of life which from its very beginning is suffering (dukkha), and from whose chain of rebirths one should incessantly strive to be free?[2]

[1] T. W. Rhys Davids and Mrs. Rhys Davids, *Dialogues of the Buddha*, London, 1899–1921, Vol. I, p. 176. It is interesting that in this edition of the *Suttanta* Rhys Davids is aware that the Buddha, in the story, is referring to a might-have-been.

[2] For the material in the last few paragraphs I am indebted to Edith Ludowyk-Gyomroi, 'Aurea Prima Sata Est. . . .', UCR, Vol. I, No. 2, pp. 43–50.

CHAPTER TWO

THE TEACHER

The life of the Buddha, as we have it today, is the legacy of several centuries of legend. The incidents depicted on the walls of ancient temples, or carved on the bas-reliefs of shrines long ago, vary from country to country; what we are concerned with here is what the Buddhist in Ceylon accepts as one or other of the stories which have grown up round the person of the wandering teacher, who in the sixth century before Christ taught a new religion in the kingdom of the Magadhas.

The Buddha of history is more or less the Buddha of legend; the historical personage whose life and teaching marked one quarter of the world for over two thousand five hundred years, is a figure composed of the successive layers of centuries of traditional lore. Of the man for whom history with its well-authenticated proofs of facts can vouch, there remain only the very faintest outlines, outlines traced so long after the event as to be of doubtful validity now. Yet as one travels over the ancient track, one arrives at last at a point, as close as it is possible now to arrive, where these ultimately started from—the memory of the Sakyan whom disciples and lay-followers once knew, and whom they recall in their remembrance of what he taught and what he had been. That is as far as one can go. It is far enough, for although legends are unbelievable, yet as they were believed in and accepted, they will tell us what the Buddha meant to his followers, the kind of personality which stamped itself on their imagination, the man whose life and teaching inspired such records.

The great figure from the past, even the great contemporary survives in the livelier colours of story than in the sober livery of history. The strongest lines in his character and personality come, not from the certainties of established fact, but from that imaginative power of human beings which loves to dower the great with the wealth of its own image-making faculties. The great man is so often better known to us by what he never said or did, but what people believed that he said or did. If one were dependent on history alone for our memories of the great, how scanty would be our garnering from the rich fields of human achievement.

38

Little is to be gained by interpreting the legends as evidence of a sun myth, or any other kind of myth. Legends are likely to be found in the most ancient and the most unimpeachable sources of information we possess about the great men of antiquity. What is interesting in the accounts of the life of the Buddha is the way in which the human personality of the teacher asserts itself over all the accompanying legendary material. This is the more remarkable when one remembers the characteristic Indian tendency to deify the great teacher. As Filliozat remarks: 'Considering how apotheosis has always been more natural in India than an equivalent rationalistic humanization, and how easily, even today, the leaders of religion are deified, we should rather think that it must have been that the human character of the Buddha was indeed a fundamental fact for it not to have been submerged by the very common Indian tendency to sublimate exceptional beings.'[1]

Of history then we have almost nothing, but of poetry everything. The legends are not only poetic in form, they express the truth of poetry, which is, after all, a more philosophic thing than history. The poetry derives its strength from that level of belief which lies below the level of consciousness. Of the several sorts of reality which the modern world offers us, the reality of poetry is not the least. The reality of the Buddha which history scarcely attests, lives more in the record of poetry which could convince of what might have been, or even of what should have been, than in the verification of history. If it does not help us to the truth, at least it brings us in our understanding closest to what was taken for the truth.

The legends are all woven into a framework of typically Indian belief— the pattern of how man thought of his world, how it had come into being; of his own destiny in it; of the aeons through which worlds evolved, dissolved, and then evolved again. All these belong to the accepted beliefs of that age in Indian thought in which the Buddha lived. The deities of that world; the spirits inhabiting wood and tree; the signs and wonders which accompany the significant crises of a great man's career, are all taken from the vast storehouse of Indian tradition. Whether the records are Tibetan, or Chinese, Burmese or Sinhalese, they disclose the great richness of the Indian poetic and popular achievement, easy to overlook in the way in which Indian traditions have been acclimatized, and established as part of the lore of the country in which they have taken root. And yet at the present day Buddhism as a great religion counts ironically enough comparatively few adherents in India itself.

The dates assigned by scholars to the main events of the Buddha's life and his final passing away are the following: he was born in 563 B.C. When he was twenty-nine he renounced his worldly life and became a wandering ascetic—534 B.C. For six years he placed himself under two teachers, and then

[1] J. Filliozat: *L'Inde Classique*, Paris, 1953, Tome II, p. 466.

practised austerities, until he discovered for himself the knowledge he had been seeking—his enlightenment or Buddhahood was therefore in 528 B.C. For forty-five years he wandered about the Magadhan and Kosalan plain, teaching the Way to disciples and lay-followers until in 483 B.C. he attained Parinirvana. His lifetime of eighty years stretched in time across the heyday of those tribal confederacies and the kingdoms coming into power in the Gangetic basin. During its span his own tribesmen were destroyed by the king of Kosala, and on his deathbed he knew that the Vajjians were going to be attacked too, for a messenger came to him from King Ajatasattu to ask whether the attack on the Vajjians would succeed. These events which mark the transitoriness of earthly power seem a fitting accompaniment to the last existence on this earth of a teacher who probed human life and found it a congeries of impermanence which man desperately strives to grasp.

In the Maha Parinibbana Sutta the Buddha speaks of four places which the believer should visit with feelings of devotion and reverence—the spot where the Buddha was born; where he attained Enlightenment; where the first sermon was preached, and the Wheel of the Law set in motion; and the spot where he finally passed away. Here then connected with sites of pilgrimage are remembered the major events of the Buddha's life, as he was supposed to reckon them, when on his deathbed he looked back on the past, and forward to the future. Round each of these events legends cluster; to gather them all is impossible, but to consider the best-known of them is to feel how the Buddha came to be regarded by those who handed down the tradition of his teaching and his life.

He was born in a Sakyan township, Kapilavatthu, to parents of noble Kshatriya blood of the Gotama clan, on the full-moon day of the lunar month of April-May (Vesak). On the same day were born five of the actors in the story of his later life: his future wife, his elephant, the horse Kanthaka on which he rode away when he renounced his life as a prince, his charioteer Channa who accompanied him that night, and Kaludayin, the son of a minister whom the Buddha's father sent to him asking him to come back home. In the graceful symmetry of the legend these five were of the same age, to a day, as Gotama, as he was known by his clan-names, or Siddhartha, the name given to him at his name-giving ceremony. Signs and wonders attended his birth, all the miraculous accompaniments of later story which spoke of six previous Buddhas. The Maha Padana Suttanta recounts the names of these six, and in telling the story of Vipassi, the first of them, broaches the legendary lore of the former Buddhas. As Gotama the Buddha relates it, the Suttanta prefaces each stage of the life of Vipassi with the remark that it is the rule that in the life of a Buddha such and such things should happen: When the *Bodhisatta* enters his mother's womb, he is fully aware of the destiny awaiting him. A great radiance is manifested in the whole cosmos. His mother bears him in her womb ten months, during which time she leads a life that is pure and is free from any kind of ailment or ill-health, but seven days after he is born, she dies. As the child is born, he stands firmly on his feet, takes seven steps as he faces north, and cries out with a loud voice—'the voice of a bull'—while the *devatas* hold the royal parasol over his head: 'Chief am I in the world, Eldest am I in the world, Foremost am I in the world! This is the last birth! There is now no more coming to be!' At his birth once again a radiance lights up the universe, and the earth quakes.[1]

So the legend of the Buddha's birth fills in the signs and wonders which are the rule when a *Bodhisatta* is born. On the body of the *Bodhisatta* are to be seen the Thirty-Two signs of the Great Man, and for him those skilled in the lore can prophesy that he will be either Universal Monarch or Buddha. And so, as mentioned earlier, the Brahmins who are called to interpret the signs, prophesy the same alternatives for Gotama, while one of them asserts that for him there can be no other destiny than that of attaining Enlightenment and becoming a Buddha. The great difference between the first of the Buddhas, Vipassi, and Gotama who was born at Kapilavatthu, was that at Vipassi's time the span of life was 80,000 years, whereas in Gotama's it was small—to have lived a hundred years or so then was to be long-lived. But for this, and other slight differences in detail, the life of Gotama repeats the legendary life of the first of the Buddhas.

Much the same account is given of the circumstances of the birth of Gotama in the Acchariyabbhutadhamma Sutta by Ananda, who asserts that he heard them exactly in the same way from the Buddha himself—the entering into his mother's womb; the heavenly radiance which even pierces the purgatories; the earthquake; the *devas* who draw near to keep watch over the four cardinal points so that nothing should harm either the *Bodhisatta* or his mother; the intrinsically virtuous life lived by her; no sickness touches her; she carries her child for ten months; gives birth to him standing erect; and dies seven days later. When he is born he stands firmly on the earth, takes seven strides to the north, and exclaims: 'I am the chief of the world, this is my last birth, I shall never be born again.'[2] The same story, very much embellished by legendary material, is told in the Jataka Nidana Katha several centuries later.

The best-known incident of his childhood, which was a presage of his later career is told by the Buddha in the Mahasaccaka Sutta. He relates quite simply how when still a boy he was sitting under a rose-apple tree, while his father's work in the fields was being carried on. He remembers attaining the first *jhana* and remaining in it.[3] This too the later commentary enlarges into a story of the miracles which mark every stage of the life of the Buddha.

[1] D. II, 15.   [2] M. II, 123.   [3] M. I, 246.

At sixteen he came of age, and soon he was married, but the next major event of his life was his abandonment of the life of pleasure he was leading in the three palaces which his father had built him for the three seasons of the year. In the Mahaparanibbana Sutta the Buddha tells his last convert Subhadda that he was twenty-nine years old when he renounced the world in his search after knowledge.

According to the legend as it is known all over the world three symbolic meetings awoke him from the dream of pleasure, and made him realize that he too was subject to human infirmities, and that the elation of his wonderful youth was impermanent. The gods took a hand in this; the three meetings were the three signs they gave the young man destined to seek enlightenment. One of their number first represented an old man, then a sick man, and lastly a corpse. The young prince saw the three figures as he drove in his chariot. Troubled by what he had seen, he receives a fourth sign—an ascetic who had renounced the world. The fated day of Gotama's renunciation of the world could not be delayed any longer. But that same day his wife bore him a son, Rahula, and the news was brought to him as he neared the city.

That night Gotama made up his mind to leave the world he had known up to that time. Looking round him in the royal apartments where his dancing girls were stretched out in sleep in attitudes which filled him with disgust, he was the more determined to go, and he ordered his charioteer to prepare his horse Kanthaka. So he left his home, his wife, and his child on the full-moon day of the lunar month Uttarasalha (June-July), riding his horse and accompanied by his faithful charioteer.

The rest of the events of that night are the common property of every school-child in Ceylon—the miraculous leap of the horse Kanthaka over the great river Anoma; Gotama's cutting off of his locks of hair which he tossed in the air, and were later miraculously enshrined in the sky; his dismissal of his charioteer and his horse which, overhearing the talk of his master who had left his home for good, died of a broken heart; and finally his robing of himself in the garb of a monk, later the traditional robes of the Buddhist mendicant. Gotama then betook himself to Alara Kalama, and studied the doctrine which that sage professed. But after a time, dissatisfied with what this doctrine had to offer, he left Alara Kalama and went to another teacher, Udakka, the son of Rama. Gotama left this teacher too, when he had seen and understood that what he offered was not enough, that it could not satisfy his desire to understand the truth.

He then set out for Uruvela, a town in the Magadha country, and here, in language which well sets out what has been recorded of the Buddha's appreciation of the natural scene, he came upon a 'delightful spot, a jungle thicket, a flowing stream, white with its beautiful banks, with a village for sustenance in the vicinity. This thought occurred to me, bhikkhus, "Delightful indeed is this spot and pleasant the jungle thicket. There flows the stream, white with its beautiful banks. . . . This spot is indeed fitting for a young man of good family who wishes to exert himself in discovering the truth." '[1] In the Ariya-pariyesana Sutta, from which the passage is taken, the Buddha described himself as 'striving after what is good, and searching for the supreme and noble state of peace'. Here he practised the known contemplative exercises of the time, and gave himself to such austerities as impressed five disciples who had attached themselves to him, believing him to be the greatest ascetic in their experience.

But all of this was of no avail. It brought him no nearer the supreme and noble end for which he was searching. He then remembered the early experience of his childhood, when under the rose-apple tree he had reached the first state of trance. So he decided to give up the way of ascetic austerities, to the disgust of the five 'disciples', and to search for understanding through the way of meditation and trance. It is during this period that the popular legend describes his temptation by the daughters of Mara who attempted to seduce him from the way of contemplation.

Gotama attained enlightenment through his own efforts of mind—with his mind purified and concentrated. 'Being myself subject to rebirth, decay, disease, death, sorrow, defilement, and seeing the evil consequence of all this, I searched for the perfect peace of Nibbana in which there is neither birth, nor decay, nor disease, nor death, no sorrow, nor defilement.' And as the *Majjhima* account continues, 'and won it.' The insight which he won was enlightenment into suffering, the cause of suffering, the destruction of suffering, and the way which leads to it. These were the Four Noble Truths, apprehension of which marked the successful conclusion of a man's intellectual struggle for truth.

E. J. Thomas points out that neither the Bodhi tree under which the attainment of Buddhahood was supposed to have taken place, nor the temptations of Mara were mentioned in the earliest accounts of the Buddha's enlightenment in the Canon.[2] The legend which attached these to the miracles which are the best remembered parts of the Buddha's life in countries of the Buddhist faith, is naturally much more elaborate and attractive to the popular imagination. The story of Sujata is but one of the acts of devotion with which the legend celebrates the triumph of the Great Being under the Bodhi-tree.

Sujata had made a vow to make a yearly offering to this tree. She tended her cows and fed them herself with the greatest care, and that day on which the Buddha attained enlightenment, she woke up early and milked them. The calves that morning did not make their way to their mothers as usual, but

[1] M. I, 166.   [2] E. J. Thomas, *The Life of the Buddha*, London, 1949, p. 68.

stayed in their stalls, and as soon as the fresh pots were placed under the udders of the cows, the milk poured into them in streams. Surprised at this omen, Sujata poured the milk with her own hands into new bowls, and set the fire alight herself. When the bowls of milk-rice were boiling, huge bubbles rose out of the food as it was cooking, turned to the right and went round, but not a single drop fell on the ground or was lost. From the fire there arose no smoke at all.

Sujata sent her servant, the girl Punna, to the sacred tree to keep watch there. The girl saw the *Bodhisatta* in all his radiance, and came back hurriedly to her mistress to report that the god of the tree was seated underneath it. Sujata then decided to send for a golden vessel in which to offer the food she had cooked. She filled it with the milk-rice which poured itself into the vessel of gold as water drops from the lotus leaf, and the bowl was filled completely with the food. The Buddha received Sujata's offering, and satisfied his hunger with it. He then bathed in the stream, and threw the golden vessel into the river and said, 'If today I shall become a Buddha, let the vessel go up against the stream; if not, let it go down the stream.' And the vessel floated with the speed of a horse against the current, sank in a whirlpool, and went down to the palace of Kala Nagaraja (the snake king). There it struck the bowls of all the previous Buddhas, and produced the sound 'Killi Killi', and stopped at the lowest of them. Kala Nagaraja when he heard the sound exclaimed: 'Yesterday a Buddha arose, today another has arisen,' and he went on to proclaim the Buddha's praises in many hundred words.[1]

Before the Buddha, as Gotama now has to be called since he had attained enlightenment, could 'set in motion the wheel of the law', or, less picturesquely, preach his doctrine, he had to decide whether he is at all going to teach the knowledge of the new insight he had gained or not.[2] The king of the gods appears and appeals to him to make known his teaching to mankind. The Buddha is persuaded, not only by the request of Brahma Sahampati, but because of his compassion for mankind. So he set out for Banarasi, to the country of the Kasi, where in the deer-park at Isipatana he preaches his first sermon. Thus the wheel of the law (the *Dhamma*) is set in motion. In the *Samyutta Nikaya* the Dhammacakkapavattana-Sutta is the Sutta of the 'Turning of the wheel of the Dhamma'.

The first sermon, as we have it, is a statement of the virtue of the Middle Way, which avoids the two extremes of the way of the world and the way of austerity. The essence of the Buddha's teaching is to be found in this sutta.[3]

[1] *Jat.* I, p. 68 ff.
[2] According to Theravada belief, there is the *paccekabuddha* who differs from the other Buddhas in not preaching his doctrine.
[3] *S.* V, 420.

That first sermon in the deer-park at Isipatana began the Buddha's life as a wandering teacher, a life which was to end forty-five years later. Round him in the course of time gathered numerous disciples who came from all walks of life. Even the members of his own noble family found their way into the order which the Buddha founded, the order which was to be the repository of his teaching and which later was to become one part of that triple support he recommended to mankind. In these forty-five years the Buddha disputed with Brahmins, contemporary wandering ascetics and teachers. Round him were disciples who through their knowledge of the doctrine and their lives were the famed associates of their master—Moggallana, Sariputta, Maha Kassapa, and, perhaps the best known, Ananda who became the Buddha's constant attendant during the last years of his life. Kings, ministers, great householders, kshatriyas, brahmins, people of all clans had heard and been moved by the doctrine which was preached.

And then the time came for the Buddha to pass away. The Mahaparinibbana-Sutta of the *Digha Nikaya* is the canonical account of the last days of the Buddha. Even in the dry and lifeless translations of the Suttas which can scarcely do justice to their originals, there appear from time to time some intimations of the variety and interest of the story and teaching they communicate. One finds in the Suttas evidence of dialectal skill; of the clearness of mind which, delighted with the opportunity for refinement, can separate and divide things seemingly alike; of insight into human character; of the charm and naïveté of story; of profundities of thought; and above all the glow with which the impression of a truly compassionate and understanding personality irradiates the text. It is this last quality which makes the Mahaparinibbana-Sutta memorable—the record of the last days of the greatest figure India produced. Quite apart from the melancholy interest attaching to the passing away of such a figure, there is a wealth of detail which presents in the lively colours of imaginative truth a man touched, even when the pangs of death were upon him, with a warmth of human affection for mankind and the transitory world of man.

The Sutta opens with the Buddha's affectionate remembrance of one of the places he had known, where some part of his life as a teacher had been spent—Vesali which he had just visited, with its shrines in the country of the Vajjis. Sitting on his mat by one of the shrines, the Buddha told Ananda that whoever had mastered the 'very heights of the four paths to *Iddhi*' could if he wished, continue to live in that life-span in which he was living for an aeon longer. He added that he himself had that power. But Ananda, slow to understand, did not ask the Buddha to continue to live an aeon longer. Three times the Buddha repeats this to Ananda, and three times Ananda failed to make the request he should have made. The Buddha then dismisses Ananda. Mara approaches, anxious that the Buddha should pass away, that his life-span should be over. Without demur the Buddha replied that he would in three months pass away. Mara could then be happy.

The rest of the Sutta recounts the events of those last three months. When Mara had gone the Buddha explained to Ananda how he had consciously and deliberately consented to his death, and when Ananda begged him three times to live longer, he is reminded that on many occasions in the past he had been told what had been told him that very morning, but he had not made the request that the Buddha's power to prolong his life should be exercized. It was too late now. The Buddha had consented to pass away. He reproved Ananda gravely but gently for not having made this request earlier, at each of those places which remained green and pleasant in his memory—the Vulture's peak at Rajagaha, its Banyan Grove, its Deer Forest, its caves, the Squirrels' Feeding Ground in the Bamboo Grove and many others—all of them spots connected with his life as a wandering teacher, spots where he had reminded Ananda of his power to prolong his life.

The Buddha and Ananda then set out from Vesali on his last journey. As he left the town, the Buddha turned round and gazed on it, saying to Ananda, as he looked back upon it: 'This will be the last time, Ananda, that the Tathagata shall behold Vesali.' How the account reminds one of the night when Gotama rode out from his native town. As he then hurried swiftly away from it he had a great desire to look on the sleeping town once more, but the gods, determined that he should be put to no exertion, had the earth turn round, so that he should not have to turn round himself. How similar in its expression of the essential humanity of the Buddha, yet how much simpler and more natural is the sentence which describes his turning to look back upon Vesali. The translator renders it as 'he gazed at Vesali with an elephant look' —'an elephant look' because, according to the commentator, a Buddha would have to turn round with his whole body as an elephant does, since the bones in the neck of the Buddha are so firmly fixed. The phrase suggests the great deliberateness and the solemn gravity of the movement, as the Great One who is soon to die turns to look back for the last time on a township which was dear to him.

They journey through various places where the Buddha meets the members of the order and addresses them, and at last they come to Pava, where Chunda invites the Buddha and his followers to a meal in his house. This is his last meal. As he journeyed on after the meal he was attacked by sharp pains, but he bore them without complaint, and decided to go with Ananda to Kusinara in the country of the Mallas.

As his pains increased he went aside from the path and asked Ananda to spread out his robe at the foot of a tree where he would rest. Here he was given some water from the stream, and soon after a young Mallian, Pukkusa, conversed with him, and was instructed. With the last remnants of his physical strength the Buddha set out with Ananda for the Sal-tree grove at Kusinara. When he reached it, accompanied by a large number of monks, he asked Ananda to spread his robe over the slab of stone which lay between the twin Sal trees, for he wished to rest there. With the curiously shaped circular flowers of these great trees blooming out of season above him, and heavenly Mandarava flowers dropping out of the skies to the strains of celestial music, the last hours of the Buddha's life ran out their course. Beautiful as the flowers were, and miraculously as they dropped out of reverance for the successor of the Buddhas of old, to Gotama the Buddha neither in the fragrance of the flowers, nor in the accompaniment of the heavenly music was true reverence done him, but in his followers' fulfilment of the precepts he had taught.

Two incidents marked that memorable full-moon night of the month of Vesak when the Buddha passed away—his consideration for the smith Chunda at whose house he had partaken of his last meal, and Ananda's grief at the passing away of his master. The Buddha was anxious that the smith should not be blamed, and that he should not feel remorse that the meal he had prepared for the Buddha had been the cause of his death. He insisted that the food which had been given him by Chunda the smith should bring him not grief, but the consciousness of having laid up for himself good *karma*. Here again is to be noted the depth of the Buddha's feeling for mankind. Among the last things which crossed his mind as he lay dying was the likelihood of the reproach that might be cast at the humble smith who had hospitably entertained him.

The second incident relates of Ananda's grief. Soon after the Buddha had left directions about his cremation, and the cairn which should be erected over his remains, Ananda, unable to bear the thought of the Buddha's approaching death, went out, and leaning his head 'against the lintel of the vihara' wept bitterly. The Buddha called for him, and on being told that Ananda was outside weeping at the thought of his passing away, he asked Ananda to be seated beside him, and tells him to be neither troubled nor to weep, for it is in the nature of all things to be impermanent. Even from those near and dear to us we must one day be parted. And then the Buddha goes on to recall the love and kindness which had bound him to his faithful attendant for many years. He praises Ananda for his devotion, but urges him to persevere in his efforts until he is free from craving, and reaches that stage which the Buddha has reached.

This episode with its delicacy of sentiment and its deep feeling both for human weakness and the need for human striving to transcend that weakness, is typical of the character of the man whose sayings and life are given us in the Suttas. The Buddha does not reproach Ananda for his tears, he knows and accepts their human reason, and he values them as evidence of the unvarying affection which Ananda has shown him. Yet there is something more, something of more importance even than such human love which is to the Buddha 'beyond all measure'. The necessity to strive to pass beyond these attachments; to know them, to value them, and yet to know that which was of greater value—this was the significance of the way of life which the Buddha had both preached and lived. The Buddha recognized the depth and quality of Ananda's attachment to him, but his insight into life had shown him that of far greater value was the knowledge that at the root of all human achievements and all the wonder of human happiness and love lay suffering, and that it was therefore man's duty to strive earnestly in the way that led to the cessation of suffering.

The Buddha's last words were: 'Behold now bhikkhus I exhort you saying: "Decay is inherent in all component things. Work out your salvation with diligence." '[1] His whole life with its pattern of the renunciation of all that a man might hold most dear, and the strenuousness with which he had striven to understand, and having understood, to teach, illustrated the relevance of those last words.

So the Buddha passed away, and in that passing away attained the state of Nirvana.[2] His remains were ceremonially cremated by the Mallas of Kusinara, and the bones which remained were divided among the kings and tribesmen who claimed a share in these relics which were sacred to them. Over them were built the cairns or *stupas* which were the characteristic architectural monuments of the Buddhist world, and which still recall the passing away of the great teacher since they too enshrine relics sacred to the believer.

[1] D. II, 156.

[2] E. J. Thomas, *India Antiqua*, Leyden, 1947, points out that *parinirvana* does not mean 'final nirvana or nirvana attained at death with the complete dispersal of the skandhas (aggregates)', although there is a distinction made between 'nirvana at enlightenment' and 'nirvana at death'. 'The real distinction between nirvana and parinirvana,' he writes, 'is a grammatical one,' where 'pari' grammatically distinguishes completed action from action in process.

CHAPTER THREE

THE TEACHING

There is a tradition that immediately after the death of the Buddha a council of his disciples defined all his discourses which Ananda recited as being the authentic teaching. But they were not written down for four hundred years. The teaching developed variously in various parts of the East, and schools once powerful have passed away leaving no adherents. What the teaching was taken to mean, how it developed, and how it came to be regarded by men have been considered in enquiries such as only scholars and philosophers could make.

Several generations of *bhikkhus* and lay persons have given to the teaching of the Buddha its well-known character of lore moulded through its process of oral transmission by all those who passed it on. Its convoluted and balanced repetitions, its pattern of question and counter-question, its transparent mnemonic schemata, its lists, verses and numbers are the pressure and form of this process. The Four Noble Truths, the Five Components, the Six Sixes, the Eightfold Noble Path, the Ten Fetters—they are the moulds into which discourse was poured for the benefit of hearer and reciter. So they were stored, and so they were conveniently retailed.

The world as the Buddha saw it in his discourses was in a continual flux, and characterized by transitoriness and impermanence, with world systems coming into being and passing away. It was the world of *Samsara*. In the Ratthapala Sutta there are four qualities attributed to the world, and each of them is given an interpretation: The world is in continual flux and change; the world is no protector or preserver; the world owns nothing, we must leave everything behind; the world lacks and hankers, being enslaved to craving (*tanha*).[1] Man in this world of impermanence was himself merely a grouping together of five components (*skandhas* or *khandhas*), transiently united: Matter, Sensations, Perceptions, Mental Formations and Consciousness. Connected with all of these is craving or grasping. Yet the Buddha did not term this grouping of components as *individuum* or an entity, nor did he attribute to it, or identify it with, a soul or an eternal principle. As craving

[1] M. II, 35.

49

was inherent in these components, the human being was committed to an endless chain of rebirths, the group of components constantly changing in the life-term of one person as his life waxed or waned, death being a moment in the process which continues. This continuous kaleidoscopic movement was no creation of a God. No personal creator brought it into being. The Buddha's teaching required no such hypothesis. There were gods, the gods of those times whom he accepted, but these gods themselves were involved in the process of change, they were themselves subject to rebirth.

This notion of rebirths was, like contemporary notions of the gods, taken by the Buddha from the sacrificial religion of his times, but he humanized and moralized its determining dynamism by making *Karma*, the cause of the effect and kind of rebirth, not a blind necessity, but itself the effect of the volition of the sentient being. *Karma* was not the mathematical result of a sum in addition and subtraction of various kinds of actions, it was the result of the human being's moral choice. This marks the difference between the Buddha's valuation of *Karma* and earlier accounts of it. The endless chain of rebirths and *Karma* were things to which the gods had to submit.

The Buddha's quest was after an understanding of how man might escape from what was incidental to all this. He investigated the causes and not the symptoms, and his teaching was both a philosophy and an ethical code of conduct. As *Karma* was a moral law, the Buddha recommended a course of moral action, which would help a man to pass beyond a process which committed him to being born again into a world of impermanence. To put an end to *Karma* was not enough. The Buddha probed into the causes of *Karma*, and formulated his own law of causation.

It is the logical formulation of this law which is distinctive in Buddhism. The Buddha himself said that the disciple who understood its successive stages could rightly be said to have mastered it. He even went further and said: 'He who sees the Chain of Causation sees the Dhamma, and he who sees the Dhamma sees the Chain of Causation.'[1] 'Take, Ananda, an Almsman who knows the following: If this is so, then that comes about; if this is not, then that does not come about; when *this* is laid to rest, then *that* passes to rest. Factors are conditioned by ignorance, consciousness by the factors, Name-and-Form by consciousness, organs of sense by Name-and-Form, contact by sense-organs, craving by feelings, attachment by craving, existence by attachment, birth by existence, and by birth come old age and death, with sorrow and lamentation, pain, suffering and tribulation. And this is how all that makes up Ill is laid to rest: by the cessation of ignorance with no trace of passion left behind the factors cease, by the cessation of factors consciousness ceases, by the cessation of consciousness Name-and-Form ceases, by the cessation of

[1] Chalmers, *Further Dialogues of the Buddha*, p. 138.

Name-and-Form the organs of sense cease, by the cessation of the organs of sense contact ceases, by the cessation of contact feelings cease, by the cessation of feelings craving ceases, by the cessation of craving attachment ceases, by the cessation of attachment existence ceases, by the cessation of existence birth ceases, by the cessation of birth old-age and death cease, and therewith disappear sorrow and lamentation, pain, suffering, and tribulation, so that all that makes up Ill is laid to rest. At this point an Almsman can rightly be described as having mastered the Chain of Causation. . . . Now the Master has laid it down that whoso sees the Chain of Causation sees the Doctrine, and whoso sees the Doctrine sees the Chain of Causation. It is the Chain of Causation which entails all that makes up these Five Attachments. The Origin of Ill is the yearning for and the resort to these Five, the appetite for them, and the cleaving to them. And the cessation of Ill is the avoidance and the rejection of all such yearnings and appetites.'[1]

In the passage in the Ariyapariyesana Sutta, already referred to in the last chapter, one sees how the Buddha describes the successful issue of his quest as the moment of insight into the condition of life in the world. He himself differs only in degree perhaps from the rest of mankind, he is himself a party to the fate man was born for—the endless chain of rebirths, but he strives to know and is enlightened: 'Bhikkhus, being myself subject to rebirth . . . decay . . . disease . . . death . . . sorrow . . . defilement . . . and seeing the evil consequences (of all this), I searched for the perfect peace of Nibbana in which there is neither birth . . . nor decay . . . nor disease . . . nor death . . . nor sorrow . . . nor defilement . . . and won . . . (it). And there arose in me the realization and the insight that now my release was assured, that this was my final existence, and (for me) there was no more rebirth.'[2]

In the dramatic repetition of all the suffering and sorrow life and rebirth are identified with, and the assurance that release is possible to the man who strives to realize and understand this, is the kernel of the Buddha's teaching. He claimed nothing more than the status of a teacher who had seen, understood and preached. He was no god, and the state of enlightenment he had arrived at was the end of a path which others, too, could, and did take. As all the attributes of life in this world are stressed in repetition, so it is necessary to see the importance of the keywords 'realization' and 'insight'. The perfect peace of Nirvana is the visionary state, both the hard-won moment of intellectual clarity, and the extraordinary transcendental state of well-being and serenity, when a man knows that he is free from the necessity of being born into the world again. As we shall see, the Buddha refused to indulge in

[1] *Ibid.* Bhikkhu W. Rahula points out to me the unsatisfactory nature of this translation. The word 'nirodha' which Chalmers translates as 'laid to rest' should be rendered as 'cessation'.

[2] M. I, p. 166.

speculation about the nature of this state. But throughout his life as teacher he was proclaiming a knowledge which would assure for others the same mode of release which he had achieved.

The simplest statement of this is in the very first sermon he preached, which might be looked upon as a manual of instruction for the beginner. This, the sermon called the *Dhammacakkapavattana*—the turning of the Wheel of the Law —is, in spite of the profundity of the insight the Buddha attained and every-thing later criticism has read into it, admirably clear in its outlines. The way recommended is neither this nor that—neither the path of pleasure, nor that of austerity—but the Middle Way. It brings the Wayfarer to enlightenment. And what is this Middle Way but the Noble Eightfold Path, the fourth of the Four Noble Truths which are the Truths of Suffering; the arising of Suffering; the cessation of Suffering; and the Way which leads to cessation of Suffering.

To claim that this alone is the *Dhamma* is to be foolish. But these were the words attributed to the Buddha in his first and simplest exposition of the *Dhamma*. The Four Noble Truths are wisdom. In the fourth of them the seeker after truth has to proceed on the way of Right View, Right Aims, Right Speech, Right Action, Right Mode of Livelihood, Right Effort, Right Mindfulness and Right Concentration.

In the Buddha's discourses, or in those of the great disciples, one returns again and again to the clear enunciation of what the teaching insisted upon. Throughout the great range of these discourses, from their simplest illustra-tions through their amplitude of reiteration to the subtlety of their dialectical procedure, one is aware of the practical end the Buddha, the expounder of the *Dhamma*, sought. The teaching was addressed to an audience, and in that audience there would be varying levels of intelligence and ability. The Buddha himself discoursed, preached, and argued for the benefit of kings, rival philosophers, sages and also humble herdsmen. He could, and did, adapt his sermon to his auditors, and he never overlooked anything which might inter-fere with their receptivity. There is the eloquent story of the poor man at Alari in the *Dhammapadatthakatha*, which illustrates his attitude to his dis-course. The Buddha knew through his superhuman power that this poor man possessed the faculties requisite for *arahatship*. The poor man longed to hear the Buddha's teaching, but he lost his ox, and had, before he could go to hear the Buddha preach, to find it. He spent the whole day in the search, and when he at last found his ox, it was so late that he feared he would miss the dis-course. He went off to the assembly straightaway, having eaten nothing at all that day. The Buddha, however, waits for him, and does not begin until he arrives. Seeing the poor man approaching, the Buddha enquired whether there was some food at hand, and asked that the man be given to eat before the discourse began. The *Dhammapadatthakatha* remarks of this: 'We are told that with this single exception there is no other instance on record in the three *Pitakas* of the Tathagata's having in this way enquired about the supply of food.' It is only after the poor man has eaten that the Buddha expounds the *Dhamma*. The *bhikkhus* displeased at what had happened murmured that there had never been a thing like this before—that the Buddha had asked about rice gruel and similar things, and wanted them given to the poor man. Overhearing them, the Buddha replies that he was concerned about these things, for he had come there himself 'thirty yojanas through the wilderness', because he saw the condition for *arahatship* in the poor man who had set out that day oppressed through excessive hunger to wander in the forest in search of his ox. 'I thought to myself,' said the Buddha, 'that suffering through hunger he will not be able to comprehend it if I expound the *Dhamma*. That is why I did this. Bhikkhus, there is no affliction like the affliction of hunger.'[1]

This reflection would not only prove the Buddha's compassionate understanding of the weakness of the flesh, it would show too the orator's proper concern with the effect of his discourse and his audience. As the expounding of the *Dhamma* was clearly intended to afford the practical means of release from the suffering and ills of existence, it had by its very nature to be easily comprehensible and memorable. Buddhism has been variously described—as a philosophical system, an ethical code, a religion with no super-natural sanctions, and a complex psychological investigation into states of supernormal experience. However one regards it now, one notices at numerous stages in the discourses attributed to the Buddha, the urgency with which its practical character is stressed, and the clearness with which its practical effects in the hearer who has had ears to hear, are described. Dogma may be conveyed through language which in its attempt to utter the ineffable can only resort to paradox, but the hard core of any teaching could often be grasped through its use of simile.

There may be in existence a collection of the figures and tropes used by the Buddha. If there is not, it surely is an omission which could rewardingly be remedied. What any such collection is most likely to show is that the figure, as the Buddha used it, always had a forensic character—it proved, with the greater illumination of the illustration taken from the context of ordinary life, a doctrinal truth which it was necessary for the hearer to accept. Necessary, because without it the means by which release from the bonds of suffering which the Buddha's *Dhamma* provided, were scarcely available.

Two such forensic figures portray the Buddha's attitude to the intensely practical nature of his teaching. They are well-known, and if they are repeated here, it is only because they illustrate so lavishly the efficient character

[1] *Dha* III, p. 263.

of Buddhism as its first teacher offered it to the world. The first is the image of the man wounded by a poisoned arrow. It is to be found in the Cula-Malunkya Sutta of the *Majjhima Nikaya*: 'If a man were transfixed by an arrow heavily coated with poison, and his friends and kinsfolk were to get him a leech expert in dealing with arrow-wounds, but the man were to declare he would not have the arrow taken out until he knew whether the archer who had shot him were a Nobleman, or a brahmin or a middle-class man or a peasant—what the archer's name and lineage were—whether he was tall or short or of medium height—whether he was black or dark or fair—what particular village or township or city he hailed from—whether his bow was a long bow or a cross-bow—whether his bow string was made from swallow-wort or bamboo or sinew or hemp or the leaves of Caleotropis gigantea—whether the shaft of the arrow was a wild reed or planted shoot—whether the shaft was feathered with the plumage of a vulture or a heron or a falcon or a peacock or other fowl —whether the gut binding that shaft came from an ox or a buffalo or a hart or a monkey—whether the arrow was a plain arrow or was barbed with horn or iron or a calf's tooth or with an oleander thorn. The man would never get to know all this before death overtook him. And just in the same way if a man were to say he would not follow the higher life under the Lord until the Lord had answered him his pack of questions he would get no answer from the Truthfinder before death overtook him.'[1] The zest with which the Buddha multiplies the number of pointless questions until they reach the hyperbolical proportions of fantastic absurdity is surely an integral part of the success of the figure. By contrast, the simplicity of what has to be done is thrown into greater relief.

Irrelevancies, the fine spinning of questions which ingenuity might essay as compliment to its powers, were at all times rejected by the Buddha. There is, both in his repudiation of certain subjects of speculation and his readiness to accept what might have been concluded about others, the singleness of purpose of the man resolute to deal with the one thing only—helping humanity to work out its own salvation. He refused to allow himself to be exercized with speculations about what he called the unknowable or unde-termined questions. These are referred to in various places in the Canon, the four being:

(*a*) whether the universe is eternal or not
(*b*) whether the universe is finite or not
(*c*) whether the vital principle (jiva) is the same or other than the body
(*d*) whether after death a Tathagata exists or not, whether he exists and does not exist, whether he is neither existent or non-existent.[2]

---

[1] Chalmers, *op. cit.*, p. 305.   [2] D. I, 187, M. I. 431.

To all these questions the Buddha makes the same reply: 'That is a matter on which I have expressed no opinion.' His reasons for this are admirable: 'This question is not calculated to profit, it is not concerned with the *Dhamma*, it does not redound even to the elements of right conduct, not to detachment, not to purification from lusts, nor to quietude, nor to tranquillization of heart, nor to real knowledge, nor to the insight (of the higher stages of the path) nor to Nirvana. Therefore is it that I express no opinion on it.'[1]

Another figure—the parable of the raft—shows plainly that an important test of the good is strictly pragmatic. The parable is sharply pointed with a question which is answered: 'It is like a man, who after travelling a long way finds the floods out, with danger and peril on the hither side, and with security and safety on the further side, but with no ferry or suspension bridge; and to him comes the thought to win his way across the floods to safety from the perils which encompass him by collecting grass and sticks and branches and boughs wherewith to fashion a raft on which to paddle himself safely across with his hands and feet; and to him when he has done all this, and has paddled himself safely across, the thought comes that the raft had been so useful that he would do well to take it along with him, packed on his head or shoulders. Think you he would be doing the right thing with the raft?—No sir—How should he act so as to do right with his raft? Well suppose that when he was safely over, he, recognizing how useful the raft had been, were to deem it well, before going on his way, either to beach it or leave it afloat;—clearly thus he would be doing the right thing with the raft.'[2]

Through this image could be indicated that the great and sole justification of the good—even of the *Dhamma*—was its effective use. The raft which delivered one from peril and conveyed the wayfarer to security had to be judged as efficient aid, and it was to be valued as such.

With the same economy and devotion to the cause of acquainting humanity with the results of his speculations, the Buddha accepted, as we have seen, certain notions about the universe which belonged to his time—notions about the cosmos, about aeons of time, and about the gods, because apparently they were not important enough to matter one way or the other. His teaching did not require the hypothesis of a personal creator god, so he does without it. The Maha Brahma he refers to is one of the many gods of the religion of his time who find a place in what he took over from it. This was, after all, one of the inhabitants of the worlds of the gods, and as they appear in the Buddha's cosmology, he appears too. Why he makes one of his appearances is interesting. When the Buddha achieves enlightenment, this knowledge he might, according to the legend of his life, have withheld from mankind. He is

[1] D. I, 188.   [2] Chalmers, *op. cit.*, pp. 94–95.

therefore entreated by Brahma to reveal his *Dhamma* to men, as there were some who would understand it. The Buddha consents, but even so he casts about in his mind to whom the new teaching should, or could, be imparted. What is to be noted here is the appraisal of the *Dhamma*. Brahma who entreats the Buddha to preach it, and the Buddha who reflects on how best it might be imparted, are concerned with making available to mankind a practical benefit, the value of which both of them understand. However complicated and profound the *Dhamma* might have been in later statement and in commentarial exegesis, it is thought of realistically as a door which opened the way to a specified goal. Both gods and men could benefit from it.

It is true that the Buddha first addresses himself to the five disciples who had originally set out with him in his search for the truth, since they could be expected to follow what might have been too difficult for the generality of men. But soon the *Dhamma* was preached to the mass of men, and as it was offered, it was the communication of knowledge which the speaker is determined that his hearers should apprehend. Other things besides able expository power must have contributed to the appeal of this teaching. More important than this alone must surely have been the person of the teacher, and the compelling example of an ethical system demonstrated by his life. But what is important to stress is that the Buddha was accepted as a teacher in whom the masses had confidence.

What was offered was not dogma which had to be taken on trust, seen by the special eye of faith miraculously implanted in the hearer, but knowledge —as the story of the poor man at Alari illustrates. The uninhibited mind perceiving what was preached accepted it, and the attitude in the satisfied mind of the hearer who was converted is expressed in Pali by the word *pasidati*, which the English translators have rendered by 'faith', colouring with the great Christian virtue a totally different set of emotions in another system. For the Buddhist it is knowledge which leads to the supreme goal of enlightenment, not faith which moves mountains, but understanding which aids in the scaling of mountains of the mind with its cliffs of fall no-man-fathomed. 'The man who heard the Buddha's discourse and accepted it takes delight in its clearness of thought. He is pleased, satisfied, with the attribute of the highest intellectual appreciation which turns into ecstatic delight. This would be a fairer rendering of *pasidati*. There is a recurring passage in the Suttas repeated by the person to whom the Buddha expounded his doctrine, whether he is an adherent of another sect or an educated Brahmin or a layman. It expresses this delight and the enthusiasm for the clearness of the exposition which makes it possible for him to understand the teaching and attain through this understanding that clearness of mind (like clear water or a bright sky) which is the result of calming down after the tension and excitement accompanying the passionate search for truth: "Excellent Gotama, most excellent! It is just as if a man should set upright again what has been cast down or reveal what had been hidden away or tell a man who had gone astray what was his way, or bring a lamp into darkness, so that those with eyes to see might discern things about them—even so, in many a figure has the reverend Gotama made the Doctrine clear.' The hearer is obviously *pleased* with the quality of the logical discourse. This attitude is found not only towards the Buddha himself. Any teacher is treated with the greatest reverence, and the 'fellows in the higher life' appreciate each other's intellectual attainments in the same way. There is no need to import the idea of Faith into this phenomenon.'[1]

There was material at one level of the Buddha's discourse for learned commentators to adorn and schismatics to wrangle over. All its doctrinal difficulties of no-soul, and its mystery of Nirvana, differ in degree from the clarity of its central truths. All levels of the discourse are offered to the intellect, or were offered to those ready to undergo the intellectual discipline of submitting themselves to the rigours of thought. The second, third and fourth categories of the Noble Eightfold Path were borrowed from the Wanderers, but, 'the significant departure is in the first of Gotama's categories—right outlook—deliberately placed in the forefront in order to affirm the sovereignty of mind and thought. Right thinking was the preface and key to everything else in the higher life, and ignorance or lack of understanding, was the root of all evil.'[2]

One of the most learned Indian Buddhologists of recent times, himself a Buddhist, made the following claims for the *Dhamma* of the Buddha. 'The world got a religion without the belief in a personal God, but which fully functioned to create the ideals of character and conduct and to awaken and establish faith in their reality, and also a vigorous missionary religion, which was destined to become a living force in Asiatic and world civilization. A sound system of ethics was built upon psychological foundations, defining and raising the standards of human conduct and heightening the values of human life, efforts and experiences. It gave rise to a system of philosophy, critical in spirit, dialectical in its mode of argument, analytical in its method, synthetic in its purpose, positivistic in its conclusions, mystical in its practice but rational in its structure.'[3] All this, and more too probably was intended for the élite—both the élite of thinkers and the élite of those undervaluing life in such a way as to withdraw from it into the ascetic discipline of the monastery. But there was something else which, as the religion developed, survived on a lower and humbler level, the level at which the very weaknesses of the flesh,

---

[1] Edith Ludowyk Gyomroi, 'A Note on the Interpretation of *Pasidati*', UCR, April 1943.

[2] Chalmers, *Dialogues of the Buddha*, Part IV, p. xxiii.

[3] B. M. Barua, *Buddha's Greatness and Role*, Ceylon, 1944, p. 15.

from which the Buddha was careful to secure the poor man at Alari, could ask for and receive the protective talismans of a world religion. These were extended to the Buddhist after the establishment of the *Sangha* in what is still called the Triple Gem—the three supports of the 'believer'. Their repetition could be regarded as the simplest 'rite' of Buddhism:

> *I take refuge in the* BUDDHA
> *I take refuge in the* Dhamma
> *I take refuge in the* Sangha

Perhaps one can see the change coming in the nature of the attitude expressed towards all three in one of the most moving stories in the commentaries—that of Kisa Gotami.[1] The Buddha faced with the same situation as Christ, when he was met by the widow of Nain at the funeral of her son, or entreated to go to the house of Jairus where his daughter lay dead, performs no miraculous raising from the dead, but tells the grief-stricken Kisa Gotami, who carries her dead child about with her, asking passers-by for some cure for its sickness: 'Go enter the town, and from any house where no man has yet died, from there bring me some white mustard.' She goes from house to house on a fruitless errand until her distraction leaves her, her normal state of mind is restored, and she says to herself: 'So it will be in the whole town. The Master knew this in his compassion and knew it would be for my good.' She went out to the burial ground, and understanding the impermanence of all things, left her child there, and went back to the teacher. He asked her: 'Gotami, did you get the white mustard?' And she replied: 'Accomplished, Lord, is the work of the white mustard. Be you my support.' At this the teacher said:

> *To him whose heart is pleased with sons and cattle*
> *To him death comes just like the mighty flood*
> *That sweeps away the sleeping village.*

As she understood the central truth of Buddhism, the first of the Four Noble Truths, she is already on the way to enlightenment. But it will be noted that in the commentary she is made to say: 'Be you my support.' The heights and profundities of the Buddha's thought might have been out of the range of inferior intellects. For them, as for others in the course of time, the reiteration of the formula of the Triple Gem was both assurance and restorative.

On those who lived as householders in the world of men and affairs, the ethical system laid the duty of practising the four cardinal virtues of Buddhism —universal love towards all living things, compassion, joy, and serenity. At

---

[1] *Thig A.*, p. 75.

the simplest level of all there were the five moral precepts enjoined upon all Buddhists. These were the *Panca silani*: the Buddhist should abstain from taking life, from theft, from adultery, from lying, and from intoxicating drink. For the devotee were added five others, which made up the ten precepts—to eat only at certain prescribed times, to refrain from worldly pleasures, to use neither unguents nor ornaments, not to sleep on a high or decorated bed, not to handle gold or silver.

Sariputta in the Samma-ditthi-Sutta repeats what the Buddha had forbidden as wrong: 'Killing is wrong; theft is wrong; sensuality is wrong; lying is wrong; calumny is wrong; reviling is wrong; chattering is wrong; harmfulness is wrong; and wrong ideas are wrong.'[1] Even here the emphasis falls on the importance of the intellectual process—'Wrong ideas are wrong'.

What can the peasant who toils in the rice-fields of South East Asia know of 'wrong ideas'? What can the teaching mean to those who in those parts of the world where the *Dhamma* spread not long after the Buddha's death still call themselves Buddhists? The honour paid to the visual representation of the teacher—the conventional image in temple—the *cetiya* which enshrines some relic, the priesthood which a man may enter if he will; and the imperfect tendance of the five precepts, almost too fragile to bear successfully through a lifetime. Does the Buddhist who prostrates himself before the statue in the temple worship the Buddha? Are the words he mumbles a prayer? To whom should he pray? The Buddha whose memory and example he reveres attained Nirvana two thousand five hundred years ago. The words repeated now are not an act of prayer, but merely recall some phrases of the sacred text in which the believer has confidence. As he lies stretched out on the floor of the temple, there may be invoked, by the atmosphere and by the conscious mind, some hazy notion of the wished-for state of Nirvana, the incomprehensible condition of ceasing to be involved in the endless chain of birth, and death, and birth again.

[1] Chalmers, *Further Dialogues of the Buddha*, p. 33.

CHAPTER FOUR

THE EMPEROR

Within two hundred years of the Buddha's death the face of the India he had known during the years of his wanderings and his preaching had been completely changed. Indian mercenaries had fought in the wars which finally broke up the great Persian empire; Alexander of Macedon had led his victorious army across Persia to India, and on the plain watered by rivers famous in classical story had defeated an Indian king whom the Greek chroniclers called Porus; the kingdom of Magadha had come into being under an able ruler, Chandragupta; and the successor, in fact if not in theory, to the eastern dominions of Alexander found it more prudent to enter into a treaty with this Sandrokottos (as he was known to the Greeks), than to dispute a claim to one part of the empire with him. Once again, as so often in the past, the permanent process of the meeting of East and West reveals itself. The empire Chandragupta Maurya founded, met on its borders the paramount power of the Western world of the time, and the kingdom of Syria acknowledged the suzerainty of the Mauryan empire over the whole of the north of India.

Chandragupta's empire in a hundred and fifty years went the way of all empires, but the memory of its power and glory and of its great emperor Asoka remained in the consciousness of later generations of Indians as Alexander's did not. It has been stated that the eastern adventure of the latter left no record whatsoever in the later history and literature of India. As far as the Indian continent was concerned it was as if Alexander had never existed. Not that the east had not known or celebrated world conquerors. The term 'universal monarch' *Cakravartin* was, as we have seen, one of the destinies which might have confronted a youth whose birth had been blessed by unusual portents. But somehow the eastern mind—Indian and Chinese—was not fired with the exploits of the young king who became in Western medieval legend a paladin of chivalry, and in Renaissance literature a symbol both of man's aspiring mind and equally of his subjection to the tyranny of death. What could Alexander mean to the east in whose vastness he had been involved as a result of his determination to destroy the empire of the Persians? Faced with the unknown, he turned away, and not long after he died on his way home. He could only be an incident in the career of a successful general to those who opposed him on the field of battle.

How different it was with Asoka, the hero of the Mauryas. Eastern legend would love to concentrate its attention on the remarkable break between the two halves of his career. The transformation of the warrior into the devotee— what a theme for the mythopoeic faculties of both East and West, and how characteristically the East lavished itself upon it. The tidier West would have furbished its dramatic sequence with a moral, the Eastern imagination, seized apparently with the central fact of the moment of enlightenment in the career of the hero, neglects the drama and accentuates the miracle of the two contrasted sides of his nature— his cruelty and his piety, his ruthlessness and his devotion to Buddhist law—so resolutely, that the legendary portrait of the emperor seems, in the oft-quoted words of Kern, that of a person half-monster, half idiot. Jules Bloch reflecting on one of the legendary tales of Asoka, that of Kunala, concludes: 'We may subscribe to Kern's verdict: "If we only know Asoka through Buddhist sources, from North to South, we shall have to conclude from them that he was a ruler of rare insignificance; remarkable only in so far as he was half monster, half idiot. His coreligionists have transmitted from him neither a good deed, nor a noble sentiment, nor a striking utterance." '[1]

It is refreshing therefore to turn from the accumulations of Buddhist legend to the 'words' of the man himself, as they are found in lithic records. Scattered all over the Indian sub-continent they have borne witness, in a sense their author never intended, to a principle of mutability which both East and West, in different ways, have accepted. Much more than this, to those who were able to decipher what they recorded, they inscribe, not what emperor and kings have so often desired to preserve for posterity—a memorial of their pride and greatness—but the resolutions and avowals of an earnest human being, often bewildered, but persistent in his recommendations of right conduct. Besides everything else these records demonstrate the extent of the empire over which his authority ran—from the far north-west to Mysore in the south. His friends and vassals were Greek rulers and the king of the island of Ceylon.

Born about 269 B.C., Asoka was the grandson of Chandragupta, who was assigned the government of Ujjain. On the death of his father Bindusara, he slew his ninety-nine brothers and usurped the royal power. His career followed lines which have by now become almost classically Indian in the imagination of the world—the life of strenuous action, the moment of awareness both of self and of the fruitlessness of all previous action, the years of devo-

---

[1] Jules Bloch, *Les Inscriptions d'Asoka*, Paris, 1950, p. 17.

tion to the new understanding, and the final withdrawal from the world. The same progress could be traced in the careers of Indians in legend and history. One could recognize it in the lives of persons as diverse as Yudishtara, Mahatma Gandhi, and even the Buddha. Jules Bloch points out that the main lines of the emperor's career, as lithic records attest it, would be sufficient to make their author unrivalled among the monarchs of the world. He calls the thirteenth edict which contains his remorse at the death and destruction of the Kalinga war a document which remains unique, in spite of some Tibetan and Chinese analogies apparently turned out in imitation of it.

The *Devanampriya Priyadarsin* of these edicts was identified by Western scholars as the Mauryan emperor Asoka not much longer than a hundred years ago. The first of the honorifics used in the inscriptions is translated as 'dear to the gods' and was used of royalty both in India and in Ceylon. (The king of Ceylon, contemporary with Asoka, was known to the chroniclers as Devanampiya Tissa.) As for the other, Priyadarsin—'he who glances amiably' —it too was a royal title. It is fitting that the emperor in his edicts should have used as titular descriptions of himself, not such grandiloquent blazonings of his supremacy as conqueror as Darius vaunted of himself, but ethical valuations in which he must have delighted. 'At Behistoun,' writes Bloch, 'Darius celebrates his own glory, his conquests and his rigorous rule at the top of a cliff, almost beyond the reach of the human eye. Asoka, who imitates him, addresses his people directly or through the intermediary of his officials; he seeks to help them to their salvation and boasts of setting them an example; further, his inscriptions as a general rule are in frequented places and within view.'[1]

The thirteenth rock edict at Kalsi records the first stage in the spiritual quest of Asoka. It is inscribed on a boulder of quartz on the western bank of the river Yamuna, and as it was 'first found by Mr Forrest early in 1860, the letters of the inscription were hardly visible, the whole surface being encrusted with the dark moss of ages; but on removing this black film, the surface becomes nearly as white as marble'.[2]

'When King Devanampriya Priyadarsin had been annointed eight years, (the country of) the Kalingyas was conquered by (him).

'One hundred and fifty thousand in number were the men who were deported thence, one hundred thousand in number were those who were slain there, and many times as many those who died.

'After that, now that (the country of) the Kalingyas has been taken, Devanampriya (is devoted) to a zealous study of morality, and to the instruction (of people) in morality.

'This is the repentance of Devanampriya on account of his conquest of (the country of) the Kalingyas.

[1] *Ibid.*, p. 43.   [2] Cunningham, *Inscriptions of Asoka*, p. 12 ff.

'For this is considered very painful and deplorable by Devanampriya, that, while one is conquering an unconquered (country), slaughter, death and deportation of people (are taking place there).

'But the following is considered even more deplorable than this by Devanampriya.

'(To) the Brahmanas or Sramanas, or other sects or householders, who are living there, (and) among whom the following are practised: obedience to those who receive high pay, obedience to mother and father, obedience to elders, proper courtesy to friends, acquaintances, companions, and relatives, to slaves and servants, (and) firm devotion—to these men then happen injury or slaughter or deportation of their beloved ones.

'Or if there are then incurring misfortune the friends, acquaintances, companions, and relatives of those whose affection (for this latter) is undiminished, although they are (themselves) well provided for, this (misfortune) as well becomes an injury to those (persons) themselves.

'This is shared by all men and is considered deplorable by Devanampriya.

'There is no country where these (two) classes (viz) the Brahmanas and the Sramanas, do not exist, except among the Yonas; and there is no (place) in any country where men are not indeed attached to some sect.

'Therefore even the hundredth part of the thousandth part of all those people who were slain, who died, and who were deported at that time when (the country of) the Kalingyas was taken, (would) now be considered very deplorable by Devanampriya.

'. . . desires towards all being . . . self-control, impartiality, (and) kindness.

· 'But this . . . by Devanampriya, viz. the conquest by morality.

'And this (conquest) has been won repeatedly by Devanampriya both (here) and among all (his) borderers, even as far as at (the distance of) six hundred *yojanas,* where the Yona king named Antiyoga (is ruling), and beyond this Antiyoga, (where) four—4—kings (are ruling) (viz. the king) named Tula-maya, (the king) named Antekina, (the king) named Maka, (and the king) named Alikyashudaka, (and) likewise towards the south, (where) the Cholas and Pandyas (are ruling), as far as Tamrapani.

'Likewise here in the king's territory, among the Yonas and Kambojas, among the Nabhakas and Nabhapanktis, among the Bhojas and Pitinikyas, among the Andhras and Palades,—everywhere (people) are conforming to Devanampriya's instructions in morality.

'Even those to whom the envoys of Devanampriya do not go, having heard of the duties of morality, the ordinances, (and) the instructions in morality of Devanampriya, are conforming to morality and will conform to (it).

'This conquest, which has been won by this everywhere, causes the feeling of satisfaction.

'Firm becomes this satisfaction, (viz) the satisfaction at the conquest by morality.

'But this satisfaction is indeed of little (consequence).

'Devanampriya thinks that only the fruits in the other (world) are of great (value).

'And for the following purpose has this rescript on morality been written, (viz) in order that the sons (and) grandsons (who) may be (born) to me, should not think that a fresh conquest ought to be made; (that), if a conquest does please them, they should take pleasure in mercy and light punishments; and (that) they should regard the conquest by morality as the only (true) conquest.

'This (conquest bears fruit) in this world (and) in the other world.

'And let all (their) pleasure be the pleasure in exertion.

'For this (bears fruit) in this world (and) in the other world.'[1]

Could one not, extracting from this edict Asoka's objections to war, regard this as a situation to which later literature of Hinduism provides a parallel? Are not these the objections of Arjuna to fighting against his kinsmen? But as history (or even legend), with the characteristic quality of the by-product of human institutions, never quite reproduces the same situation in the course of its infinite vagaries, so there is to be noted, if we compare the experiences of Asoka and of Arjuna, a world of difference. Arjuna, appalled at the prospect of the destruction of family and kinsfolk, proceeds to the battle only when the god had overcome his reluctance, and imparted to him the validity of a philosophical distinction. Asoka, at the conclusion of a successful war, appalled by its fruits of slavery and slaughter, remembering the words not of a god but a teacher, turns back upon all warfare because he is convinced of the superiority of another way of life. The morality, or the law, or the teaching, however the key-word Dharma (Dhamma) is rendered, as the emperor Asoka offered it, was based upon a simple rule of conduct.[2] Whatever Krishna may have meant on the plains of Kurukshetra, the simple difference between the course he recommended and the resolution of Asoka is clear. The latter, as Asoka derived it from the teacher of his Dhamma has continued to remain one of the distinctive strands of Buddhistic ethical teaching. The law Asoka invoked is the Dhamma the Buddha had preached in the Magadhan kingdom two centuries previously.

The tolerance of all other sects and beliefs the emperor recommended on various occasions to his subjects was no specific personal trait on Asoka's part,

---

[1] E. Hultzsch, Inscriptions of Asoka, Oxford 1925, pp. 47–49.

[2] Bloch, op. cit., p. 31 notes of the word dhamma: 'mot traduit par "Loi", entendant par ce mot à la fois (loi) sans implication dominante juridique, et (religion) sans implication de dogme et de culte (ordre) qui correspond bien à la notion fondamentale hérédetaire manque pour nous de résonance religieuse: (moralité) qu'on a également employé, souffre du même defaut.'

Mihintale: Ruined stupa on the hill

7.

Left:
Anuradhapura:
Naga Guard-
stone

Right:
Anuradhapura:
Guardstone with
Naga King—see
P. 96

8.
Above: Mihintale:
Nagapokuna. The
carving of the five-
hooded snake—see
p. 99

Right: Anuradhapura:
Detail of moonstone—
see p. 115

9.
Anuradhapura:
Jetavana Stupa—
see p. 114

Anuradhapura: Royal Baths below the Tisa Vava, with bas-relief of elephants—see p. 114

Anuradhapura: Detail of bas-relief above—see p. 115

11. Anuradhapura: Sedent Buddha on the present-day Outer Circular Road—see p. 117

it belonged to the common ethical tradition of both Hinduism and Buddhism, and has certainly survived as a portion of the *Dhamma* known as Buddhism in the course of its history. It is known from the inscriptions that the emperor showed favour to the Ajivakas, to the Jains, and to various other believers, in the way in which later kings, in both Ceylon and India, were known to have behaved.

Hultzsch points out that, 'epigraphical and literary records show that Hindu kings considered it their duty to build temples and to make grants to other gods and denominations than their own. The same tolerance was practised by Asoka. As a pious Hindu he acknowledged the debt (rina) which every king owes to his subjects in return for the revenue (shadbaga) levied from them, and which consists in offering them protection (palana).'[1] However he might have been denominated by his subjects—whether he was a Buddhist or a Hindu (alternatives which scarcely could have been posed in this way in his time)—Asoka's Twelfth Rock edict at Girnar is replete with a tolerance which has long been associated with the tenets and practice of Buddhism. In this edict, and elsewhere too, Asoka lays down the excellence of wise tolerance, and refers to his institutions of state officials whose duties were the propagation of 'morality':

'King Devanampriya Priyadarsin is honouring all sects: both ascetics and householders; both with gifts and with honours of various kinds he is honouring them.

'But Devanampriya does not value either gifts or honours so (highly) as (this), (viz.) that a promotion of the essentials of all sects should take place.

'But a promotion of the essentials (is possible) in many ways.

'But its root is this, viz. guarding (one's) speech, (i.e.) that neither praising one's own sect nor blaming other sects should take place on improper occasions, or (that) it should be moderate in every case.

'But other sects ought to be duly honoured in every case.

'If one is acting thus, he is both promoting his own sect and benefitting other sects.

'If one is acting otherwise than thus, he is both hurting his own sect and wronging other sects as well.

'For whosoever praises his own sect or blames other sects,—all (this) out of devotion to his own sect, (i.e.) with the view of glorifying his own sect,—if he is acting thus, he rather injures his own sect very severely.

Therefore concord alone is meritorious, (i.e.) that they should both hear and obey other's morals.

'For this is the desire of Devanampriya, (viz.) that all sects should be full of learning, and should be pure in doctrine.

[1] E. Hultzsch, *op. cit.* p. xlviii.

c

'And those who are attached to their respective (sects) ought to be spoken to (as follows).

'Devanampriya does not value either gifts or honours so (highly) as (this), (viz.) that a promotion of the essentials of all sects should take place.

'And many (officers) are occupied for this purpose (viz.) the *Mahamatras* of morality, the *Mahamatras* controlling women, the inspectors of cowpens, and other classes (of officials).

'And this is the fruit of it, (viz.) that both the promotion of one's own sect takes place, and the glorification of morality.'[1]

The frequency of these edicts may be explained by the wide extent of territory over which they had to be promulgated. Their tone does seem to indicate that the way was difficult. The law, whether it was only *ahimsa* and tolerance, or even the much simpler and smaller matter of abstention from the sacrifice of animals, was not easy of fulfilment. State institutions, like those of 'overseers of morality' (*Mahamatras*) may have helped, but even in his own imperial household Asoka felt that he had fallen far short of his ideal. The First Rock edict at Shahbazgarhi records the frank confession of the man striving to work a change among his subjects, and a trifle dashed at the recalcitrance of things to subdue themselves to the ideal:

'This rescript on morality has been caused to be written by King Devanampriya.

'Here no living being must be killed and sacrificed.

'And also no festival meetings must be held.

'For King Devanampriya Priyadarsin sees much evil in festival meetings.

'But there are also some festival meetings which are considered meritorious by King Devanampriya Priyardarsin.

'Formerly in the kitchen of King Devanampriya Priyadarsin many hundred thousands of animals were killed daily for the sake of curry.

'But now when this rescript on morality is written, then only three animals are being killed (daily), (viz.) two—2—peacocks (and) one deer, (but) even this deer not regularly.'[2]

Before his death Asoka visited two of the major sites associated with the life of the Buddha: Buddha Gaya where the Buddha attained enlightenment, and Lumbini where he was born; and according to the Ceylon tradition he became a Buddhist lay worshipper (an *upasaka*).

His grandfather who had founded the empire was a man of whom the legends had related such wonders as clearly marked him out to be the great ruler of a state. The empire he left, his grandson, also a great warrior, elected to rule differently after his 'conversion'. Within fifty years of Asoka's death it passed out of the hands of his dynasty and a new line ruled over his

[1] *Ibid.*, p. 21 ff.   [2] *Ibid.*, p. 51.

domains. Whether or not the empire crumbled because of the new teaching Asoka enjoined on his subjects, it is fitting that it should not have remained with its upholders, for the 'law' Asoka devoted himself to was itself unconcerned with the conquest of kingdoms and the maintenance of power. It had its roots in the conquest of oneself, the right understanding of how that conquest was to be achieved, and in the acceptance of the basic truth that all things were transitory.

Hsuan Tsang, who visited India eight hundred years after the time of Asoka, tells a story of the Buddhist sovereign Harsha, which illustrates that king's acceptance of this truth. The king saw the tower of the *sangharama* he had built in flames, but at his prayer the flames were extinguished. Looking on the ruined building he asked the assembled princes what they thought of the strange catastrophe which had destroyed the crowning work of his religious life. Unable to do more than to lament the destruction of the work on which the king had lavished so much zeal, a work which they confidently hoped would be handed down to posterity, the princes throw themselves at the feet of the king. But he, better grounded in the law than they, tells them: 'By this, at least, we see the truth of what Buddha said; the heretics and others insist on the permanency of things, but our great teacher's doctrine is that all things are impermanent. As for me, my work of charity was finished, according to my purpose; and this destructive calamity (change) does but strengthen my knowledge of the truth of the Tathagata's doctrine. This is a great happiness (good fortune), and not a subject for lamentation.'[1]

The law Asoka wished his subjects to be governed by was that form of Buddhism handed down orally as the practical wisdom of a teacher, whose precepts the emperor accepted as a sufficient guide as to how life could be lived. It could be, in the form in which it appeared at his time, neither an articulate philosophical system, nor the world religion it was later to become as a result of the impetus Asoka himself gave it. At this stage—to be sure one is considering the evidence of some few edicts and not the available teaching—what was stressed was not the doctrinal character which distinguished Buddhism then, and even more strongly at a slightly later date, and continues still to differentiate it from other religions. In the Bhabru edict certainly Asoka expresses his veneration and his faith in the Buddha, the *Dhamma,* and the *Sangha,* and he goes on to recommend certain texts to the attention of the priest, the nun, and the lay disciple of both sexes:

'The Magadha king, Priyadarsin, having saluted the Sangha, hopes they are both well and comfortable.

'It is known to you, Sirs, how great is my reverence and faith in the Buddha, the Dhamma (and) the Sangha.

[1] S. Beal, *Buddhist Records of the Western World,* London, n.d. Vol. I, p. 220.

'Whatsoever, Sirs, has been spoken by the Blessed Buddha, all that is quite well spoken.

'But, Sirs, what would indeed appear to me (to be referred to by the words of Scripture): "thus the true Dhamma will be of long duration" that I feel bound to declare.

'The following expositions of the Dhamma, Sirs, viz., (1) the *Vinaya-samukasa*, (2) the *Aliya-vasas*, (3) the *Anagata-Bayas*, (4) the *Muni-gathas*, (5) the *Moneya-sutta*, (6) the *Upatisa-pasina* and (7) the *Laghulovada* which was spoken by the Blessed Buddha concerning falsehood—I desire, Sirs, that many groups of monks and (many) nuns may repeatedly listen to these expositions of the *Dhamma,* and may reflect on them.

'In the same way both laymen and laywomen (should act).

'For the following (purpose), Sirs, am I causing this to be written, (viz.) in order that they may know my intention.'[1]

But Hultzsch notes that the inscriptions make no mention of Nirvana, and concludes that in this one important point 'Asoka's inscriptions differ from, and reflect an earlier stage in the development of Buddhist theology or metaphysics than, the *Dhammapada*: they do not yet know anything of the doctrine of Nirvana, but presuppose the general Hindu belief that the rewards of the practice of Dharma are happiness in this world and merit in the other world.'[2]

What is of significance is not what Asoka believed in, the exact dimensions and extent of his conceptions, but what he, as the ruler of a state, attempted to do. Could one find here in embryo the conception of the idea of a Buddhist king and the Buddhist state? Could one differentiate such an idea, and isolate it from what was currently believed about state and king? One can only turn to the famed Buddhist kings of Indian history to decide.

The kings the Buddha knew—Bimbisara, his son Ajatasattu—were patrons, friends, and even champions of the *Dhamma,* but this interest did not apparently extend to any specific difference in the way in which they ruled the state. Nor was Pasenadi very different from these two. Nearly two hundred years after Asoka, the Scyth Kaniska, a doughty warrior who accepted Buddhism, was, even as a defender of the faith, somewhat eclectic in his own beliefs. Those of his activities which receive great stress in later Mahayanist literature are his sallies against heretical doctrine on behalf of an equally uncertain orthodoxy. Both Fa-Hsien and Hsuan Tsang celebrated him as a great builder of *sangharamas.* They repeat, with varying details, the same legendary prophecy about him, and the temple he built on the spot where he was told of it. Fa-Hsien tells of how the Buddha, while he was travelling in former times with his disciples in the country of Purushapura (Peshawar), told Ananda that after his death a king of the country called Ki-ni-kia (Kanika or Kaniska)

---

[1] Hultzsch, *op. cit.*   [2] Hultzsch, *op. cit.*, p. liii.

would raise a *stupa* on that particular spot. Centuries after the event Kaniska was going round on a tour, and Sakra, king of the devas, wishing to put this into the mind of the king, took the form of a little shepherd boy engaged in building a tower by the roadside. The king passed by and asked the boy what he was doing. 'Making a Buddha-tower' he replied. The king was pleased with the boy's devotion, and proceeded to have built over the boy's tower 'another adorned with all precious substances'. Of all *stupas* and temples seen by travellers, says Fa-Hsien, 'none can compare with this for beauty of form and strength. Tradition says this is the highest of the towers in Jambudvipa (India). When the king had completed his tower, the little tower forthwith came out from the side on the south of the great tower more than three feet high.'[1]

Later legends speak of both Asoka and Kaniska as great builders of *stupas*. Of Harsha we know more. Hsuan Tsang who met him and resided at his court, gives a very sympathetic picture of a man who, from all accounts, must have possessed amazing energies and versatility. His interests ranged from amateur dramatics to philosophy and the administration of a large state. The manner of his selection as king, on the death of his elder brother, as Hsuan Tsang relates it, contains a great deal of what one would be inclined to accept as typical of the Buddhist Monarch. The chief minister Po-ni (the poet Bana) advises the assembly of ministers to invite the dead king's younger brother to assume the royal authority. 'The destiny of the nation is to be fixed today. The old king's son is dead: the brother of the prince, however, is humane and affectionate, and his disposition, heaven-conferred, is dutiful and obedient. Because he is strongly attached to his family the people will trust in him. I propose that he assume the royal authority: let each one give his opinion on this matter, whatever he thinks.' They agree and the prince is invited to become king.

The prince replies: 'The government of a country is a responsible office and ever attended with difficulties. The duties of a prince require previous consideration. As for myself, I am indeed of small eminence; but as my father and brother are no more, to reject the heritage of the crown, that can bring no benefit to the people. I must attend to the opinion of the world and forget my own insufficiency. Now, therefore, on the banks of the Ganges there is a statue of Avalokitesvara Bodhisatva which has evinced many spiritual wonders. I will go to it and ask advice.'

The case is put to the statue and the *Bodhisatta* tells the prince: 'In your former existence you lived in this forest as a hermit (a forest mendicant), and by your earnest diligence and unremitting attention you inherited a power of religious merit which resulted in your birth as a king's son. The king of the

[1] Beal, *op. cit.*, p. xxxii.

country, Karnasuvarna, has overturned the law of Buddha. Now when you succeed to the royal estate, you should in the same proportion exercise towards it the utmost love and pity. If you give your mind to compassionate the condition of the distressed and to cherish them, then before long you shall rule over the Five Indies. . . .'[1]

Fortified, the prince assumes the royal office, and after he has destroyed his enemies fulfils in his career all the demands which allegory might have made on any monarch. In Hsuan Tsang's eulogy of his patron are the clear marks of the mould in which the qualities of the ideal king had been cast in Brahmin tract and exegesis. Harsha possesses the virtues that statesmen and poets demanded of the ideal king: he is a successful warrior; he punishes his enemies; after his 'righteous' wars are over he is foremost in the arts of peace; he is temperate and religious; a great builder of temples, and a patron of the priests; he is defender of the faith; like any good Erastian he exercises his kingly right to control the priesthood; he governs his empire himself; he is tolerant of other religions and sects, and, like scores of other monarchs both Eastern and Western, proceeds against their adherents only when religious beliefs threaten the political *status quo*: at all times he is ready to deal graciously with his subjects.

But it may be objected that all this relates to a period long after the great Asoka, and that the eight hundred years which elapsed since the Asoka edicts were graven on pillar and rock altered out of recognition what he said. Could it be that one should find in such late adulatory accounts of a monarch something of what might be implied in Asoka's rescripts on such subjects as the Buddhist king and the Buddhist state? It may not be sufficient to aver that Asoka never intended to formulate any notions of Buddhist polity, and to state that his notions on these subjects could not have differed from the commonplaces of his time on the role of the king in the state.

We might turn to his own times then. He sent his son, or his nephew, Mahinda, on a spiritual mission to a country whose king had, in accordance with Asoka's wishes, been consecrated a second time. This second coronation of the king of Ceylon, Devanampiya Tissa, was perhaps 'a gesture both of intimate friendship as well as an admission of Asoka's supremacy and influence over Ceylon'.[2] In return for the costly treasures sent him by Devanampiya Tissa, Asoka sent the king of Ceylon 'all that was needful for consecrating a king, marvellous in splendour', and also the special gift of the true doctrine. Of the two sorts of treasure the rarer is the second. The Pali poet's account of it has to be read: 'He (Asoka) took counsel with his ministers considering (what should be sent as) a return-gift; and he took a fan, a diadem, a sword, a parasol, shoes, a turban, ear-ornaments, chains, a pitcher, yellow sandalwood,

---

[1] *Ibid.*, Vol. I, p. 212.
[2] Bhikkhu W. Rahula, *History of Buddhism in Ceylon*, Colombo 1956, p. 33.

a set of garments that had no need of cleansing, a costly napkin, unguent brought by the nagas, red-coloured earth, water from the lake Anotatta and also water from the Ganges, a (spiral) shell winding in auspicious wise, a maiden in the flower of her youth, utensils as golden platters, a costly litter, yellow and emblic myrobalans and precious ambrosial healing herbs, sixty times one hundred waggon loads of mountain-rice brought thither by parrots, nay, all that was needful for consecrating a king, marvellous in splendour; and sending these (things) in due time as a gift to his friend the lord of men sent envoys also with the gift of the true doctrine, saying: "I have taken refuge in the Buddha, his Doctrine and his Order, I have declared myself a lay-disciple in the religion of the Sakya son; seek then even thou, O best of men converting they mind with believing heart refuge in these best of gems!" '[1]

The two things are thus seen to be one—the consecration of the king and his establishment in the 'true doctrine'. When Mahinda goes to Ceylon, he sets out to perform a religious task which has important political implications. In the island whose king, according to the story, 'annointed' in accordance with the wishes of Asoka, had been recommended to accept the gift of the *Dhamma*, the conversion of king and people to Buddhism and the establishment of the *sangha* were now to take place. Buddhism was probably known in Ceylon already, but the Pali chronicle in choosing to identify the official establishment of Buddhism in the country with the mission of Mahinda, stakes a claim for the special character of the island as a Buddhist realm. To poets and to the ordinary man it was *Dhammadipa*—the island of the *Dhamma*.

If the distinctive features of a Buddhist kingdom then are to be sought anywhere, surely they are more likely to be discovered in Ceylon, an island cut off (if one wished to exaggerate the obvious geographical distinction) from the subcontinent in the throes of continual military alarms and excursions, and among a people at all times made conscious and mindful of their peculiar heritage.

[1] *Mbv.* p. 79 ff.

CHAPTER FIVE

THE ISLAND

Ceylon in the middle of the third century before Christ when Buddhism, in the official record, was first preached in the island by Mahinda—what was this island like, the island to which Asoka's son miraculously travelled? There are Pali chronicles compiled long after the event, nearly eight hundred years after, which must have relied upon local traditions and stories for their material; in the absence of any other written material of greater reliability what they chose to set down has to be weighed as evidence. For the rest studies yet to be completed must reveal as much as could literally be scraped together of ancient Ceylon.[1] Out of the labours of archaeologists, ethnologists, folklorists, historians and countless other savants is still to be reconstructed a picture of the past, which will fit in with the impressions one derives from later chronicle and poetic reference.

The older literature of both India and Ceylon conjures up an island filled with beings of a supernatural character—*Yakkhas* and *Nagas*—regarded as mostly malevolent. We have already seen how the Buddha on one of his legendary visits to the island struck terror into their ranks and banished them to the central mountainous region. These were the aboriginal inhabitants of the island whom Vijaya, in the legend, met, and from whom he won the kingdom. Reference has been made earlier to the legend of Vijaya. Descended from a lion, and expelled from his country by his father, he landed in Ceylon on that very day on which the Buddha finally passed away. With his exiled companions on the copper-red beaches of Ceylon he met a *Yakkhini* who was also a princess. Like another Jason in search of the golden fleece he had to marry his enchantress before he could gain his object, and, like Jason once more, he deserted her. But, unlike Jason, he suffered no retribution for his misdeed. The ancient chronicle to which we have referred already writes that the hapless woman's children fled to the central region near the mountain which the Buddha had visited, and over which the guardian deity Sumana

[1] S. Paranavitane, 'The Shrine of the God Upulvan at Devundara', MASC Vol. VI, p. 22—'We know nothing definite of any people who inhabited this island in pre-Sinhalese times.'

presided, and that they lived there, and from them were descended the Veddah tribes.

Of the Veddahs who have been called the first settlers in the island, hardly any trace remains now, so effectively have they been assimilated into the various strands of the population from whom they were once distinguished by their jungle habitat and their wandering life as hunters. Whence these people originally came to Ceylon is yet disputed; their connection with the island has left little record, except perhaps in folklore and in the remnants of ancient custom—more particularly in propitiatory rites still associated with hunting, and charms against wild animals.

Vijaya was succeeded by princes who came from India and who were as-signed localities where they settled and 'ruled over small communities'. In this way is picturesquely communicated what must have been an observed fact—how settlers from India came in various waves, colonizing areas in the north-west, the country near the modern Kelaniya, and in the south-east near Kataragama and Tissamaharama. They gradually exerted pressure upon the original inhabitants, and drove those unwilling to accept their rule into mountain fastness and forest. These settlers came from a more highly developed culture, they were familiar with the use of iron, they were both agriculturists and herdsmen, they had a knowledge of various crafts, and they kept contact with their Indian homeland. They were the Sinhalese of the legend of Vijaya and the later Panduvasudeva, his nephew.

These were the tribes who settled the country and made it their home, some of them marrying with the people of the island. They brought the agricul-tural and village culture of Ceylon to such a point that Buddhism fertilized it and caused it to bear flower in the old Ceylon which the Pali poets of the sixth century A.D. knew. The great dynasty of Sinhalese kings they write of was the successor of the Vijayas and the Pandukhabhayas, whom the same chronicle celebrates as kings ruling over prosperous domains and married to daughters of kings over the sea.

The greatest contribution of these early sovereigns—in truth they could hard-ly have been other than local chieftains, heads of village communities, tilling their fields and protecting their people—is mentioned in the same chronicles, and we are left in no doubt of it from the much later story of a much later king, Dhatusena, who when he was threatened with death by his son if he did not divulge the hiding place of his treasure, asked to be brought to the banks of the great artificial reservoir he had built for the irrigation of the fields, and after he had bathed in it, said, 'This here, my friends, is my whole wealth.'

It is not to be doubted that the basis of the security and prosperity of the regions which the Indian settlers colonized was the rice-field irrigated from a man-made source of supply, which tapped the flow of streams which were not perennial, but yet when the monsoon rains fell on the central highlands could become torrents pouring themselves uselessly into the sea. If nothing else but these man-made sources of conserving the water which the rains brought to the central massif of Ceylon, remained as memorials of the people who tilled the fields of the north-central regions of Ceylon for some two thousand years, they still would prove to the highest degree the skill and genius they inherited from their forbears. These 'tanks', as they are called, range from the small village reservoir to immense lakes. The great builders of these tanks were kings who reigned in Ceylon centuries after the first colonists from India must have come to the island. But it is impossible to believe that such monuments of engineering skill could have been the work of any but a people who had already learnt to know, not only the country, but also how to develop the science of ascertaining gradients, planning the disposition of channels, impounding waters and regulating their flow.

In fact the earliest chronicles do state of one of the mythical princes who settled in the island, Anuradha, that he built a tank, and when he had built a palace to the south of this, he took up his abode there. He had come here with his sister when she married the king. The chronicler's sequence is instructive: he first built a tank, he then built a palace. And of another prince it states that he was on the point of reaping a field measuring a hundred *karisas*, when his nephew, the heir-apparent, came to his fields with his band of soldiers. It is indeed difficult to believe that the precision and mastery of the knowledge which went into the construction of these tanks was not the painfully won inheritance of centuries of man's struggle with his environment and his solution of its problems. Later builders built on sites once essayed and vindicated, and restored and enlarged earlier works. We know—again from the chronicle —that the capital city of Anuradhapura had its tanks before Mahinda came to Ceylon, and that each of these tanks had its tutelary deity. Cittaraja was, according to Dr Paranavitane, the water-spirit who guarded the Abhayavapi, and the Tissavapi had 'an unnamed genius as its protector'.[1] If at this early time these spirits were associated in the popular mind with these two tanks, then it is natural to suppose that the cults which paid them honour as guardian deities were of long standing.

However one regards them, these tanks scattered all over the north, the north-western and north-central, and south-eastern parts of the island do leave on the spectator the feeling that such a level of human achievement could have been attained only in the course of centuries of slow growth. There were gods and heroes before Agamemnon, but they in their time were mortals too, performing human exploits which later ages celebrated as heroic.

[1] S. Paranavitane, 'Pre-Buddhist Beliefs in Ceylon', JRAS (CB), Vol. XXI, No. 52 from which the above is taken is a valuable and lucid examination of the whole subject.

In a passage fragrant with the flowers of Macaulayan rhetoric, Sir Henry
Emerson Tennent—whose two volumes on Ceylon have yet to be replaced
as compendious records of the island—salutes these great irrigation works:
'The stupendous ruins of the reservoirs are the proudest monuments which
remain of the former greatness of the country. . . . Excepting the exaggerated
dimensions of Lake Moeris in Central Egypt and the mysterious "basin of
Al Aran" the bursting of whose embankment devastated the Arabian city
of Mareb, no similar constructions formed by any race whether ancient or
modern, exceed in colossal magnitude the stupendous tanks in Ceylon. The
reservoir of Kohrud at Ispahan, the artificial lake of Ajmeer, or the tank of
Hyder in Mysore, can no more be compared in extent or grandeur with Kala-
wewa or Padivilcolam (Padawiya) than the conduits of Hazekiah, the kanats
of the Persians, or the subterranean water-courses of Peru can vie with the
Elahara canal, which probably connected the lake of Minneri and the "Sea of
Parakrama" with the Anban-ganga river.'[1] Of the site of an ancient tank in
Ceylon, the folklorist and engineer Parker writes: 'The next work for storing
water, of which any information is given in the histories, is of an entirely
different class from the village tank of Anuradha. Possibly it was the first
reservoir ever made with an embankment of any importance that must have
required special acquaintance with the principles of reservoir construction.'[2]
'This ancient tank', continues Brohier, 'is popularly identified by some ruins
on the Wariyapola-Chilaw road, about a mile and a half to the south east of
the modern village Hettipola; which Modder considers to be the city known
in ancient times as Panduwas Nuwara. This city, said to have been founded
by Upatissa, Prime Minister of Wijaya (505 B.C.), who later gave it up to
Panduwas after whom it is called, is said to be the oldest in Ceylon excluding
Tammana Nuwara. The magnificent tank, now in utter disrepair, lies to the
north of this ancient city, with the present day PWD road traversing its bed.
It is supposed to have been built by king Panduwas during his reign. This
tank appears to have been originally formed by throwing an embankment
across the valley of the Kolamunu-oya. There is a large gneiss rock in the line
of the embankment which is to this day known as Deviyannekanda, meaning
"God's Hill" or "King's Hill". Local tradition believes this spot to be haunted
by the spirit of King Mahasen, to whom is also ascribed the construction of
this tank. Undoubtedly it has been repaired and enlarged over the ages which
have passed since it was originally built. The bund, 24 feet in height and a
mile to a mile and a half in length, is said to have flooded a superficial area of
1,000 to 1,200 acres.'[3] Parker thought that this tank, if it was, as he was

---

[1] Quoted by R. L. Brohier, *The Ancient Irrigation Works of Ceylon*, 3 Parts, Colombo, 1934,
Part I, p. 1.

[2] H. Parker, *Ancient Ceylon*, London, 1909, p. 353.   [3] Brohier, *op. cit.*, Part I, p. 4.

inclined to believe, the work of Panduvasadeva (fourth century B.C.), 'may be the first great reservoir ever constructed, if we omit from consideration the great lakes of Egypt, since they were merely immense natural hollows into which water was turned.' Actually later research has shown that the ancient Pandavapi or Pandavava was restored by Vijayabahu I (eleventh century A.D.) and greatly enlarged by Parakrama Bahu I (twelfth century A.D.).[1] The remains Parker saw were therefore of a much later date than he imagined, but the site and the magnitude of the work were possible on account of the skill and experience of the older builder of the fourth century B.C.

So great were those irrigation works that even from the earliest times legend connected their construction with giants and demi-gods. One of the tanks in the North-west of the island still bears the name of Giant's Tank. Brohier remarks that 'Sinhalese histories say that Minneriya tank was built by the conjoint labour of men and demons.'[2] The same authority rather wryly suggests that if one were asked by what method of haulage the ancient Sinhalese brought their immense monoliths to the irrigation works they constructed, 'when facts fail we are compelled to fall back on legends which maintain that the blocks were moved by giants—there having been Anakim in the land of old—of the measure of whose strength an idea may be formed when we are told that one of them with his right hand compressed the head of the king's chief elephant, and thus shaped the two hollows now to be seen at the temples of all animals of the species.'[3] The dam built across the Walawe Ganga near Kalota is still called the Yodaya (Giant's) Dam because legend ascribes its construction to a young man of gigantic strength. So, too, names like Yoda Ela, Yoda-bemma, and Yoda Wewa illustrate the superstition which rationalized the achievements of these engineers of old. The more massive these works seemed in retrospect, the more difficult it would have been to credit their origin to any but Titans. Even those monarchs during whose reigns in historical times great tanks were built were raised to the level of the gods and worshipped as such. Mahasena (fourth century A.D.) was one of these. He is now worshipped as Maha Sen Deviyo. A little devale not far from the present roadway which connects Minneriya with Polonnaruva is his shrine. In the uncertain light of this humble little temple one can see offerings still made to the deified king who built the tank of Minneriya. On the bund of this tank, as on so many others, there is a number of broken images supposed to be images of the king, his consort and his ministers. 'Such is the veneration and awe in which these relics are held, that not infrequently, law-suits and family disputes are settled, even up to the present times, by one or the other party

---

[1] C. W. Nicholas, 'Irrigation Works of King Parakkama Bahu I,' CHJ, Vol. 4, Colombo 1956, p. 56.

[2] Brohier, *op. cit.*, Part I, p. 20.   [3] *Ibid.*, Part 2, p. 30.

undertaking to swear to the truth of their statement in the presence of these images.'[1]

Round these tanks in ancient times, as still in many places in Ceylon, would cluster the fields and houses of the village. Village and tank were almost synonymous. For the cultivator the rhythm of life would be set by the seasonal work in the rice-fields. Besides there were cattle to feed, and some hunting to be done for at hand was the jungle. The village had its various craftsmen who made it self-sufficient, and it had its council of elders to regulate its affairs and to settle disputes. Important among the tasks of the community was the duty of keeping embankment and channel in repair, and of building new works when need arose. This labour undertaken by the community for its own benefit becomes in the course of time the institution of *Rajakariya*, or work performed for the king. The builders of tanks like Mahasen and Parakkama Bahu I could put their vast schemes into effect only because the labour which went into them was service rendered by the community. Of course such service could be either voluntarily performed or forcibly exacted. It is a well known fatality of institutions that the best in them is subject to decay and corruption, and it may be that some of the labour of the community needed for construction of tank and channel was arbitrarily demanded and tyrannously enforced in later times. But one can see that the prosperity, nay the survival, of these village communities, each of them grouped round a tank depended on the voluntary labour of the whole unit. As long as the community remained intact, the water on which it depended could provide it with the means for survival. Equally true is the reflection that as long as the system of irrigation works remained intact, the community could survive. As long as the life-giving water was conserved in the tank, or the channel undamaged which brought it from its further source, the village prospered and could maintain, in spite of the variability of seasons of drought and rain, its simple standards of decent well-being.

Across the strait and the seas were the Indian kingdoms. There was trade along the coasts and overland between the various divisions of India, and there was trade too between India and Ceylon. In the north of the island the present Mantota, now a ruin in a desert, flourished as the port of Mahatittha. From it must have gone the pearls and gems which made Ceylon famous as the island of precious stones, and claimant, in the opinion of many an antiquary in the last century, to the title of both Solomon's Ophir and Sindbad's valley of gems. Perhaps it was the lure of these riches which drew invading bands which kept pushing further and further down the rivers and deeper and deeper into the Sinhalese kingdom. Or it may have been another kind of treasure, like that of king Dhatusena, which brought the invader—

[1] *Ibid.*, Part I, p. 20.

the wealth of rice-field and tank with the air of seemly peace which ruled over them.

How can one measure the quality and specific artistic excellence of these ancient Sinhalese craftsmen? It is to be sought in a range of work in moulding stone, from simple drip-ledge of caves to the engineering feat of the *Biso-kotuwa*. All these would be the by-product of handling the practical day-to-day necessities of living, they are nonetheless artistic achievements. The *Biso-kotuwa*, or valve-pit, must be regarded as a rare piece of industrial design, for economically and functionally it made possible the greatest industry of those times—the growing of rice. Who invented it, or when the community through a long process of trial and error discovered this 'tool' which solved their difficulties, will never be known; but it was a discovery as effective for its purposes as any similar construction which present-day techniques and present-day materials can produce. The *Biso-kotuwa* is the counterpart of our sluice which regulates the flow of water from a reservoir. A British Governor of Ceylon in the middle of the last century was impressed that there appeared to be no visible outlet at the point at which the stream irrigating the fields issues from the tank. He felt that the run of the water was regulated by an ancient sluice placed under the bed of the lake. Parker an irrigation engineer who spent thirty years working in Ceylon between 1873 and 1904, compares the *Biso-kotuwa* to the valve-towers or valve-pits which have been built at numerous reservoirs in Europe: 'Their duty is to hold the valves, and the lifting-gear for working them, by means of which the outward flow of the water is regulated or totally stopped. Such was also the function of the *Biso-kotuwa* of the Sinhalese engineers; they were the first inventors of the valve-pit, more than 2,100 years ago. It will be readily understood that in an age when iron-casting was unknown, and even the smallest plates of iron could be heated only with difficulty in the early forges, no iron or iron-bound sluice valves were made, and that it must have been no easy task to control the outflow of the water at reservoirs which had a depth of thirty or forty feet, as was the case at several of the larger works. Yet the similarity of the designs of the *Biso-kotuwas* at all periods proves that the engineers of the third century B.C., if not those of an earlier period, had mastered the problem so successfully that all others were satisfied to copy their designs.'[1]

Time in the course of a thousand or two thousand years has made both the ruined tank against which one nudges in the jungle, and those which restored still conserve the volume of water they used to impound, so much a part of the natural landscape that it is hard to think of them now as the work of men and women. They lie so naturally in the fold of the land, and resemble lakes in pleasant hollows with grassy and treed banks that the mind sees them as

[1] Parker, *op. cit.*, p. 379 ff.

existing from the beginning of time. To one who has wandered on their banks and gazed over their sheets of water, it would seem that the serenity they have inherited enforces something more than a philosophical commonplace, and that the extraordinary feeling of calm they seem to bestow on the beholder mirrors in some way one of the contemplative virtues the Buddha preached.

These people who toiled in the mud of the rice-fields, working with their hands on the bund and on the moulding of earth, were people physically linked with the earth in the way all early agriculrual communities have been. To call them 'primitive' would be unfortunate, because that word might imply a value judgement entered against them. Round them, not quite tamed or subservient, was the earth they knew, manifesting itself through various presences on knoll, river, lake, hill and grove. These were the gods of the earth to whom offerings were made and whose aid was sought in every activity of the community. The *Yakkhas* of the later chronicles were these earth-gods worshipped by the inhabitants of these village communities of ancient Ceylon. Not a tank but had its own water-spirit, not a grove but had its guardian god. Reference has already been made to tutelary deities which the 'Aryan' invaders must have known in their home on the mainland. The cults of some of these would have been brought over and have been acclimatized in the new island home.

The god of these immigrants were the Vedic gods of the legends of their forefathers. Rama, the powerful, who, bending the bow Varuna gave Janaka, won Sita as his bride, must have been a special object of worship, for these immigrant tribes would associate Lanka in the legends of Rama with the island to which they came. As they came over the seas and must therefore have been a seafaring people, they would hold the god Varuna in special honour. He was worshipped in Ceylon as the god Upulvan, the dark-complexioned one. The Buddha on his deathbed had spoken to Sakka, the king of the gods, who stood nearby, and told him that Vijaya had arrived in Lanka with seven hundred followers. In Lanka Buddhism was going to be established, so Sakka was asked to protect Vijaya and the island. Sakka gave charge of Lanka to Upulvan. Vibhisana, another guardian god of Ceylon, had his fane at Kelaniya, and like Sumana, was specially venerated.

The fame of some of these gods prospered, and of some declined. Upulvan, or Varuna, was, among other things, ruler of the sea. Not long after his cult was gradually forgotten, as Paranavitane good-humouredly remarks, 'Ceylon, for the first time became politically subject to a maritime power from the West'.[1] 'This same god, Varuna, was worshipped by "Aryan" speaking

[1] Paranavitane, *The Shrine of the God Upulvan at Devundara*, p. 52. This monograph is a masterly survey of all the available literary, archaeological and epigraphical evidence relevant to this ancient shrine.

peoples in the Indo-Iranian and Indo-European stages. He figures in the earliest document so far known (c. 1,400 B.C.) in which there is mention of an Aryan god.'[1] He corresponds both to Uranus, the father of the Greek Chronos, and to the Ahura Mazda of the Iranians.

From the peoples the settlers in Ceylon displaced they must have borrowed animistic beliefs too, so that their natural world was inhabited by beings palpable in the ripples of a tank, the rush of a stream, the branches of a tree, or the peculiar indentation of a rocky crest. Tree-worship, in a somewhat altered form, survives in the Ceylon of today. There are groves still associated in popular belief with powerful gods, who have it in their power to help the devotee who lights the wick of cloth floating in the clay saucer of coconut oil. The woods and the jungle are still sacred to deities whom the hunter and the traveller still find it necessary to propitiate. The act of propitiation is a simple offering, with, perhaps, the murmuring of a few words of a charm.

As we have seen, Buddhism, which came long after these primitive cults were established, did not oust them. The old rites existed, and the deities they honoured were transformed into adherents of the Buddha with an allotted place in the scheme of things. Dr Paranavitane who argues that Upulvan is the same as Varuna, concludes that 'the worship of that god was probably widespread among the Sinhalese before Buddhism won for itself a pre-eminent position among them. It was not the policy of those who spread the Buddha's message to wage war against such popular cults, provided that they did not go counter to the Buddhist way of life. Rather were such popular gods enlisted as allies to help in the furtherance of the Buddhist cause. The more benignant among the ancient gods of India, such as Brahma, Sakra, and Vaisravana, are represented as enthusiastic supporters of the Buddha, ready to acknowledge, by their attendance, the momentousness of the main events in the career of the Great Sage. Some of the gods are even represented as sufficiently developed in intellect to realize the more subtle points of the Buddha's doctrine.'[2]

That species of tree (*ficus religiosa*), under which the Buddha attained enlightenment, became a special object of worship. It was before his time worshipped as the abode of a god, as the story of Sujata would have shown. It will be remembered that she sent her servant to the tree with an offering, and the girl having seen the Buddha there came back to her mistress with the information that the god of the tree was sitting beneath it.

Bhikkhu Rahula, in his account of the religion of the ancient Sinhalese, speaks of the belief in the living properties of every inanimate thing which grew. Not only were special trees invested with this *ekindriyan jivan* (life with

[1] *Ibid.*, p. 58.   [2] *Ibid.*, p. 50.

one sense faculty), every plant, even grass, was according to the popular mind similarly endowed.[1]

The tiller of the field had the gods of his particular locality whose altars he tended; the king, on ceremonial occasions, to exhibit his power and grandeur, sat on an equal eminence with the images of two of the *Yakkhas* beside him. The king of the *Yakkhas*, Vaisravana or Kuvera, the god of wealth, had his own places of worship, and long after Buddhism was introduced into the island his cult continued, and still to be seen at Anuradhapura are the guardstones in which his stocky figure is featured, with his protuberant belly and his formal geniality of expression.

Dance forms whose origins lost in antiquity have yet to be traced, by their persistence speak of times when the gods of the earth were powerful beings to be placated then, and still to be placated now. The *Kohomba Kankariya*, one such form, is a propitiatory rite performed in honour of *Kohomba Yaka* and its origins are connected with the legendary story of the ancient king Pandu-vasudeva, sick and infirm as the result of the curse laid upon him by the *Yakkhini* Kuveni whom Vijaya deserted.[2]

More frequent and almost commonplace in the village are 'devil dancing' ceremonies, performed to exercise the devils responsible for afflicting men with sickness. The *kattadiya*, or exorcist, is still a figure in the village community, and his services are often called upon by a people still responsive to the existence of malevolent demons and spirits around them. The activities of these agents have to warded off or nullified according to the prescribed mode. Robert Knox, who lived as a prisoner for eighteen years in the Kandyan country in the second half of the seventeenth century, compassionately regretted the dread of the devil in which the villager lived. 'And indeed it is sad to consider, how this poor People are subjected to the Devil, and they themselves acknowledge it their misery, saying their Country is so full of Devils, and evil Spirits, that unless in this manner they should adore them, they would be destroyed by them.'[3]

Sickness, impotency, droughts, harvests, natural calamities, had their special rites. Exorcist and devil dancer, and the services they provided were regulated, as in fact were all the activities of the village, by astrological computation and the 'science' of interpreting the stars, lunar mansions and the position of the planets relative to the lives and work of men. This lore was pre-Buddhistic, and we have seen how the erudite Brahmin was consulted to forecast the destiny of the Buddha. On the subject of this lore the Buddha had

[1] Bhikkhu W. Rahula, *History of Buddhism in Ceylon*, Colombo 1956, p. 42, n. 6. I am indebted to this book at several points in this chapter.

[2] E. R. Sarathchandra, *The Sinhalese Folk Play*, Colombo, 1954, p. 47 ff.

[3] Robert Knox, *An Historical Relation of Ceylon*, Glasgow, 1911, p. 123.

expressed himself unequivocally. He condemned it. But it continued in his time, and still continues. Paranavitane notes the frequency of astral names in the earliest inscriptions of Ceylon. After Buddhism was introduced proper names would have changed, but the belief in the old lore was not destroyed.

D. H. Lawrence who visited Ceylon in 1922, and spent a few months living in a house overlooking Kandy Lake and the Dumbara Valley, felt very sensitively the force of the underground stream of the old beliefs. Living as he did, close to the most celebrated object of worship of the Buddhist masses—the sacred tooth of the Buddha—he felt much more strongly than the elevated philosophy and the ethical fineness of Buddhism, the presence of the gods of the earth, to him a much deeper and more powerful stratum than any system of thought. As he looked at rice-fields, the men and women who worked in them, the buffaloes who gazed at him from the mud, and the elephants like huge prehistoric beasts padding along village paths, he was filled with the consciousness of the immanence of the older gods of the earth, and the secret of the 'mystery of the dark mountains of blood'. Sensitive to all this he was revolted and angry at the expense of all this passion and energy in the old rite of the Perahera performed before the tired and dispirited English Prince of Wales. Lawrence instinctively grasped a truth about the ancient cults of Ceylon which folklorist and culture historian seek to establish through a sober citation of sources, bequeathing to the reader as the pallid end product of their researches the lifeless fact instead of the full-blooded reality.[1]

Contact with India brought into the island all the emissaries of newer faiths and newer disciplines. Ascetics of various kinds are referred to in chronicle and inscription, Brahmin teacher and priests, and even followers of Mahavira the Jain teacher. The exponents of all these faiths were apparently free to practise what they believed, some even enjoyed royal favour. With so many different kinds of religious devotion known and practised in the island, is it not possible that the mendicant priests of the *Dhamma* taught by Gotama the Buddha had not arrived in Ceylon too? Yet the chronicle clearly insists, as it is important for its purposes, that Buddhism was preached in Ceylon only when in the fulness of time the moment for its propagation had arrived. Only when the great *thera* Moggaliputta had looked into the future and had seen how the Buddha-word was to be taken into various countries near by, then and only then did he lay the special charge upon Mahinda that he should, with our others, 'found in the lovely island of Lanka the lovely religion of the Conqueror'. And Mahinda sets out only when he knows that the moment is ripe, and when Indra the god seeks him out and bids him go.

So did Mahinda, waiting for the full moon day of the lunar month of May-June, depart on his mission. The importance of his journey to Ceylon is

[1] See D. H. Lawrence's poem 'Elephants'.

thus enunciated by the chronicle: 'He who was foretold by the Sage, in the hour of death, as bringing salvation to Lanka, by his merit in converting Lanka, he who for Lanka's salvation had become like to the Master, alighted there, extolled by the gods of Lanka.'[1] This event was no mission such as any wandering ascetic or mendicant could have undertaken. Mahinda's arrival in Ceylon was the fulfilment of a prophecy made by the Buddha as he lay dying in the Sala grove of Kusinara. It was, furthermore, the wish of his father the great king Asoka; it had been enjoined on him by the *thera* Moggaliputta; and the gods of the island welcomed him with their praise. What is more—when Mahinda came to Ceylon he was, like his master who had visited the island on the invitation of one of its gods, bringing it salvation. If there had been any known trace of Buddhism existing on the island before this time, the chronicle chose to ignore it, since the visit of Mahinda was an event of such importance for the development of the history and culture of Ceylon that the chronicler whose heart was in these things, gave it the aura of preternatural significance it demanded.

[1] Geiger, *Mhv*, trsl. p. 90.

CHAPTER SIX

THE THERA AND THE KING

The meeting of the *thera* Mahinda and the king of Ceylon, Devanam-piya Tissa, took place on the Missaka mountain on the full-moon day of the lunar month of April-May. The *thera* with his powers of perception divined that the king would on that day go to the mountain; so, travelling through the air with his companions, the *thera* anticipated him. The Missaka mountain, later Cetiya-pabbata, and now Mihintale, after Mahinda with whom it is associated, in one of a group of hills which thrust themselves out of the plain, some seven miles to the east of the city of Anuradhapura. Between it and the city low scrub jungle now hides what even at that time must have been wooded country, for in that direction from the ancient site of Anuradhapura were the quarters assigned to the hunters, and there on that day the king went hunting on the slopes of the hill.

As the *thera* had come of set purpose to meet the king, the god of the hill naturally took a hand in arranging the rendezvous. He appeared to the king in the shape of a deer feeding in a thicket. Unwilling to infringe the rules of the game, Tissa twanged the string of his bow, so as to give the animal a fair chance. The deer sprang towards the hill and the king followed, until it disappeared when it came near the *thera* standing there in his yellow robe. Out of consideration for the king, that he should not be put out at the unaccustomed sight of a number of yellow-robed priests, the *thera* stood there alone.

The *thera* and the king now stood face to face. Seeing him the king was rooted to the spot, and not even the voice of the *thera* calling to him by name would make him advance. It was only when the *thera* told the king that he was a *Samana*, a follower of the Buddha, and that compassion for the king had brought him thither from India, that discarding his bow and arrows the king greeted the *thera* and sat down beside him.

The *thera's* companions appeared when the king and his company were assembled on the grassy plateau of Ambatthala, just above which the hill gathers itself up to its crest. The king was told of the spread of Buddhism in India—'the country gleamed with yellow robes'—and that the *theras* had come travelling through the air.

84

What followed is so much in keeping with the ancient tradition and the valuation placed upon intellectual comprehension (knowledge), that it would be best to quote this passage from the *Mahavamsa*, since it illustrates a point made earlier. Before the *thera* could be sure that the king was receptive, and that he could understand the teaching of the Buddha, he had to satisfy himself by putting the king through a test of intelligence. The questions the *thera* asked the king enabled him to decide whether his mind was ready to discriminate between words and things and to apprehend distinctions: 'To test him that most wise (thera) now asked a subtle question, and even as he was questioned the monarch answered the questions severally.

"What name does this tree bear, O king?"

"This tree is called a mango."

"Is there yet another mango besides this?"

"There are many mango-trees."

"And are there yet other trees besides this mango and the other mangoes?"

"There are many trees, sir; but those are trees that are not mangoes."

"And are there, beside the other mangoes and those trees which are not mangoes, yet other trees?"

"There is this mango-tree, sir."

"Thou hast a shrewd wit, O ruler of men!"

"Hast thou kinsfolk, O king?"

"There are many, sir."

"And are there also some, O king, who are not kinsfolk of thine?"

"There are yet more of those than of my kin."

"Is there yet anyone besides the kinsfolk and the others?"

"There is yet myself, sir."

"Good! thou hast a shrewd wit, O ruler of men."[1]

'When he had known that he was a keen-witted man,' the chronicle goes on, 'the *thera* preached his first sermon to the king.' It would be well to insist here on the similarities between the story of the Buddha and this follower of his: like the Buddha, the *thera* gave up his life in a royal palace to don the yellow robe of the mendicant; like the Buddha, he travels miraculously to Ceylon; and like the Buddha, before he can preach the *Dhamma,* he has to assure himself that he has an audience fit though few. The Buddha bethinks himself of his 'disciples', the *thera* examines the king with questions which have something of Socratic guile in their seeming simplicity.

The king and his retinue were converted to Buddhism on hearing the sermon, and the *thera* and his group of priests were invited to partake of the royal evening meal. This they declined, as they also refused to accompany the king to the city that very day. However, the *thera* was made to promise that he would

[1] *Mhv.* xiv, 16 ff. p. 92.

enter the city the next day. Before he left the Ambatthala plateau, the king drew aside one of the *thera's* followers who had not as yet been ordained, and did not therefore wear the yellow robes, and asked him what the *thera's* name was and what his intentions were. When he had been told, the king for the the first time realized that he had been conversing with human beings and not with *devas*. As he sat at his evening meal by the pond now called Nagapokuna, he heard the miraculous summons to the *devas* all over the island to assemble on the mountain to hear the preaching of the *Dhamma*. Not understanding what the summons was, he sent a message to Mahinda asking whether anything untoward had happened, to which he received the reply that the time had arrived for preaching the word of the Buddha.

Mahinda's second sermon that day was preached to an audience of countless *devas* from all parts of Lanka. They too, like the king, were converted to Buddhism, and a second stage in the mission of the conversion of the whole island had been achieved. Legend assigns as the site of this second sermon of Mahinda's a rock on the plateau. Now that this sermon had been delivered, and the island deities had taken refuge in the Triple Gem, could it be doubted that soon the whole island was to pass under the sway of the *Dhamma*?

The next day the *theras* who had miraculously travelled through the air to the Missaka mountain, proceeded in the same way to the royal capital, the waggon the king had sent for them being needless. Received with every mark of attention by the king, served by him with the food which had been specially prepared for them, it was no wonder that the soothsayers foretold that these *theras* would soon be lords upon the island. To the king and his court Mahinda preaches his third sermon, choosing as two of his discourses texts which dealt with the spirit world. The fame of his preaching spread in the city, and in order to enable as large a crowd as possible to hear him, the elephant stable—the hall of the state elephant—was cleaned out and specially prepared for the *theras* and the crowds expected to hear them. Here Mahinda preached his fourth sermon in Ceylon, and the townspeople were converted.

Bhikkhu Rahula[1] draws attention to the appropriateness of the sermons preached in Ceylon by Mahinda on his first two days there. The Sutta he preached to the king—the Culahatthipadupama Sutta—'the lesser discourse on the simile of the elephant's footprint', would have explained to his auditors what the life of a monk was, how a man is converted to Buddhism, and what its Four Noble Truths are. To the *devas* he preached on spiritual calm, placing before these gods a Buddhist ideal which would recommend to them benignity. To the court he introduces a subject which must have gone more than half-way to meet their belief in the world of spirits. The *Petavatthu* and the *Vimanavatthu* deal with such beings as the Sinhalese, in pre-Buddhist times

[1] Bhikkhu W. Rahula, *History of Buddhism in Ceylon*, Colombo 1956, p. 50 ff.

and later, accepted as part of the world in which they lived—the ghosts and spirits of the dead. If these sermons enforce no lesson, they yet result in a reflection which would be doubly comforting: the existence of these beings was confirmed, and it was shown that while there are some spirits who are punished with torments, there are others who are rewarded with heavenly mansions. Belief in the world of spirits is thus validated, but it is placed in a different framework. *Karma* rationalizes what was taken on trust, and a logic of cause and effect accounts for what must previously have been accepted as superstitious belief. To the townspeople the Devaduta Sutta would recommend, through its illustrations of the retributory misery which attends the criminal, the practice of a morality finer and nobler than any these people had known up to that time. Finally, in his choice of the Balapandita Sutta for the women of noble families who thronged the royal park in order to hear him, Mahinda paints the picture of the man whose wisdom enables him to live uncorrupted by vice, sure of happiness and the fruits of his good life in this world and in future existences.

In these sermons, Mahinda, besides acquainting his audience with the new *Dhamma* he preached, lays stress on the practical results of the good life lived in this existence. When one considers his position—the evangel of a superior message conveyed to listeners in a stage of development as yet far from his own—one can understand how his zeal to make himself understood takes into account the preconceptions of his hearers and uses them in order to produce the desired effect: acceptance of the new *Dhamma* as practical good. As a propagandist of Buddhism, Mahinda was no less skilled than the Buddha.

Yet the purpose of the visit of Mahinda to Ceylon was not alone that of preaching sermons and converting the inhabitants of the island to Buddhism. There were two specific objects he had in mind, without which institutionalized Buddhism could not exist. The establishment of Buddhism in Ceylon would demand the foundation both of an order of monks in the island, and of a monastery where the monks would not only live, but where the sacred functions devolving on them as members of the *Sangha* would have to be performed.

So the next day the king presented to his visitors, as to the *Sangha*, the royal park named the Mahamegha (the Great Cloud), and accompanied by Mahinda traversed its extent, marking each spot where the future buildings of the monastery were to stand: the space where the sacred functions were to be carried out; the tank for baths; the enclosure for the Bodhi-tree; the *uposatha* hall; the place for the distribution of gifts for the community of monks, the refectory; and the site of the great *stupa*. At each spot the *thera* marked as future site, the earth in affirmation of his choice, quaked. No wonder the king trembled with joy, and assisted at the proceedings with jubilation. What is more, in selecting these sites for the future monastery, Mahinda recounted to the king that he was only reviving the old connections of those very places with the lifetime of previous Buddhas. Here quite obviously we see how the new religion is presented—it is a repetition of the ancient archetype. In accepting the *Dhamma* of Gotama the Buddha, Lanka was remaining true to its earlier role in the years of the previous Buddhas. At each of the chosen sites Mahinda expounds to the enthralled king the relation between past and present, and at the place where the *cetiya* of the Mahavihara was to stand, he looked back into the past and saw how that very spot had been hallowed by four previous Buddhas. 'Thus was this place, O king, visited by four Buddhas; on this spot, O great king, will the thupa stand hereafter, with the relic-chamber for a *dona* of the relics of the Buddha's body; it will be a hundred and twenty cubits high and will be known by the name Hemamali.' To the king who vowed in the excess of his zeal to build the *thupa* himself, Mahinda replies that this task is not for him. He then looks into the future, and prophesies that Duttha Gamini, the hero-king of Ceylon, 'great in glory, wondrous power and prowess, will build the thupa here.'

How satisfying this union of past, the significant moment of Mahinda's progress through the park selecting the various sites, and his prophecy of the future, must have been to the later chronicler, who composing hundreds of years after these events a record of the siting of the great monastery to which he belonged, could not have refrained from illuminating the page of history. Whether he was the monk Mahanama, or whether the record was the product of multiple authorship, it was yet sponsored by the Mahavihara, and it must have been undertaken at a time when that community was engaged in a struggle against the monks of the Abhayagiri. The *Mahavamsa* goes back to the fourth century A.D. In that century the king Mahasena, who was under Mahayanist influence, destroyed the Mahavihara. Later in the same century the Mahavihara was deserted for the second time. In this background of strife, with its threat to the very existence of the community, everything which belonged to its past history, in legend and in commentary, would tend to be glorified, the miraculous called in to dignify the historical, and both adorned in epical grandeur. In the story of Mahinda's selection of the site for the monastery, the Mahavihara celebrates not only 'the splendour and majesty of the Buddhist order', but also its own origins. It recreates itself.

It was the home of Theravada Buddhism in Ceylon. For hundreds of years it had stood firm against heterodox deviations. It had been and was going to be, long after the chronicle was first set down in writing, the symbol of Buddhist Lanka. What wonder then that the occasion was improved and a poetic tribute paid by the chronicler to his monastery, to the heroic king who built the *thupa*, to the island, and to the *thera* whose action so graphically made past, present and future one continuous stream of the fulfilment of a special destiny.

The selection of the sites was not enough, the boundaries had to be assigned for the monastery, and the king himself ploughed a furrow enclosing the circular area in which the various buildings were to stand. At his own desire the royal city was included in this area. With this setting out of the boundaries a third stage in the founding of the religion had been reached. The king and his people had been converted, the *devas* had been enlisted as adherents of the new religion, the boundaries which took in the city and made it part of the sacred ground had been marked out. It only remained now to inaugurate the order of priests in the land.

The commentary explains that when he was asked by the king whether the religion (*sasana*) had been established in Ceylon, Mahinda replied that it had, but that its roots had not gone deep. 'When will its roots go deep?' asked the king. The *thera* replied: 'When a son born in Ceylon, of Ceylonese parents, becomes a monk in Ceylon, studies the Vinaya in Ceylon, recites the Vinaya in Ceylon, then the roots of the sasana are deep set.'[1] This statement, which Bhikkhu Rahula characterizes as 'most remarkable', because it claims a peculiar condition for the establishment of Buddhism in a particular geographical unit, must surely be taken again as part of the legitimate pride of the Ceylon commentator surveying the past and mindful of the particular destiny of the island as the home of the authentic teaching of the Buddha. To one imbued with devotion to this ideal of Ceylon as the *Dharmadvipa*—the island of the *Dhamma*—such a statement as Mahinda is credited with, departure though it may be, as Bhikkhu Rahula points out, from the teaching of the Buddha in the earliest writings, is emotionally a necessity.

It may be that we see here not the self-effacement of the *thera* who coming to the island from another country claimed no special privilege for himself, and was anxious to make over to the priests of the country to which he came rights which were duly theirs, but the commentator's claims for the practical advantage of the recognition of a national religion. These words of the commentator, it should not be forgotten, written long after the event, reflect the attitudes of his own time. In the fourth century A.D. Pali Suttas, had for the first time been translated into Sinhalese, and throughout that century there had been bitter dissension between the community of the Mahavihara and monks of other sects who had come to Ceylon from India. It is understandable therefore that the commentator, when he considered Mahinda's task in Ceylon, should have been unsatisfied with earlier accounts which confined it to the preaching of the *Dhamma*, the establishment of the boundaries of the monastery, and the acceptance of the relics in the island. To the author of the *Samantapasadika* the foundations of the religion could only have been well and truly laid when a Sinhalese monk recited the Vinaya in Ceylon. When the

---

[1] *Samantapasadika* (S.H.B.) p. 60—quoted by Bhikkhu W. Rahula, *op. cit.*, p. 54.

king's nephew, therefore, who had formerly been a minister of state, did this, then the *sasana* was finally established in the island.

Both chronicle and commentary relate how relics of the Buddha, and a branch of the original Bodhi-tree under which the Buddha attained enlightenment were brought to Anuradhapura. Without these relics the practice of the religion, as it was known to a later age, would scarcely have been possible. Asoka sent to Ceylon the right collar bone of the Buddha and his almsbowl, and as these remained on the Missaka mountain till a fitting place was prepared for them in the city, the mountain came to be known as Cetiya-pabbata, the hill of the *cetiya*, since a *cetiya* enshrined relics. For the collar-bone relic the Thuparama was built at Anuradhapura, the first of the *stupas* to be built in Ceylon.

The Bodhi-branch was brought to Ceylon by Mahinda's sister Sanghamitta, who was herself a *theri* or nun. Miracles attended its progress to the island. The south bough of the tree needed no cutting, its branches vanished, and when the emperor Asoka had drawn a line about the bough with a pencil of red arsenic mounted in gold, the bough severed itself at the mark and deposited itself in the golden vase the emperor had prepared for it. A hundred roots sprouting from it made a fast net in the earth of the vase. Before the *theri* Sanghamitta set out for the island, the miraculous bough was worshipped, and when it travelled across the waves in the ship, the seas were stilled and heavenly music resounded in the air. It was received by Devanampiya Tissa on the seashore. He waded neck-deep into the water to receive it, and bore it, as every relic is borne, on his head, to the pavilion which had been specially built for it. The king in honour to the Bodhi-bough served as door-keeper in the pavilion during the three days it remained there. It was conducted to Anuradhapura with great solemnity, and planted in the special enclosure in the Mahamegha grove. The various saplings which issued miraculously from it, were planted in various parts of the island, one of them as far away as Kataragama in the south. Sanghamitta had in the meantime ordained those women of the royal household wishing to be nuns, and an order of nuns was thereby instituted.

Of the original enclosure for the Bodhi-tree—the *Bodhi-ghara*—at Anuradhapura nothing now survives. The tree, probably the oldest historical tree of which record is extant, is still there, surrounded by a modern structure of a distressing ugliness. Vogel writing more than twenty years ago commented on the difficulty at the present time of mediating between the claims of the zeal of the devout and the demands of an aesthetic sensibility.[1] It is pleasant to record in this connection the work of the Archaeological Department of Ceylon; it has been noteworthy in the care of its restoration, and its resistance to the misguided enthusiasm so often accompanied by bad taste. What that

[1] J. Ph. Vogel, *Buddhist Art in India, Ceylon and Java*, Oxford, 1936, p. 75.

ancient *Bodhi-ghara* must have looked like has recently been revealed in the beautiful restoration of the only one so far discovered in Ceylon—at Nillak-gama in the Kurunegala district, not far from Galgamuwa and Maho.

This handsome example of eighth or ninth-century work, perhaps the site of one of the saplings of the original branch, demonstrates how strong and true both the architectural and sculptural traditions of the Sinhalese were. The square enclosure to which two entrances are provided—east and west— is of moulded stone with a frieze of elephants running round the base at the level of the landing. The door-jambs and lintels are ornamented. Inside, on a raised platform in the centre, also ornamented, are lions carved on the vertical slabs which must have surrounded the tree. The four altars on the four sides indicate the presence of the specific object of worship.

As one comes upon this chaste and modest structure, not far from the village tank in the jungle, its yellowish stone—an effect which its long burial under-ground may have produced—is the first intimation of its unusualness. The linear rhythm of the walls with their moulding and the coping is relieved by the sweep of the carving—the creeper on the door-way, the naga-king with his multiple hoods, and the cherub bestriding a horse. The simple dignity of the lions on the vertical slabs of the upper platform is in keeping with the general restraint of the whole structure. The elaborate ornament on the door-frames is not felt to be excessive, it is held in poise by the gravity of the lines of the stone-faced wall and the upper platform.

Of this beautifully integrated work of art Dr Paranavitane writes: 'In its ornamental character, the structure at Nillakgama is not surpassed by any other monument at the *prasadas* of Anuradhapura. No door-frames so elabor-ately ornamented as those at Nillakgama are known from any other site as early as the ninth century. A structure on which so much of artistic effort was lavished must have been dedicated to an object of great religious veneration. It is not impossible that the Bodhi-tree which stood at the centre of the upper platform was one believed to have sprung from the seeds of the Anuradhapura Bodhi-tree immediately after it was planted in the reign of Devanampiya Tissa.'[1]

The preaching of the *Dhamma*; the conversion of *devas*, king and people; the establishment of a monastery; the arrival of the relics; and the founding of an order; all these conditions for the institution of the religion in Ceylon had been fulfilled. Nothing was wanting for the existence of the institutionalized religion as it was known in the fourth century A.D. but images, the adoration of which was common at that time. Yet in the story of the choosing of the site for the future Mahavihara, no reference is made to the position of the image-house, which becomes about the fourth century A.D. a regular feature of the

[1] A.S.C.A.R., 1954, Colombo, 1955, G 28.

plan of a monastery. Attention has already been drawn to the absence of any representation of the Buddha in early reliefs and carving. Certainly in the time of the emperor Asoka, according to later tradition the builder of some 84,000 *cetiyas*, no images of the Buddha were known. The cult of the image of the Buddha is a later development, and it must have grown with the growth of Mahayanist belief and practice. Bhikkhu Rahula holds that it is possible that Buddha-images were known in Ceylon in the third century B.C., on the strength of an allusion made to 'the great and beautiful stone image that was placed of old by Devanampiya Tissa in the Thuparama'. But of this there is no proof.

Throughout his long lifetime in Ceylon Mahinda resided on Mihintale. He refused to live anywhere else, preferring the caves lying scattered about the rocks on the hills which form the historic Cetiya-pabbata. A great monastic site grew up later on the hill where the *thera* met the king. Its fame as the spot where Buddhism was first preached in Ceylon inspired later monarchs to adorn it with numerous *cetiyas*, and everything needed for a large community of monks. Yet the reputation of those early *theras* who lived on the hills as cave-dwellers continued throughout all the vicissitudes of Cetiya-pabbata, and many a later writer invokes the true simplicity and the devout life of meditation lived by them in times long gone.

Mahinda survived his friend the king, and died at the age of eighty, sixty years after he had been ordained priest. His body laid in a golden chest and placed upon a golden bier was conducted in solemn procession to Anuradhapura, and cremated near the Mahavihara. Half of the relics were collected and distributed at various places at Cetiya-pabbata, and *stupas* built over them. The Ambatthala *Stupa* is supposed to be one of them. It stands on the little plateau where the *thera* and the king had met.

Their meeting was, in its consequences for the island, one of the most fateful events in its history, for with the *thera* Buddhism officially made its spiritual conquest of Ceylon. In the two thousand years and more which have passed since then, no other single event could be placed beside it in its epoch-making results, except perhaps the first contact of feudal East with commercial West in the sixteenth century, when the caravels of the Portuguese appeared off the coast of Colombo. But even this event, impossible to assess as yet in all its implications, for the process of that contact still continues to be one of the greatest solvents of cultural change, could hardly be reckoned as significant in the development of Ceylon. For Mahinda brought not only a new religion, through this the island was given a consciousness of its peculiar destiny. Besides, in the institution of the priesthood and the formal mode of practising the new religion, a new impulse was given to the skill of the architects and sculptors of Ceylon, and a new literature of Buddhism came into being.

Mahinda was received in Ceylon by the king of a small agricultural community, who in some vague way had owed allegiance to the emperor Asoka. So humble was life in this community and so far from the norms established in the Asokan court, that before Mahinda's arrival in Ceylon the emperor had had the king of Anuradhapura consecrated anew as king, and on his arrival there was no fit place for the *thera* to reside in the royal city until a building in brick had hastily to be put together. One of the consequences of the meeting of *thera* and king was the flowering of an architectural style in stone and brick, which following the contemporary Indian mode yet achieved great distinction of its own. The great *stupas* or *cetiyas* of Ceylon followed upon the need created by the institution of Buddhism in the island.

In the order which Mahinda had established was created a new class of *religieux*, devoted somewhat fanatically, as their records will show, to the ideal of Ceylon as the island of the *Dhamma*, and proving their loyalty to this cause by their work in commentary and poetry, as well as in the religious life they led. Mahinda, when he is reported to have decided that the *Dhamma* was not firmly rooted in the island until a Sinhalese monk recited the *Vinaya*, was something more than the prototype of the nationalist. He was responsible for the development of the Sinhalese language and its use for creative and artistic purposes. The Buddhist monk is reputed to have taught the Sinhalese how to write, and the religion kept monk and layman in touch with some of the best thought of the time through the medium of the prakrits and Pali.[1]

Besides, Buddhism was a liberating force. Through its ethical code and its contemplative ideal it gave the member of the small agricultural community hemmed in by sacrificial rite and the punitive vengeance of the gods of the earth, the nobler conception of the wise man who strives to free himself through his own understanding and his good actions. He was given, too, rites to perform, and sermons to hear which must have done a good deal to sweeten his lot, and lend purposiveness to his existence.

Finally it would not be wrong to think of the coming of Buddhism to Ceylon as insisting on the island's connection with the Indian mainland at a moment which represents one of the high levels of its development, and also ensuring that there was much which was borrowed to be transformed in modes which were going to be characteristically Sinhalese. In fact Buddhism gave to Ceylon an opportunity to prove itself; it drew out of the community something which, but for the demands it made, might well have slumbered for some centuries yet.

'Mahinda's arrival in Ceylon,' writes Bhikkhu Rahula, 'can be regarded as the beginning of Sinhalese culture. He brought to Lanka not only a new religion but also a whole civilization at the height of its glory. He introduced

[1] G. C. Mendis, *The Early History of Ceylon*, Calcutta, 1935, pp. 16 ff.

art and architecture into the island along with *sangharamas* and *cetiyas*. He can be regarded as the father of Sinhalese literature. Buddhaghosa says that Mahinda brought to the island of the Sinhalese the commentaries of the *Tripitaka* and put them into Sinhalese for the benefit of the people of the island. He thus made Sinhalese a literary language and inaugurated its literature. It is probable that he introduced the Asokan alphabet as well.'[1] It is no wonder that Mihintale is one of the most highly venerated sites in Ceylon, and that a special festival later commemorated the arrival of the thera in the island.

Most of the area of the ancient Cetiya-pabbata is in ruin now, yet the spot and its name must remind anyone who has lived in Ceylon, or seen in drawing or photograph any of its Buddhist sites ancient or modern, of the most constant feature of the landscape of Buddhist Ceylon—the *cetiya* or *stupa*. The white bell-shaped dome, which in spite of its sheer bulk leaves the impression of a mildness in its curve; the spire rising out of it, so slender in the distance as to be almost unseen; its plinth of moulded terraces; all this gives to the landscape in which it appears its characteristic associations of Ceylon. The pagodas of Burma, the *wats* of Siam and Cambodia may be more impressive, but the very simplicity of the *stupa* in Ceylon, and its easy curve speak of a cult that is basically quiet and restrained. Since Mahinda came to the island, these *stupas* have marked Buddhist Ceylon. Some of them, in the days of the ancient kings, must surely have been as ornate in their exterior, with the painting on the dome, as the exotic fanes of gods earlier and later, but in general their architectural lines are plain, harmonizing with whatever setting nature provides—coconut grove, terraced rice-field, a clearing in the jungle, or some road which winds beside the sea.

Like the religion with which it was associated, the *stupa* was brought to Ceylon from North India, where it was the counterpart of the *tumulus* erected all over the world by ancient cultures to mark the remains of heroes and great men of the tribe. Its outlines correspond therefore to the curve and the pile of the mound heaped up on the level of the earth. In the Mahaparanibbana Sutta we have seen how the Buddha spoke to Ananda of the places which would later be visited by pilgrims. The same Sutta relates how after the Buddha's cremation his relics were divided into eight parts, and *stupas* built over them. As it honoured the memory of a great man, the *stupa* would be built over some relic of his, however infinitesimal it might be; and as it was built over a relic, it would be worshipped in the same way the relic would be worshipped.

As an object of worship in ancient times, the *stupa* would be characterized by special features conventionalized by tradition. Its precincts would include

[1] Bhikkhu W. Rahula, *op. cit.* p. 59.

an outer area strewn with sand. From this a flight of steps would lead to an area paved with stone—the ambulatory—with four ornamented gateways at the four entrances. In the centre of this paved area would rise the domed structure, on its pediment of three circular terraces, originally intended for the offering of flowers. Dome was surmounted by a box-like square structure, called by its Burmese name a 'tee', out of which rose a conical spire placed on a circular drum-like support. The spire through its course of concentric rings of moulded stone (or brass as at the present time) imitated the old umbrellas of stone. On its finial would stand a large ring of crystal in which used to be set a precious stone. The dome plastered in white, crystal and precious stone, would catch the light and reflect it from afar.

Round the base of the *stupa* were places marked out for the devotee to pause in his circumambulation from left to right. Subsidiary shrines would mark these places, generally at the four cardinal points and at each of their sub-divisions, so that there would be as many as sixteen positions at which an act of worship would be made. The remains of slender monolithic columns round some *stupas* suggest that at one time a roof protected the whole domical struc-ture. This *cetiya-ghara* is not unknown in Ceylon, the finest examples—roof being of wood has long since perished—are the twelfth-century *Vatadage* or circular relic-house at Polonnaruva, and the somewhat earlier *Vatadage* at Madirigiriya.

Six types of *stupa* were known in Ceylon, all of them described by reference to familiar objects. They could be shaped like a bell, a pot, a bubble, a heap of paddy, a lotus and the amalaka fruit. Paranavitane in his study of the *stupa* in Ceylon states that the bubble-shaped was the commonest in ancient times. The architect of the Mahavihara *stupa*, when the king Dutthagamani en-quired of him what shape it was going to be, took a golden bowl filled with water, and into it dropped some water from his hand. 'A great bubble rose up to a half-globe of crystal.' This was sufficient demonstration.

Paranavitane refers to Foucher's apt comparison of the bubble form with the unreal nature of the world which is so often emphasized in Buddhist teaching. In this similitude could be noticed the frequency with which archi-tectural or sculptural detail reveals symbolical significances. This feature of religious architecture is so commonplace as to need no special illustration. On the four faces of the square tee which surmounted the dome were often sculptured or plastered discs representing the sun and the moon. These may symbolize, according to Paranavitane, the light of the Buddha's teaching. 'The moulded conical spires represented the series of umbrellas' which, as the symbol of royalty, crowned the square tee. Beside steps which led to the paved court were carved slabs of stone with a semicircular top surmounting a rectangular base, on which were represented supernatural beings who guarded the entrances to the court. These 'guardstones' as they are called lent the symbolical support of earth-deities and snake-kings to the religion of the Buddha. The commonest motif of these guardstones became that of the Naga king. He is 'shown as standing in a graceful attitude holding, in one hand, a vase filled with flowers, and in the other a flowering twig. Very often the Naga is shown as trampling, with one of his feet, the foot of a diminutive *bhuta* (evil spirit) who is looking up towards the Naga with terror-stricken face as if begging for mercy. Both objects held in the Naga's hands are symbolic of plenty and prosperity; and his attitude in trampling down a *bhuta* suggests that he averts evil influences.'[1]

The devotee at the stupa would thus receive visually confirmation in the belief he professed. Ruskin in the last century made several strictures on Indian art which he felt to be overconventionalized and far from the truth of nature which he valued. His difficulty lay in his natural ignorance both of the framework of belief which made convention and symbol pulsate with the force of a living reality, and of its setting. It is strange that the man who wrote so rhapsodically of the medieval cathedral should have turned with distaste from a style allied to it in its intention.

Even if time had spared the original form of what was built on Mihintale, the devotion of later kings would scarcely have left untouched shrines which they delighted to honour. Only the caves remain, perhaps, in a form which most resembles the ancient, yet even these, if we are to believe the commentaries, used to be pleasant places, with their openings bricked, and plastered inside, the roof sometimes adorned with paintings; quite different from the dark and noisome resorts of bats most of them now are.

In the present-day Mihintale several hundred steps of massive stone hewn and chased lead to the level below the Ambatthala plateau. The ancient drain which drew off the flow of water and prevented it from rushing over the steps in time of rain has been restored, the stones have been replaced, and the whole in its easy gradient leaves the impression of a gigantic Renaissance stairway leading to some palace. To the right, about midway on the steps, a path leads to the Kanthaka-*cetiya*, which recent excavation and restoration reveal in its loveliness and loneliness, whether one views it close at hand standing on the ruins of its paved walk, or sees it from the hillside above, on the path to the Nagapokuna where king Devanampiya Tissa sat down to his evening meal on the day he met the *thera*.

This little *stupa*—small by comparison with the great stupas of Anuradhapura and Polonnaruva—stands on a grassy knoll to the west of the main flight of steps. It may have commemorated the horse Kanthaka on which Siddartha rode away from the palace. Built not long after Mahinda took up his residence

---

[1] S. Paranavitane, *The Stupa in Ceylon*, p. 71.

. Anurdhapura: *Mithuna* couple. Sculpture in present-day Issurumuniya Vihara—see p. 117

13.
Left:
Anurad-
hapura:
The sculp-
tured Man
and Horse
near the
Tisa Vava
—see p. 118

Right:
Anurad-
hapura:
Guardstone
with the
godling
Padma—
see p. 120

14.
Sigiriya: Two
figures from
the well-known
frescoes —see
P. 124

Sigiriya: The polished wall of the Western Gallery on which the graffiti were found—see p. 134

15. Sigiriya: One of the Lion's Paws—see p. 132

16.

Left: Polonnaruva: The statue of a King, or The Statue of the King?—see p. 149

Right: Polonnaruva: The Royal Pavilion— detail of a frieze —see p. 151

17. Polonnaruva: Pillars in Nissanka Lata Mandapa—see p. 152

Above:

Polonnaruva:
Vatadage, with
statue in fore-
ground—see
152.

Right:

Mandalagiri:
present-day
Medirigiriya
statue in
Vatadage—see
153

Polonnaruva: The piers of the Lankatilaka

19. Polonnaruva: Vatadage—guardstone

on the hill, it was restored more than once by later kings, and rifled by treasure seekers several centuries ago. Its recent restoration, undertaken in the last twenty years, has allowed the present age a glimpse of the beauty of a characteristic mark of the *stupa* as it developed in Ceylon, for here much better preserved than elsewhere is the *Vahalkada*, or what the archaeologist at the turn of the last century called the 'frontispiece'.

The bubble-shaped dome of the Kanthaka-*cetiya* is built upon three terraces, the highest nearly eleven feet above the stone paving; it still preserves some of its ancient coat of lime plaster. Neither tee, nor spire remain, grass covers the top which treasure seekers must have breached. The distinction of this shrine lies in its *Vahalkadas*, at the four cardinal points, each standing behind a gneiss altar. Two of these, the ones on the East and on the North, are the best preserved of any found so far in Ceylon. The function of these structures has not as yet been definitely explained. The earlier description 'frontispiece' thought of them as decorative ornament in front of the *stupa* at the four cardinal points. To another authority of those times they provided protective backgrounds for the flower altars which stood before them. Screens which concealed the flights of steps leading to the upper terraces of the stupa, and structures containing flower altars, were other theories. The most recent suggestion is that they are the Sinhalese elaboration of the platforms which projected from the base of the *stupa* at the four cardinal points. These were known in the *stupas* of the Andhradesa in India.[1]

Whatever their purpose may have been, it is undeniable that as ornament they prove the great advance made by the Sinhalese in the plastic arts in the centuries which intervened between the arrival of Mahinda and the date of these creations. If the Kanthaka-*cetiya* was built during the reign of Devanampiya Tissa in the third century B.C., the *vahalkadas* are likely to have been an addition of the second century A.D. They may be an imitation of work carried out much earlier at Anuradhapura, and a development of that tradition, for there is a difference noticeable between those at Mihintale and those at Anuradhapura, just as there is a difference between the Mihintale ones and those at Polonnaruva nearly a thousand years later. The great skill of the artist is shown in the variety he is able to get into the conventional design while yet working within the tradition of regulated course of ornament at the regular interval, with intervening frieze with its formalized row of figures.

The symbolic significance of course and frieze, clear enough to the devotee of those days, no longer adds the satisfaction of the return of the expected pleasure as the eye travels over each element of the sculptured decoration. But even taken in complete isolation from place, time and intention, these *vahalkadas* are notable examples of Sinhalese plastic art. Not one of them

[1] *Ibid.*, pp. 59 ff.

D

remains intact, so the effect of the whole can only be surmized. In shape they resemble a large five-leaved screen in stone, the three central leaves projecting to form three sides of a square, while leaves 1 and 5 are parallel to 3. The whole stands between two stelae, elaborately carved, and on which are mounted the figures of animals. Above the pediment of the screen-like structure runs a course of elephant heads with trunks curled, in between the heads stand conventional lotus flowers. Above this, in the example at the Kanthaka-*cetiya*, are two rows of plain moulding, and then a cornice with a conventional design of dormer windows. Above this is a plain vertical face with a cornice of a floral design, another common feature of all *vahalkadas*, followed by another typical feature, the row of projecting brackets which seem to issue from the mouths of strange beasts. Above this again, after an undecorated vertical face is a frieze of *hamsas* (geese), and then a frieze of dwarfs in which the sureness of the sculptor's touch is manifested. Each of the gnome-like creatures is given a different attitude, and there is a wonderful variety and humour in the ways they are represented. Some have animal heads, others play musical instruments, while one solemnly stands on his head. Above this lively and charming frieze is again another conventional pattern—that of the Buddhist railing from the Sanchi *stupa*. Of the rest of the *vahalkada* there are the remains of the brick structure with the huge design of the window with the recessed niches in which statues must have been placed. The limestone stelae on either side of the *vahalkada* are very finely carved with floral designs, with men, animals and birds. On each of these column were the animals traditionally associated with the cardinal point in early Buddhist legends of the cosmos—the lion for the north, bull for the south, elephant for the east and horse for the west.

At the Kanthaka-*cetiya* the figures of these animals were found in positions other than those they should have been occupying. The horse, a beautiful study in repose, was discovered near the southern *vahalkada*, and not the western. The earlier symbolism was forgotten, and the animals became, like the whole of this architectural feature, another piece of decorativeness. It should not be surprising that these figures of animals are so finely executed. That of the elephant, the most frequent in ornament, is surely one of the most natural tests of the artist's skill in India and Ceylon, not only because it was well-known both in captivity and in the jungle, but in Buddhist legend it became one of the animals associated with the story of the Buddha's life. On the rock at Kalsi, beside Asoka's inscription, is inclined the figure of an elephant, 'the superlative elephant', (gajatama), as it was called. If there was an artist worthy of the name in Ceylon who claimed mastery of his craft, then as Giotto drew an O, he would have shown his skill with the drawing of an elephant. Rock-pool, river-wharf, the retaining wall of the paved courtyard of *stupa*, pediment and frieze provided opportunities for this peculiar skill. How the hand of the craftsman in Ceylon has forgotten his ancient cunning could be seen in the recent restoration of the Ruvanvelisaya *stupa* at Anuradhapura, more particularly in its elephant wall. 126356

'These *vahalkadas* are, from an architectural point of view, among the most important features of the Ceylon stupas and supply the earliest examples of plastic art in the island.' So Paranavitane.[1] Whether they were integral parts of the *stupa* or not, one feels that in their composition, particularly in the way in which the eye is made to travel from one element in the whole decorative structure to the other, they combine a high degree of skill in the intricacy of detail and an understanding of balance and order. There is no reckless profusion of decoration in these stone façades. Even if the stone faces of the *vahalkada* had been painted, and its niches filled with statues, the plain moulded courses would have relieved the eye and balanced the grandeur of the whole composition.

Mihintale has one other piece of evidence over which it is worth while to spend some time. On the terrace above the flight of steps is a stone bath, cut into the rock on one side and completed with carved stone slabs on the other three. The originality of the whole design can scarcely be appreciated now, for all one sees is a depression on which the dressed slabs irregularly define the area of the bath. But the beauty of each of the carved stones, and the lion spout through which the waste water of the bath flowed, cannot fail to impress the spectator with their vitality and freshness. Here again the Sinhalese artist using the conventional—the lion—has contrived to inspire it with great vigour of movement. What seems realistic in the lion which rears itself up as if to spring is due to the freedom with which the sculptor has modified the formal. The lion gets its dynamic effect, weathered though the original lines are, through the flexibility with which the paws and the mass of the body of the stereotyped figure are presented.[2]

On the stone slabs which make up the sides of the bath are represented lions, dwarfs, dancers and wrestlers. Here we have such a mixture of the conventional (lions, dwarfs) and the living contemporary (dancers and wrestlers), that we can understand how the artist could invigorate his work through the interaction of the two. Dancers and wrestlers were conventional motifs, but like elephant, bull and horse, they could be living models too. Formalism could be offset by reference to the natural. In the Nagapokuna the gigantic

---

[1] *Ibid.*, p. 47.

[2] P. E. P. Deraniyagala, 'The Human and Animal Motif in Sinhala Art.' JRAS (CB) Vol. IV (New Series) 1954, p. 21 suggests affectingly that the earliest sculptures of lions in Ceylon are truer to life than the later ones because the earlier artist better remembered 'the animal that once inhabited Ceylon'. This allusion to race-memory is highly interesting, to say the least.

cobra carved in the projecting rock has the conventional five hoods, but its concentrated tenseness over the pool it seems to guard is surely the result of the artist's observation of natural life around him. The cobra (Naga) appears to hold in the poise of its attitude the weight and mass of the rock overhanging the dark water.

At the foot of the hill, along the present approach road, are the ruins of another important institution in the buildings grouped round a monastery—the hospital. Wherever a large community of monks lived, there had naturally to be a hospital. These were not restricted to the religious, the layman could be treated too. Remains of hospitals are found, distinguishable as such by descriptional evidence in default of other proof, all over the island at ancient monastic sites. At Mihintale the buildings are planned on the four sides of an inner court which contained a shrine with three images. Most interesting in the ruins is the 'medicine boat'—a monolithic trough moulded on the outside, and so shaped with depressions for head, shoulders, and buttocks, as to receive the patient stretched inside at full length in his bath of medicaments. Monolithic troughs, called 'boats', for the purpose of receiving offerings at temples, and for storing the water required for the ablutions of the devout before they entered the sacred precincts, are also found on the sites of ancient monasteries.

The hill where the *thera* met the king, with its group of three near-by hills must once have been studded with buildings for the very large monastic community living there. Fa-Hsien who visited Ceylon in the fifth century A.D. wrote that there were 5,000 monks residing at Mihintale. Only one of the four hills the Missaka mountain, has really been freed from the grip of the jungle. But all about, on the plain below, and on the hills, in cave, pillar and ruined *stupas* are the records of the past greatness of the site. Evidences of its historical vicissitudes are plain to see too, for Mahayanist shrines occur frequently, and from them have been recovered images belonging to the time when Mihintale passed into the hands of sectaries supported by schismatic kings.

CHAPTER SEVEN

SACRED CITY

King Devanampiya Tissa ploughed a furrow to mark out the boundaries of the future Mahavihara at Anuradhapura. These took in the city too, as the king insisted, in his pious devotion to the religion to which he had recently been converted, that the city should be included in the sacred precincts of the monastery. 'I will abide under the Buddha's command, thou Giver of light!' he told Mahinda, 'therefore establish the boundaries with all speed, taking in the city.' 'If it be so,' the *thera* replied, 'then do thou thyself, lord of the earth, mark out the course of the boundary.' The head of the state, of his own will and with his own hands made of Anuradhapura, his capital, a sacred city. Within a few years the presence there of the relics of the Buddha—the collar-bone at the Thuparama, the begging bowl at the royal palace, the branch of the Bodhi-tree in its enclosure—must have added to its reputation as one of the chosen sites of pilgrimage for Buddhists. As a sacred city it drew pilgrims from the West and the East of the Buddhist world. We read of travellers from India and from China, the most famous of them being Fa-Hsien who visited the city at the height of its reputation, not long after the Tooth Relic had been brought there. A king and queen from the Kalinga kingdom in India, forced into exile, spent their last days in the holy city of Anuradhapura.

The ancient Sinhalese state, inaugurated by king and *thera* when the furrow marked out the boundaries of both monastery and capital, was a Buddhist Kingdom in which the king, a Buddhist, was thereby *Fidei Defensor*. It was his right to see that the religion was kept pure and in its pristine condition. Consecrated in the ceremonial of the *abhiseka* or 'annointing' with rites at which in time the *sangha* assisted, the king was head of the state with power to purify the *sasana*, as he often did. He could, and did, when it was necessary, settle disputes within the *sangha*. He was referred to in phrases generally reserved for the Buddha and *arahants*, and, in the tenth century A.D., he was even regarded as a *Bodhisatta*. Many kings in their devotion to the religion offered their kingdoms to the *sangha*. Bhikkhu Rahula[1] quotes a number of

[1] Bhikkhu W. Rahula, *History of Buddhism in Ceylon*, p. 75 and also p. 148, cited earlier and referred to throughout in this chapter.

cases where the formal act of oblation was made, but in every case the *sangha* returned to the king what had been the vehicle of ritual gesture. Such a gesture would denote not political submission, but religious devotion. There was one king who offered his queen to the *sangha*. This embarrassing transfer was not intended to be taken literally, either by donor or recipient.

The king had his own officers of state, his ministers, his generals, and his Brahmin chaplain, or *purohita,* who was responsible for performing the domestic rituals in the royal household. Such things as the birth of a child to a queen would be attended by ceremonies typically Brahmanical. On such occasions the *sangha,* then as now, had no official status, nor did it assume any rights. The king protected the *sangha* and looked after its well-being. As head of the state he was responsible through his officers for the administration of the country, the collection of revenue, defence, justice, public services—everything which a secular state at the present time organizes through departments responsible to the government of the country. A great deal of what would now be the concern of a department of local administration was worked through village councils constituted in accordance with customary procedure. These *gamsabhava* were an old institution, going back to the Indian origins of the 'Aryan' settlers in Ceylon.

In the state, and abiding by its laws, was the *sangha;* although from another point of view, the ideals and the purpose of the *sangha* would remove it from concern with any official secular activities or interests. Its position in relation to the secular authority was never precisely defined; the normality and traditional clearness of that position precluded the necessity for exact definition. Statecraft, and the governing of a country would by definition be outside the purview of the *sangha.* It was its duty to devote itself to the religious life, and to carry out, in the precincts of the monasteries, such duties as devolved on it—preaching, meditation, and the regulation of the life of the particular monastic community.

Yet the duties of the *sangha* can hardly be thought of as sacerdotal. The Buddhist monk cannot be regarded as the counterpart of the medieval Christian monk, not even of one of the wandering orders of friars. In the process of time monasteries grew into great communities with large acres of rice-fields and tanks, and a retinue of servants, both lay and semi-religious. Into these communities the layman who desired to become a priest could enter, and out of these communities would go priests for whom the religious life was a vocation no longer. The monk who followed *Vinaya* precepts carefully would go out on his begging round every day. Others would be fed at the monastery or state refectories. Contact with the people came through the role the monk played in the performance of his obligations as a religious, through his preaching, and the layman's seeking advice of him. In the hospitals attached to monasteries, laymen could be admitted as patients. So, too, in the schools which were intended for the education of the monk, lay people could find a place.

But the significant duty of the *sangha* was that assigned to it by the Buddha —the diligent working out by each man of his own salvation. The *sangha* was not a carefully planned organization, each monastery—*vihara* or *pirivena* as it is still called—was a unit in itself. No single head controlled the various monks living in cells, meditating in the forest, or residing in the great monasteries which were the feature of the capital city. There was no spiritual pontiff who claimed the allegiance of all who wore the yellow robes. In the lifetime of the Buddha the yellow-robed mendicants would naturally look up to him as teacher, but after his death, if a council met it would only be for the purpose of deciding which was true doctrine and which false. At the time of the Third Council in the reign of Asoka, it would seem that the emperor took a prominent part in arranging for it to reform abuses in the *sangha*. He may even have taken a share in its deliberations, for in the Bhabru edict already quoted, he recommends to monk and nun special texts for study. The *Vinaya*, or the rules, which came into existence in the process of the growth of the order shows the reason for the customary observances.

After the Buddha's death when the prime minister of the state of Magadha, with the statesman's instinct for procedure, asked Ananda whether the Buddha had appointed any *bhikkhu* to be the refuge of the *sangha*, to whom it could turn after his death, Ananda answered, 'No.' To the question whether the *sangha* then had appointed such a person, Ananda again made the same reply. The statesman then propounded a question which must have been valid in constitutional law: 'Venerable Ananda, when there is no refuge what is the basis for unity?' Ananda's answer convincingly stated the Buddhist position: 'Brahman, we are not helpless (not without refuge): we have a refuge, we have the refuge of the *Dhamma*.'[1]

The *Dhamma* the Buddha preached laid stress on the individual's perceptive understanding of the nature of the world. Each individual was therefore the arbiter of his own salvation. Far from recommending, in the interests of organization, conformity to an accepted position, the Buddha advized his disciples always to question everything, and to criticize a thing before they accepted it: His words in the Kalama Sutta are the best illustration: 'It is proper, Kalamas, for you to doubt and to waver. In a doubtful matter wavering does arise. Now look you, Kalamas, do not be led by reports, or traditions, or hearsay. Be not led by proficiency in the collections, nor by mere logic or inference, nor by considering appearances, nor by delighting in speculation. Be not led by the appearance of possibilities, nor thinking: "The recluse is our

[1] M, III, p. 49 ff. Quoted by Bhikkhu Rahula, *op. cit.* pp. 170.

respected teacher." '[1] Such an admirable attitude of wise scepticism could not allow the development of an institution laying claim to the unquestioning obedience of its members, either in the name of tradition or authority.

One is forced to the conclusion that the power of the *sangha* was the corrollary of this very lack of organized strength. It was not, in relation to the state, an *imperium in imperio*. It was thereby the more influential because its members, devoted to an ideal which basically undervalued the secular, could give a place to the secular power in the scheme of things of a religious, without actually dismissing it. The life of the layman with its excitements and attractions existed outside the orbit of the life the monk chose for himself. It might be important, but it lay outside. For those who were drawn to it return to it was normal and easy. But those in the monastery had fixed their attention elsewhere, and for them the secular life was an echo and a rumour of a world apart from theirs.

In its relations with the king the *sangha*, by and large, would observe the decorum to which its importance and its necessary role in the *sasana* would entitle it. Naturally there were monks who did not scruple to admonish the king, when they felt moved against him. Some monks were very highly honoured by kings, some of whom had actually been educated by monks. Some were even the special favourites of the sovereign, and some, in the course of the thousand years in which Anuradhapura was the state capital, played a part in palace revolutions. But there is no evidence that the monk, as in Europe, ever held secular office and was statesman or adviser to the monarch. In the story of the warrior-king of Ceylon the Chronicle relates of the war between Dutthagamani and his brother Tissa, that when a *thera* had brought the warring brothers together, Dutthagamani said to him: 'If you had but sent a *samanera* of seven years our strife had not taken place (and all had ended) without the loss of men.' 'O king,' said the *thera*, 'this is the brotherhood's guilt, the brotherhood will do penance.'[2] In such matters as a dispute between two royal brothers the *sangha* could have exerted its influence, but it enjoyed no right *per se* to wield political power, or to claim any political rights. Bhikkhu Rahula refers to one instance of a monk who was made a legal officer on account of his skill and knowledge of the law. But he states that this monk is likely to have heard only ecclesiastical cases. Nor was the monk, as monk, exempt from the working of the law of the land. A monk guilty of an offence against the legal code would be disrobed and handed to the civil authority.

Ancient Ceylon was thereby saved the disputes which disfigure medieval European history, between church and state, each arrogating to itself the supremacy. As the *sangha* made no claim for itself in matters temporal, it

[1] *A*, I, p. 189.   [2] *Mhv.* xxiv, 54 ff.

enforced none. As will be seen, where it did enforce its claims, as for instance in matters of doctrine, it prosecuted them with a vigour and a single-mindedness characteristic of the devout everywhere. But ever here, it is worth noting it is not the *sangha* as a whole that we speak of, but of particular communities of monks. The bitterness of the feuds between the monks of the Mahavihara and those of the Abhayagiri or the Jetavanarama, were the results of doctrinal clashes in spheres over which the monk claimed the right to decide. In these feuds, as they spread, lives were lost, and temples razed to the ground. The king may have helped one group against another; one of them, Mahasena, was forced by the disastrous consequences of the strife to urge the monks to return to the monastery they had left. But these basically were matters spiritual over which the community of monks had jurisdiction. With these the king had no right to interfere, except when the *sasana* had to be purified.

In the great monasteries the monks would live given over to such pursuits as had in the lapse of years become characteristic of the *sangha*. The ascetic ideal would, of course, have always been a driving force in the lives of many of them, and there were movements of a puritanical kind reminding the monk of the ancient character of the order. Since the great monasteries virtually held the monopoly of learning in the land, they produced their scholars, their artists committed by *Theravada* rule and tradition to such subjects as produced the emotions proper to the member of a religious order.[1] Many of the *stupas* and monasteries must have been designed by architect monks, and adorned through the skill of other monks proficient in the arts. There would be monks who were physicians, practising for the benefit of the monastery, and the community at large. The old ascetic ideal, seemingly out of place in the changed circumstances of monastic Buddhism in medieval Ceylon, would tend to be replaced by newer ideals of the merit to be gained by knowledge and study. The *Vinaya* rules, as they had grown out of circumstances in which the Buddha was asked to prescribe a mode of conduct for the mendicant, were themselves modified to meet changed circumstances. These modifications may not always have harmonized with the original teaching of the Buddha, but then since his time the order had developed into a monastic community supported by the king and the people as the customary duty of both state and laity.

Caste, as it was known in the country, was known in the *sangha* too. Here it should be noted that the Buddha refused to recognize the justification for any distinctions of caste in the *sangha*. On the other hand, caste did exist in the Magadha of his time. In this, as in all matters, the Buddha divided the

---

[1] The most famous of these learned monks was the fifth century A.D. Buddhaghosa, who translated the Sinhalese commentaries on the *Tipitaka* into Pali.

spheres of influence of Caesar and the spiritual life, keeping out of the latter traffic with any of the institutions the state recognized in his time, but rendering unto Caesar the right to regulate the secular life as it seemed good to him. With the brahmanic justification of caste the Buddha had no patience. It might have been possible, as it was done, to rationalize caste even through an application of his teaching, but that teaching was based on more fundamental realities.

Slaves were known in the monasteries, just as they were known in the world outside. The practice grew up of devotees, in the interest of acquiring merit, offering themselves as slaves to the monastery, and then, with a sound instinct both for double merit and personal comfort, buying themselves out. Here again the monastic practice deviated from the original teaching of the Buddha, who forbad the bhikkhu from accepting slaves as servants, but other times brought other customs. It was the age of the monastery as a large estate-owning institution with revenues and wealth which often excited the cupidity and rapacity of kings. To such institutions slaves would have been a necessity, and, as ever, the tenets of religious institutions could be made to stretch obligingly to gratify the demands of those in power.

Of the country in which the *sangha* jealously guarded its rights to decide upon all matters of doctrine, and in which the king ruled, not by divine right but by traditional custom, we have a picture all too scantily delineated as yet, and still waiting for the interpretations of scholars before its outlines could be filled in and coloured. That it was a prosperous kingdom; that it drew traders from all parts of the then known world; that it displayed its prosperity in the splendour of the sacred city; is clear from the evidence of poems, inscriptions, coins, and from its surviving remains. Its history—the history of more than a thousand years—is as much a tangle as the sinuous jungle creepers which enveloped its great monuments when the sacred city ceased to be the capital of the kingdom. Hardly any trace remains of its palaces, the dwellings of its nobles, its merchants who were organized in trade guilds, and its common folk, largely because wood has not resisted the tooth of time as well as gneiss and limestone. To search for the clue which will make its invasions by the South Indian kingdoms, its strife between rival claimants to the throne, its palace revolutions, its roll of assassinations intelligible, must remain the work of a later generation. It is not an uninteresting history, but to the layman it must seem wanting in the traces of that clear development with which historians neatly tie up the result of their labours. From across the sea—the narrow strait which divided India from Ceylon—there was always the threat of the marauding band. Kings reigned, built tanks endowed the *sangha* with tanks, *stupas* and images; were followed by kings who were neglectful of these obligations; or were slain by generals or rival princes; and the country was either at peace or in the toils of civil war or invasion. Of the great mass of people in the country we have little first-hand information. Most of what we know about Ceylon for more than a thousand years of its history comes from the very partisan assessment of the monks of the Mahavihara of the events of times past.

To these monks it was the excellence of the teaching they alone preserved which gave not only the capital city, but also the whole island, its fame. Its old reputation as the stronghold of *Theravada* Buddhism still clings to Anuradhapura. For over a thousand years it had been the capital of the kings of Ceylon, for close upon nine hundred years after, it gradually sank deeper and deeper into the jungle which closed over it, despite the attempts made by two or three kings to arrest its downward plunge. As far as one can see it is not likely to reassume its dignity as capital; but this at least is certain, to the Buddhist of Ceylon it will always remain the sacred city of the past. If all of its twenty-five square miles were reduced to the rubble of brick and stone which marks most of its area now, even if all its *stupas* were obliterated, and their sites forgotten, it would still survive as the honoured city of Buddhism in Ceylon, because the community of the Mahavihara celebrated it as such in their epical chronicle, the first part of which was written between the fourth and fifth centuries A.D.

The *Mahavamsa*, or the chronicle of the great line of kings, celebrated Dutthagamani, the great warrior-king of old Ceylon. How such a poem with its subject matter of war, civil strife and crime, came to be composed by a monk or a group of monks, is interesting. True, the poetic record in its references to kings, speaks of their acts of piety, their donations of land and tanks to monasteries, the building of *stupas*, and the presents of treasure to shrines. It is regrettable that as history, in spite of all its authenticity, it is mainly hieratic, for out of its annals very little could be gathered of how people lived and how they managed their affairs. Yet even as religious chronicle of the development of a religion, its material seems far removed from the subjects of a monk's contemplation or study. The Buddha, according to the Suttas, directed the attention of monks away from such subjects of talk as 'battles long ago' and the excitements of the secular life. He denounced such things as 'animal talk'. Yet the author of the *Mahavamsa*, in order to survey the history of the Sinhalese race up to the fifth century A.D. had to repeat such talk. With a masterly power, characteristic of the religious determined to have the best of both worlds—the secular and the spiritual—the pageant of history is unfolded as a topic for the contemplation of the devout. The chronicle was compiled 'for the serene joy and the emotion of the pious'. What better theme for meditation than the crimes and follies of mankind. If history had no other lesson to teach, scanning its pages or rather hearing its sad stories of the deaths of kings, was to fortify oneself anew in the knowledge of the transiency of all things, and to savour, by contrast, the joy of the mind directed towards the Four Noble Truths. Each chapter of the *Mahavamsa* ends with the edificatory flourish: 'Here ends the . . . chapter of the *Mahavamsa*, compiled for the serene joy and emotion of the pious.'

The Chronicle even when it deals with the time of the Tamil ruler, Elara, the Hindu 'who knew not the peerless virtues of the most precious of the three gems', makes its didactic point. The just king had secured rain in due season for the country through the intervention of the god Pajjuna. The Chronicle notes: 'Only because he freed himself from the guilt of walking in the path of evil did this (monarch), though he had not put aside false beliefs, gain such miraculous power; how should not then an understanding man, established in pure belief, renounce here the guilt of walking in the path of evil?'[1] History, as in medieval Europe, is given the justification of a moral sermon, its actors and catastrophes are *exempla* for the contemplation and self-examination of the devout.

Yet the *Mahavamas* is more than a sermon which takes the history of a people as its text. It is, not surprisingly, the national epic of the Sinhalese. Not surprisingly, because ancient epic in its ritual origins, and modern epic, out of political considerations, have lent themselves to the process of creating a national self-consciousness. Virgil successfully hymned not *pius Aeneas*, but imperial Rome, while the revival of legendary material in the Wagnerian rodomontade of music and spectacle contributed not a little to the theory of a master race in our own time. The *Mahavamsa* is no exception. Its Pali lines must have fired the imagination of the clerics of its time. Ungainly translation into prose removes from it every vestige of either inspiration or rhetorical excellence. Even so, one can see in such maladroit prose renderings as we possess the ore out of which was fashioned a nation's pride in its achievements. Serene joy there may have been in it for the pious, but for those whose ears were attuned to other harmonies, it must have communicated emotions only collaterally related to those of 'calm of mind all passion spent'. Surely the writer's quickened feelings as he recounts, for instance, the war between Dutthagamani, the national hero of the epic, and the Tamil prince Elara, create something of his own excitement and the intensity of pride in the victory of the Sinhalese, which comes through the most literal of translations: 'When the battle began the mighty and terrible Dighajantu seized his sword and shield for battle, and leaping eighteen cubits up into the air and cleaving the effigy of the king with his sword, he scattered the first body of troops. When the mighty (warrior) had in this manner scattered also the other bodies of troops, he charged at the body of troops with which king Gamani stood.

[1] *Mhv.* xxi, 34.

But when he began to attack the king, the mighty warrior Suranimila insulted him, proclaiming his own name. Dighajantu thought: "I will slay him," and leaped into the air full of rage. But Suranimila held the shield toward him as he alighted (in leaping). But Dighajantu thought: "I will cleave him in twain, together with the shield," and struck the shield with the sword. Then Suranimila let go the shield. And as he clove (only) the shield thus released, Dighajantu fell there, and Suranimila, springing up, slew the fallen (man) with his spear. Phussadeva blew his conch shell, the army of the Damilas was scattered; nay, Elara turned to flee and they slew many Damilas. The water in the tank there was dyed red with the blood of the slain, therefore it was known by the name Kulantavapi.'[1]

The poem is characterized by a strong national sentiment which, identifying religion with nation, claims a state of predestinate grace for the people and the island. The emotions which colour a great deal of the poem are those of a national fanaticism with strong religious components. The stories of its battles and wars must have come from lays and ballads extant earlier. That they found a place in this chronicle compiled for 'the serene joy and emotions of the pious' would illustrate not the well-known observation of the development of epical poem from popular song, but much more the depth of the writer's feelings which could overwhelm the specificity of his intention. How sterile beside passages like the one quoted above are the conventional lists of the meritorious works of pious kings. Saddhatissa, who succeeded his brother Dutthagamani, was one of the most righteous kings who ruled in the island, but how flat the lines which commemorate his reign:

. . . 'Dutthagamani's brother, Saddhatissa, annointed king after his death, ruled, a peerless (prince) for eighteen years. He finished the work on the parasol, and the plaster-work and the elephant-wall of the Great Thupa, he who won his name by his faith. The magnificent Lohapasada caught fire from a lamp; he built the Lohapasada anew, seven stories high. And now was the *pasada* worth (only) ninety times a hundred thousand. He built the Dakkhinagiri-vihara and the (vihara) Kallakalena, the Kalambakavihara, and the (vihara) Pattangavalika, (the viharas) Velangavitthika, Dubbalavapitissaka, and Duratissakavapi, and the Matuviharaka. He also built viharas (from Anuradhapura) to Dighavapi, one for every yojana (of the way).

'Moreover, he founded the Dighavapi-vihara together with the cetiya: for this cetiya he had a covering of net-work made set with gems, and in every mesh thereof was hung a splendid flower of gold, large as a waggon-wheel, that he had commanded them to fashion. (In honour) of the eighty-four

[1] *Ibid.,* xxv, 58 ff. Basham's unrhymed verse translation of the storming of Elara's stronghold in the *Mhv* in *The Wonder that was India* p. 457 certainly gets spiritedness and vigour into his four-line stanzas.

thousand sections of the *Dhamma* the ruler commanded also eighty-four thousand offerings. When the king had thus accomplished many works of merit he was reborn, after his death, among the Tusita gods.'[1]

The epic, like tragedy, seems to have become an anachronism in the West. A settled faith, the proneness of a race to see itself fulfilling some supernal destiny, would seem to be as demodé now as the fashions of last year. Instead of the passionate colours of heroic poetry, the West seems to favour the common greyness with which the statisticians of the welfare state have silvered everything. The epic is no longer a political necessity in a world which strives to order its chaotic affairs aright through the unification of its diverse parts. The ideal of one world can find no room for the partisans of small national entities. One wonders whether the survival of a public for the epic in the East is indeed a virtue. Few epics are written now, but they are frequently cited, and they may be invoked by the fervour of a people anxious to grasp at a past which it only vaguely understands. The age of epics, like that of miracles, may long be past, but among communities not quite caught in the toils of our industrial civilization, some life obstinately lingers in them yet. The devotee who looks backward to the past as the ideal to which the present development of Ceylon should approximate, is only repeating what the *Mahavamsa* must have inculcated. Call back that world again, and content oneself with the infinite space it encloses in its nutshell, and the emotions engendered by the poem might still seem valid. Where this fails, where time cannot bring back the age of gold, to use its pages for political sortilege is in effect to mount the high horse Homer left riderless and to tilt against atomic reactors.

The ideal king of the poem, Gamani, was a prince of Ruhuna, the southern division of the island. Incurring the displeasure of his father because of his determination to fight against the Tamils who ruled over Rajarata with its capital of Anuradhapura, Gamani left his royal home and levied a band headed by ten champions possessed of supernatural powers. When his father forbad him to wage war against the Tamils, he sent him a woman's ornament in derision of his lack of manly spirit. This act earned him the name of Dutthagamani, Gamani the enraged. After a series of campaigns he defeated the Tamil king, Elara, and entered the capital in triumph. He made Lanka one kingdom, defeated all the enemies opposed to him, and paid signal honour to the tomb of the King Elara he had killed in single combat: 'On the spot where his body had fallen he burned it with the catafalque, and there did he build a momument and ordain worship. And even to this day the princes of Lanka, when they draw near to this place, are wont to silence their music because of this worship.'

The great conqueror whose epical story repeats, in some of its details, that

[1] *Ibid.*, xxxiii, 4 ff.

of other Indian epics, is then stricken with remorse at the numbers killed in his wars. On the night of his victory when he had slain all the Tamils, as he sat in his palace and looked out on his dancing girls like nymphs, and his ministers, his heart was troubled. The occasion immediately recalls many others. But as the monk improves it, one is filled with disappointment. Dutthagamani is comforted by eight *arahants* who knew the thoughts passing through his head, and determine to soothe his conscience. Miraculously they travel through the air, and come to the palace gates at midnight. They tell the king that they have come to comfort him. But what is it they say to him when he refuses to be comforted and asks: 'How shall there be any comfort for me, O venerable sirs, since by me was caused the slaughter of a great host number-ing millions?' The king's heart is not to be troubled, his path to heaven is un-obstructed, not a million men were slain, but only one and a half! 'From this deed arises no hindrance to thy way to heaven. Only one and a half human beings have been slain here by thee, O Lord of men. The one had come unto the (three) refugees, the other had taken on himself the five precepts. Un-believers and men of evil life were the rest, not more to be esteemed than beasts.'[1] In brief, only one and a half of those slaim could be regarded as Buddhists. How grievously religious fanaticism expresses itself in these verses. Here is the sign in which sophistry has always conquered.

The rest of his life the king spent in good works, building *viharas* and atoning for every single action of his which might have been thoughtless of the *sangha*. As he had once upon a time forgetfully eaten some sweet peppers without giving a share of them to the priesthood, he expiated this by building for the Mahavihara a monastery and a *stupa* which was called Maracavatthi-vihara, or the vihara of the pepper in the pod. For this community he likewise built the Lohapasasda, its *uposatha* hall which gleamed in its magnificence like the hall of the thirty-three gods. The *pasada* was covered over with plates of copper, from which came its popular name of the Brazen Palace. His last great work was the building of the great *stupa* (now the Ruvanvelisaya) on the spot consecrated by the Buddha, and marked out later by Devanampiya Tissa—the *stupa* which that king wished to build, but which Mahinda told him was not for him, but for Dutthagamani to build later.

He did not live to see his *stupa* finished, but on his death bed was carried in a litter to see the dome covered with white cloth, and painted over to look as if it had been completed. As he lay there dying the book of his meritorious deeds was read to him—all the *viharas* he had built, all the money he had spent on the religion. The king took up the tale of his benefactions himself, and as his strength ebbed out the priests chanted in chorus, and at his death he passed into the Tusita heaven where the *Bodhisatta* waits to be born as Maitreya Buddha.

[1] *Ibid.*, xxv, 108 ff.

Of the sacred city of the time of Dutthagamani little trace survives now. It would be surprising if any did, for the history of the city since that time includes, beside the story of its greatness, the records of successive pillagings and nearly a thousand years of neglect. It suffered at the hands of rival claimants to the throne and foreign soldiery no less than six times. It was plundered and despoiled by Sinhalese, Pandyans, Cholas, and other marauders, until in the reign of the great king of Polonnaruva, Parakkama Bahu I, the chronicle writes of it that 'the temples were overgrown with great trees and bears and leopards dwelt there'. In its oblivion it did not escape the attentions of treasure seekers who rifled *stupas* in search of the valuable objects deposited in ancient relic chambers. Its remains are chiefly of the tenth century A.D. And even today, despite the best efforts of the Archaeological Department, inartistic and tasteless restoration has in places effectively obliterated what was graceful even in its ruins. The *Mahathupa* of the national hero, the Ruvanvelisaya degoba, was taken in hand by a society which in restoring the ancient *stupa*, provided for all to see an index of the bad taste and the decadence of the plastic skill of modern craftsmen in Ceylon.

It is a relief to turn from these melancholy reflections to the record of Anuradhapura in one of its periods of glory—that of Fa-Hsien who visited it in the early years of the fifth century A.D. He spent two years in Ceylon in search of texts which he carried back with him to his own land of Han. In his time Anuradhapura was a fine city in a prosperous and flourishing countryside, with its shrines of the Tooth-relic and the Bodhi-tree, its monasteries, the imposing dwellings of the head-merchants, its level side-streets, and its well-kept main thoroughfares with lofty dais for preaching the *dhamma* wherever four roads met. Most interesting in his account of the city are his references to the numerous *bhikkhus* in monasteries in the city and in caves: 'The people of the country say that there are between fifty and sixty thousand priests altogether, all of whom get their food from a common stock. The king separately provides within the city a common stock for five or six thousand more; and those who want food take their own bowls and go to fetch it, returning with them filled according to the capacity of each.'[1] At the Abhayagiri—it was one of its great periods too—there were five thousand priests in residence; three thousand at the Mahavihara, and two thousand at Mihintale. His description of the Buddha image in green jade at the Abhayagiri, the image referred to in the first chapter, will give the reader some idea of the splendour of the sacred city.

Two centuries later the city was despoiled during wars between rival claimants to the throne. When order was restored, it came only through the result of the help given to the son of Kasyapa II by a Pallava king of India,

[1] H. A. Giles, *The Travels of Fa-Hsien*, Cambridge, 1923, p. 70.

whose forces in Ceylon were responsible for the architecture of Nalanda near Matale. Only one brief period of revival in the ninth and tenth centuries held back the increasing tide of invasion from South India. In 1017 Rajendra I, the king of the Cholas, invaded Ceylon, captured the king and all his royal treasures and devastated the country. Ceylon was annexed by the Chola empire, and governed by a Chola who resided at Polonnaruva. A period was over, the period of Anuradhapura's fame as capital of the island. It ended in a desolation from which the city never recovered.

Of its splendour in its hey-day, both in ancient and medieval times, there could be no doubt. Discount all the fanciful projections of the enthusiast, all that has been claimed for the ancient Sinhalese kingdom—its wealth, its idyllic Buddhist character, its prosperous rice-fields which were the granary of the East, its sturdy and incorruptible village institutions—as insubstantial dreaming, and yet one has to concede magnificence to its ruins and the culture they represent. What brought about its decline, whether one or other of the causes currently cited—whether the diastrous breaching of the ancient tanks (a stratagem of war resorted to by both sides), and long periods of disrepair caused the decay of the village communities, malaria completing what war began; whether the fault was in the Sinhalese kings who not only involved themselves in the wars of the South Indian kingdoms, but were also dependent on South Indian mercenaries to help them in their own dynastic broils; whether the pressure from the South Indian kingdoms was the consequence of economic drives independent of the part played by Sinhalese forces on the mainland; whether it was the critical disunity of the Sinhalese at a dangerous juncture in their history—it is difficult to say.

The clear outlines of the ancient past survive so tenuously at Anuradhapura that numerous sites are confused, and even official societies, devoted exclusively to the preservation of the sacred places, add their misapplied zeal to the confusion. The Abhayagiri and the Jetavanarama are obstinately mistaken for each other; the Dakkhinagiri *stupa* is popularly supposed to be Elara's Tomb, which now, alas, lies buried somewhere in the garden of the quarters constructed for the Medical Officer of the district; what is now called the Isurumuniya is really the Meghagiri vihara; the sentimental believe that Dutthagamani died on the monolithic slab in the middle of what is called the Dhatumandiriya; the ruins now called the Vessagiriya are really the ancient Issarasamana vihara; and the *uposatha* hall of the Abhayagiri is miscalled the Elephant Hall.

Least changed are perhaps the tanks of the sacred city. It is altogether fitting that they should remain the most gratifying features of a countryside mainly in jungle which the State is trying to reclaim. They are the memorials of the village communities on which the ancient kingdom was based. As we have already seen, the great builders of tanks developed the fortunes of the island to which Mahinda brought the message of Buddhism. The growth of the capital was facilitated by one of them, Dhatusena, who dammed a river fifty-five miles away and from it led a channel bringing water to the capital. The gently undulating stretches of land with its frequent outcrops of stone, and these man-made lakes with their fields nearby, are the familiar features of the countryside of the old Rajarata of which the broken columns of *stupas* stand out.

Tanks, restored or extended, are now being utilized for schemes of colonization in areas once supporting populations much larger than these districts know. But these old irrigation works in their modernized form, feed fields still laboriously tilled with simple plough and buffalo, as they used to be two thousand years ago. The newer divinities of electrical power and the internal combustion engine have not as yet displaced the gods worshipped on tank bund and in sylvan shrine. There may be some comfort in this, but it is cold cheer for a land which has to provide more food for its rapidly increasing population. More definitely than ever now the well-known landscape will be changed.

But the ancient *stupa*, as relic of old times, will survive such change. Once upon a time the glitter of their spires with the crystal in the sunlight, the brightness of the white-plastered dome, the brilliance of the glazed tiles covering the roofs of monasteries and palaces, would have given the traveller the first tidings of the capital he was approaching. Now with the exception of the very few which have been restored, a knoll of green surmounted by ruined tee drum, and broken spire, mark all that is left. Yet in their desolation they accord with the landscape, and remain in greater harmony with both place and time than the brashness of the restored *stupas*. The Abhayagiri and the Jetavana are now man-made hills crowned with a simple structure of box-shaped tee out of which rises the fragment of the spire. They leave the impression of an architectural feature, which having travelled full circle from its earliest beginnings, has come back into a position of rest in the original *tumulus*. The Jetavana *stupa* was 400 feet in height, while the Abhayagiri was 350. Both of them were taller than the third pyramid at Gizeh, and were the wonders of their time, the Jetavana probably being the largest *stupa* in the whole Buddhist world.

The ancient skill in handling the familiar medium of stone is abundantly displayed in the ruins of the old city. There is a graciousness of design in the royal baths just below the Tisa Vava which shows how a natural feature has been treated. In the royal park, near the western boundary of the bund of the Tisa Vava is a mass of granite which was turned into a pleasing feature. Two separate baths and one fountain have been cut out of the granite mass as it descends to the shallow rocks at its base. The first of these baths was provided with a stone seat cut into the rock-face, on which the bathers must have reclined. Steps, with elegantly moulded balustrades, descended into the bath. On either side of the seat the sculptor allowed his fancy to sport with a bas-relief of elephants enjoying themselves in a lotus-covered tank. On the one side there are three amiable looking pachyderms at play in the water, on the other they seem to be leaving it in good order. The carving is so happy in its line that a dramatic change is seen by one writer between the elephants on the left and those on the right. The latter, to him, seem alarmed, one of them scenting danger, while the other two are in full flight.

The skill in stone shows itself again in the moulded and carved capitals of columns which stand askew, or lie half-buried in the earth; the stone steps leading to the porches of shrines, with their balustrades, guardstones and that characteristically Sinhalese feature, 'the moonstone'. These are also found at Nagarjunakonda, and in the opinion of Dr Sivaramamurti, must have found their way there from Ceylon.[1] These semicircular stones, placed at the foot of steps, with their sculptured features of concentric bands of design spaced round the half-lotus at the centre of the semi-circle, reveal not only the artistry of the sculptor, but the typical character of practically all Indian religious art—its inherent tendency to use both architectural and sculptural feature to communicate symbolical significance to the worshipper.

Recent research into the moonstone[2] has high-lighted what must have been a dramatic element in the act of worship at the time when the Buddha image came to be a regular feature of the shrine in Ceylon, as well as the kinship of Indian and Ceylon art in their inevitable symbolism. Deprivation of the know-ledge of what the artist has intended to portray through the forms he has represented, may not interfere with the aesthetic effect of moonstone or *vahalkada*; it would even be wrong to state that only the savant, fortified at all points with his knowledge of Indian texts, could appreciate the work of the Indian artist. But with our attention directed to what has been intended, and the meaning of the representation, the object is invested with a new depth, and what was peripheral ornament becomes central in the design.

Dr Paranavitane's study of the moonstone in Ceylon restores to what used to be thought of as excellent added ornament the element which integrates it with the whole unit of the shrine to which it leads. The sculptured feature of the moonstone, placed before steps leading to shrines where a statue of the Buddha stood, with its details, together with steps, guardstones and balus-trades, represents symbolically the various stages through which the Buddha

[1] C. Sivaramumurti, 'Nagarjunakonda', *Marg*, Bombay, 1956, Vol. IX No. 2.

[2] S. Paranavitane, 'The Significance of Sinhalese Moonstones, *Artibus Asiae*, Vol. XVII, 3-4, 1954.

passed when he reached enlightenment, and from the height of the palace of truth surveys those subject to the world of *samsara*. The devotee, when he enters the shrine, re-enacts through the successive stages of his approach, these different phases, his mind being directed dramatically through the symbolizm of the sculpture to the Master who recommended a similar course to him. It is, in this way, a re-treading of the path the Buddha trod, as in the fourteen Stations of the Cross, the Christian is invited to relive again the traditional events of his God's passion and death on the cross. (It is true that the worshipper steps in a moment on the central lotus, but the carved details are there to attract his attention to the stages they symbolize.)

The successive stages lead through the phenomenal and human world which the Buddha saw as being continually aflame with the fires of craving—the outermost band with the tongues of flame; through the cycle of the four perils which beset all existence—the four animals on the next band signifying birth (elephant) decay (bull), disease (lion) and death (horse); the creeper of desire—the scroll with the undulating design of leaves and flowers, the state of existence in which discrimination is attained, signified by the *hamsa* (goose) with its ability to separate the good from the bad, as it was one of the mythical abilities of this bird to drink the milk in a mixture of milk and water, and to leave the water behind; through a further stage, signified by the water-lilies, of desire brought under control, and then to the central lotus signifying 'firm establishment among the possibilities of existence', or 'birth and manifestation primarily in the intelligible, or also and consequently in the sensible, world'.

At this stage the devotee is faced by the ascending levels which have brought the Buddha to the height of the palace of truth. Standing on the lotus, with his back to the world so beautifully represented as evil by the sculptor, he is reminded of the four trances which led the Buddha to enlightenment. The four steps—(sometimes they are five by another classification)—lead to the landing of the shrine, which stands for the wisdom of insight. These immense monoliths at this stage are not functionally necessary to the structure, their presence aided the graphic intention of the sculptor in the completion of his symbolical scheme. A further step, signifying compassion, leads from landing to the pedestal on which the statue was placed.

Beside steps were balustrades and guardstones, each with its symbolical meaning too. The Naga king with the pot in his hand standing for time which produces all things, and the *makara* on the balustrades for time which destroys. So 'the flights of steps of these Anuradhapura shrines thus symbolize the Path to Purity along which the Buddha has ascended to the Palace of the Dhamma—which Path all Buddhists have to tread in order to attain their goal. The devotee who steps over the moonstone, ascends the flight of steps to the landing, and enters the shrine through the doorway, symbolically performs this act in order to obtain the qualification that would enable him, under favourable circumstances, to follow the course which would by degrees lead him to the Supreme Insight.'[1]

If the Kanthaka-*cetiya* is the chief glory of Mihintale, sculpturally the finest product of the Sinhalese artist at Anuradhapura is the richly composed union of the symbolistic with the naturalistic of these moonstones. The rhythmical sweep of the procession of animals, the divagations of the creeper design and the tongues of flame, all repeat graphically the simile of the persistent whirl of a world of craving from which the Buddhist has to free himself. The vigour and clarity with which movement has been depicted in the hard mass of the stone; the nobleness of the conventional design of the lotus; and the expressive benevolence on the face of the Naga king; are the work of an artist inspired by the majesty and beauty of his theme. The world of observed natural life, as usual in the hands of a great artist, is made to revivify the world of convention, and out of both is produced the original work of art.

This same originality is seen too in the statue of the Buddha found in the entourage of the Mahayanist Abhayagiri monastery. The present-day Outer Circular Road takes in, between the site of the Twin Baths of the Kuttam Pokuna and the Abhayagiri *stupa*, no less than three statues of the Buddha. The first is a remarkable piece of sculpture—a sedent Buddha with the hands in the position of the *dhyana mudra*—the meditative pose. (The nose of this statue was damaged and has been restored, affecting through its slight disproportion the serene aspect of the teacher in *samadhi* (meditation).) The strength and placidity of expression on the face, the simplicity with which the triangular mass from head to folded feet has been rendered, cannot fail to move the beholder. Here could be seen the triumph of a tradition which using, as it would normally, the durable medium of stone for the sublimest level of religious devotion, produces out of the hard mass of the rock an impression of refined spirituality. If the style here is reminiscent of Amaravati sculpture, then to the credit of the Sinhalese sculptor must be put down the greater strength and majesty he has been able to convey.[2]

Allied to the Indian in inspiration and style are two pieces of sculpture in the present-day Issurumuniya Vihara, one on a slab of the wall supporting the terrace below a modern shrine; the other on the rock as it rises steeply above the surface of the water of the pool. The former is reminiscent of the *mithuna* of the Gupta period—a couple in the stylistic idiom of this school,

[1] *Ibid.*, p. 230.

[2] E. B. Havell, *A Handbook of Indian Art*, London, 1920, p. 155, comparing it with the famous Sarnath statue of the Buddha at the preaching of the first sermon, praises 'the beautiful rhythmic flow of the Ceylon image' by contrast with the 'rather woodeny plastic treatment of the Indian'.

with its details of drapery and ear ornament, the roundness of face and lips, and the smooth contours of the human body, depicted in much the same way as in the sculptures of the fourth and fifth centuries in the Andhradesa of India. The Indian inspiration of the Sinhalese artist is definitely not Dravidian, the contacts generating fresh creation are with the central Indian kingdoms and the northern.

Different, both in intention and in execution, and yet akin to the work of the sculptors of the Pallava period in Indian art, is the second of the sculptures, that on the rock-face above the pool. Here is carved in a cavity of the rock the figure of a man seated in the pose *maha-lila-raja* (kingly ease), his right leg bent at the knee, the outstretched right arm placed negligently upon it, the left leg bent back on the ground, the left foot meeting the right thigh. The left hand with palm stretched out on the floor of the cavity supports the weight of the figure on the left side. His gaze appears to be directed outwards and towards the left, where, in the middle distance, are the rice-fields irrigated by the tank built by king Devanampiya Tissa. The lower half of the body of this figure is clothed. His hair, massed on his head and arranged in a broad fillet which falls down to his shoulder, appears to be a crested helmet. Large earrings are in his ears. Behind him, issuing out of the mass of the rock is the figure of a horse, with head slightly turned to the left. The suggestions of the body of the animal disappear into the mass of the boulder. The modelling of the face of the man gives him a look of supreme confidence, even of disdain. Eyebrows in the regularity of their curve, the fine line of the nose and the slightly parted lips suggest the hauteur of a god for everything but the objects towards which his imperturbable gaze is turned.

This beautiful piece of work, regarded by most connoisseurs as wonderfully distinguished in its expression,[1] was long thought to be a representation of a warrior with his horse, the bracelet worn on the right arm being taken for the horse's halter. Coomaraswany later suggested that the figure was of the sage Kapila. It was objected to this that the gracefully proportioned man was hardly an ascetic, nor was the posture assumed characteristic of the ascetic, who would have been represented in the *yoga* pose. In a recent reconstruction of the probable history and purpose of this piece of sculpture,[2] Paranavitane suggests that the two figures are those of Parjanya (Pajjuna, to whom we have referred already,) the cloud-god to whom was entrusted the bringing of rain, and of his steed Agni, the god of fire or of lightning. The composition must be taken as a later attempt to restate one of the royal functions of the Sinhalese kings,

[1] Vincent Smith, *A History of Fine Art in India and Ceylon*, revised by K. de B. Codrington, Oxford, 1930, calls it (p. 149) 'one of the most remarkable productions of Indian Art, whether on the mainland or in the island of Ceylon'.

[2] S. Paranavitane, 'The Sculpture of Man and Horse near Tisavava at Anuradhapura' *Ceylon Artibus Asiae*, Vol. XVI, 3, 1953.

that of providing the rain needed for the crops. The site of the composition marks the special place in the park below the Tisa Vava, where the group of seven boulders was sacred to the god who was well known in ancient Ceylon, with his honoured cult.

The function of the sculpture was to demonstrate dramatically the god's association with the tank and the fields he must have been invoked to bless with rain. His horse is behind him, and his eyes are fixed on the rice-fields irrigated by the tank. In the same representation are included the elephants carved in the cleft of the rock where it meets the pool down below. The elephants, four of them outlined in the round, and one on the boulder opposite playing in the water, with the whisking tail of another just disappeared under the water, are thus the proof of the supply of water in which they are shown. 'The sculpture of the man and the horse, assuming that they represent Parjanya and Angi, was intended to indicate to one familiar with the religious lore of the period, that the rock on which they are carved was a Cloud Rock, even more explicitly than the figures of the elephants.'[1]

Here we have the sculptor's art directed towards the purposive end of vitalizing an ancient practice. As in the case of the moonstone, the rock-carving of the two gods, once we have understood the sculptor's intention, recapitulates on the durable mass of the rock the chief figures in the drama of an old fertility rite with which Buddhism came to terms, for the same group of rocks in the park housed a Buddhist shrine to which the Tooth Relic was brought from India. Both moonstone and these divinities could not escape paying the penalty of time, their significance was forgotten and both came to be regarded as exhibitions of the sculptor's skill in decoration.

Other rites and other cults are now honoured in times of drought. Kings no longer exist, the *kattadiya*, or exorcist, taking upon himself the role of mediator between the devotee and the gods. The Hindu cults of South India later overpowered the remains of the primitive heritage the Sinhalese were endowed with when they migrated from their north-central Indian homeland. The objects of devotion and the practices of the devotee may have changed, but the sense of insecurity which confronts man in a world in which he is expected to confront fate alone, has never left him. To the peasant belief in the old gods whose names he now confuses, to the reader of the mass-circulation newspaper in Ceylon the forecasts of the syndicated astrologers, work with the force of a universal religion.

Sometimes the old gods fulfil other functions. In Anuradhapura anthropomorphic representations of two of the treasures of Kuvera show that he must have been worshipped in ancient Ceylon. There are guardstones of various sizes with the familiar features of two of the god's treasures. Excavations of

[1] *Ibid.*, p. 186.

the eleventh century A.D. palace of Vijayabahu I brought to light two more—
godlings with protuberant bellies, scantily clad but richly decked with ornaments and jewels, their sensuous lips wearing a satisfied smile. Quite apart
from the iconography of the representation, they might be, naturalistically
conceived, the bankers and tycoons of their time, and were therefore appro-
priately placed at the entrances to palaces and the homes of the wealthy. They
are the godlings Samkha and Padma, known by the headgear they effect—
the former with the two conch shells minus their whorls forming a hat on
which the spiralled whorl is superposed, the latter with a lotus petal cloche
hat on which the flower stands. The specific cult associated with them has
now been forgotten, but the guardstones at the gateway of the Abhayagiri
stupa are still resorted to by the peasant of those parts on the solemn occasion
of swearing an oath or making a vow.[1] Their services are often invoked in
securing the election of members to local bodies and to Parliament, this being
in no wise an ironical reflection on contemporary modes of amassing wealth.

After the havoc of the eleventh century Polonnaruva became the capital,
and there the Tooth Relic was moved. This relic—the left eye-tooth of the
Buddha—was brought to Ceylon in the fourth century A.D. by a Kalinga
princess and prince, and, according to its fabled history, was first taken to the
Meghagiri Vihara—the Cloud Rock vihara which has been referred to above.
It was secured by the king, specially enshrined, and an annual exposition
arranged by the sovereign at the Abhayagiri monastery. The Tooth Relic had
been specially credited with the power of making rain, and its possession by
the king of an agricultural community would guarantee king and community
the source of their life. The possession of this relic must have been a powerful
addition to the majesty and sacredness of the royal office. Fa-Hsien's description of an exposition of the relic, which he saw, would be a fitting conclusion
to a chapter dealing with the greatness of Anuradhapura: 'Buddha's Tooth is
regularly brought out in the middle of the third moon. Ten days previously
the king causes a large elephant to be splendidly caparisoned, and a man who
speaks well to be dressed up in royal robes and mounted on the elephant.
This man will beat a drum and proclaim in a loud voice, "The Bodhisatta
during three immeasurable aeons practised self-mortification and did not
spare his person or his life; he gave up his country, his wife, and his child; he
gouged out his eyes to give to a fellow creature; he cut off his flesh to ransom a
dove, and his head to give as alms; he flung his body to a hungry tigress,
stinting neither his marrow nor his brains. Thus in various ways he suffered
for the benefit of living creatures, and so he became a Buddha, tarrying on
earth forty-nine years, preaching the Faith and converting sinners, giving
rest to the weary and salvation to those who had not been saved. When his

[1] S. Paranavitane, 'Samkha and Padma', *Artibus Asiae*, Vol. XVIII, 2. 1955.

relations with living creatures had been fulfilled, he passed away. Since his entry to Nirvana, fourteen hundred and ninety-seven years ago, The Eye of the world has been put out, and all living creatures have sorely grieved. Now, ten days hence Buddha's Tooth will be brought forth and be taken to the shrine of the No-Fear Mountain. Let all those ecclesiastics and laymen of this country who wish to lay up happiness for themselves, help to level the roads, decorate the streets, and prepare flowers, incense, and implements of worship."

'When these words have been recited, the king then proceeds to make on both sides of the road representations of the five hundred different forms in which the Bodhisatta successively appeared; for instance as prince Sudana, or as a flash of lightning, as the king of elephants, as a stag, or as a horse. These representations are all beautifully painted and have a life-like appearance. The Tooth is then brought out and passes along the central street, receiving homage of offerings as it goes. Arriving at the Hall of Buddha in the shrine of the No-Fear Mountain, (Abhayagiri translated literally), ecclesiastics and laymen flock together in crowds, burn incense, light lamps, and perform the various ceremonies of their Faith, day and night without ceasing. After ninety days have elapsed, the Tooth is returned to the shrine in the city.'

This account, quite apart from the phrasing of the translation which may contribute an effect quite other than that intended, shows how far the religion had changed from the teaching of the Buddha.

CHAPTER EIGHT

ROYAL PALACE

Five miles off the main road which links the present naval base of Trincomalie with Colombo, and about one hundred miles north east of the latter, is the ancient rock-fortress and palace of Sigiriya. The name derived from *Sinha-* or *Siha-giri* signifies Lion Rock. Seen from the south this strange and isolated mass of granite, which rises almost perpendicularly out of the plain to a height of 600 feet, resembles in its ovoid shape, with a slight inclination of plane at the top, nothing so much as the petrified mass of some gigantic animal, trapped as it slowly lumbered across the plain. The area covered by the lower reaches of the rock-mass is strewn with boulders and numerous smaller rock-formations, and spreads over some 700 acres. Like almost every single mass of rock, common in the ancient Rajarata of Ceylon, it was made use of by ancient builders and masons. This particular crag was the abode of the king Kassapa I (A.D. 478–496), who built for himself upon its summit a palace resembling the fabulous mansion of Kuvera, the god of wealth and riches. For eighteen years in the troubled history of Ceylon, it was the royal capital.

It rises out of the plain almost due north of the Matale Hills, and round it, but some distance away, are the rocks and hills, split away from the central massif and marking the gradual subsidence from it to the ground level of the northern plain. Ten miles to the north-east is the tank of Minneriya built in the fifth century by Mahasena, and about sixteen miles, as the crow flies, is the city of Polonnaruva, which became the capital of Ceylon some six centuries later. The sacred city of Anuradhapura lies some forty miles north west. It must have been, in the days when the ancient road running from Anuradhapura to the principal ford across the Mahavali Ganga passed close by, a very well-known landmark. But there are no traces of any extensive use of the rock, for strategic, military, or other purposes, until the end of the fifth century. Until that time its precipituous sides, and its very mass, must have discouraged prospective architects and builders. If fortresses were needed there were other rock-masses like Ritigala and Dimbulagala.

As the ancient site has now been rescued from the oblivion into which it passed from the tenth century until comparatively recently, it comprises the remains of a fortified city with city-wall of brick, a moat and outer ramparts of earth. A tank, intended apparently more for ornament than for irrigation, lies on the south east. About the undulating grounds on the western side are a number of caves, which show that the only use to which the precincts of the rock had been put before the fifth century A.D. was to provide cells for Buddhist monks. The boulders scattered about this area had been used by ancient masons to provide a cistern, what is popularly known as an Audience Hall, and one boulder on account of the traces of socket holes has been called The Preaching Rock, because it was supposed that these socket holes supported benches on which monks may have sat to listen to preaching.

A modern flight of steps ascends on the south side of the rock to a terrace, from which another ascent is made to the spur thrown out directly west of the rock. These ascents correspond to the old stairways giving access to the main mass of the rock, but they were long in ruin, and their materials were used to build the present approaches.

From this point, at a height of some 150 feet above the level of the plain, an ancient gallery hugged the western face of the rock and worked its way serpent-wise to the northern terrace. This gallery, to which reference will be made later, is on account of its sheltered position, almost intact on the western side. But where the mass of the rock turns north-west, it had collapsed, and a modern bridge of iron with a steep ascent of iron steps leads to the northern terrace which is shored up with an impressive ancient stone rampart. Here stand the remains of the immense Lion Staircase—the forepaws of the enormous figure of the beast made in brick and plaster, through the body of which steps used to ascend the northern face of the rock and give access to the summit. It is impossible to imagine, from the ruins left, what this daring piece of engineering and plastic skill must have looked like. Some slight idea of the grandeur of its conception will be given by the dimensions of the claws of the lion. They are four feet in breadth and three feet ten inches in height, and the paws run back some thirteen feet.

Iron ladders, and rock steps provided with an iron hand-rail take one to the top now, but the rock face bears traces of the old stairway which must have been in use till the tenth century. On the summit are the remains of the ancient palace, built to rise sheer out of the edge of the rock and originally plastered in white. A large bath, two cisterns and innumerable walls of buildings, with a finely designed and simple stone seat, are all that survives of structures which as they rose in their whiteness above the beetling mass of the rock, must have seemed to dwellers in the plain below, 'the abode of a god-king'.

The rock, as traces here and there still show, bore on its surface the adornment of paintings. About 50 feet above the western gallery there is a long cave in the shape of two pockets which contain paintings on the specially prepared wall. These, less famous than those of Ajanta, are the most considerable piece of evidence extant of the art of the ancient Sinhalese painter. Havell thought that if they were 'attributed correctly to Kasyapa's court painters, they are the only extant works of the secular schools of Indian painting before Muhammadan times'.[1]

These 'frescoes' as they are called, are twenty-one portraits, sixteen of them in one pocket and five in the adjoining and smaller one. They are of richly jewelled women holding flowers or scattering them. The lower half of their bodies is cut off by painted cloud effects. As they are depicted they face, all of them, in one direction, and represent two types of personages, one lighter or golden-coloured, the other darker or olive-green complexioned. The inaccessible position in which these paintings were placed is difficult to understand at the present day, for without the aid of the spiral stairway of iron with its mesh protection rising up perpendicular from the floor of the gallery, it would be impossible to get anything but the vaguest impression of the artist's work. It seems to be clear that their sheltered position protected them from tropical rain and sun which must have destroyed others decorating the rock above the gallery and in full view of the passer-by.

With others on the rock face they were believed to be portraits of the ladies of Kassapa's court attended by their slaves (the dark-complexioned ones). It was suggested that they depicted a procession of princesses making their way to worship at the nearby shrine of Pidurugala, directly north of Sigiriya. Recent excavations at Mihintale and at the Sutighara *cetiya* at Dedigama, have supported the theory of Paranavitane that they represent cloud and lightning maidens, for in both these *cetiyas*, paintings on the wall of the relic chamber have shown that the veiling of half the form in cloud was deliberately intended. The half-figure was not the result of the painter's concern that the lower limbs of his figures should not be distorted by the curve of the cave surface on which he painted.

We have no means of knowing who were the painters responsible for them. Their affinities with the cave paintings of Ajanta have been noted by all connoisseurs of Oriental art.[2] Those very probably represent eight centuries of the art of the Indian painter. The traditions of Indian painting, the technique and its artistic theory, are likely to have been known and practised in Ceylon, since the basis of the culture of Buddhist Ceylon was Indian. But in this

[1] E. B. Havell, *A Handbook of Indian Art*, London, 1920, p. 203.

[2] See Havell, *Ibid*. V. Smith, *A History of Fine Art in India and Ceylon*, 2nd Ed. Revised by K. de B. Codrington, Oxford, 1930. P. 111, 'All critics recognize that the art of Sigiriya is closely related to that of Ajanta'.

sphere as in every other, the artist and craftsman in Ceylon must have made the Indian tradition his own, and in his practice introduced something of his own into the accepted norms. Whether it is possible to evaluate the paintings at Sigiriya with reference to those at Ajanta, is not to the point. It is sufficient to notice that there are differences between them without trying to claim on the ground of the slender evidence before one the existence of a distinctive Sinhalese style.

Besides the difference in subject matter and the total absence of blue in the Ceylon paintings, it will be observed that the line of the Ceylon painter is freer and less deliberate than that of the painters represented at Ajanta. The absence of the narrative purpose in the Ceylon paintings would account for the difference between their lucidity and their economy when compared with the Indian. The decorative intention—if this would be granted—is reinforced by what might be termed the hieratic pose of the cloud maidens in Sigiriya. Their position concentrates attention on an effect which may be deemed statuesque. The figure holds a pose, but the freedom of the outlines in contrast with this gives the paintings fluidity of design which might even approach the naturalistic in portraiture. It is not surprising that they have appealed to countless persons who, reacting both to the hieratic and the popular in their total effect, have appreciated the tension between the two which appears to characterize this. If, as has been suggested by Paranavitane, the paintings of these figures show the 'compromise (made by the artist) by representing the clouds partly naturalistically and partly in a personified form',[1] the harmony with which the naturalistic and the symbolical are integrated, is noteworthy.

They are the products of a sophisticated level of art. Behind them is a recognized civilized tradition—the art of a court—which one is aware of in the very simplicity of the means used. The presence of this tradition then and its total disappearance today can be seen in the contemporary monstrosities which copy 'the Sigiriya frescoes' on ash-tray, embroidered chairback, and painted vase. The copyist, out of touch with this tradition, can only provide evidence of stiffness of outlines, and hardness in the disposition of colour and tone which are far, very far, from the spirited drawing of the originals and their nuances of form. The graciousness of touch in the originals appears to be a lost art now.

The chronicles, as we have seen, preserve for us only such records of persons and events as are related to what we now would call an ecclesiastic's history of Ceylon. The kings, generals, and nobles who feature in it, are recalled to assist in what is predominently the story of the Mahavihara and its vicissitudes. Even the monuments speak more of the religious than of anybody else. We have already pointed out that it is natural that this should be so, for the more

[1] S. Paranavitane, 'Sigiri, The Abode of a God-King,' JCBRAS, Vol. I. (New Series) p. 155.

durable material of granite and limestone was used to build shrine and monastery. In various parts of Ceylon there are remains of palaces, in Anuradhapura there is the palace of Vijayabahu, and at Polonnaruva and at the earlier headquarters of Parakkama Bahu at Panduvasnuwara considerable remains of royal residences. It is curious that medieval Ceylon should show more of these than the mainland of India. Basham, writing on this subject, remarks that 'remains of pre-Muslim secular buildings are few. In the Middle Ages kings and chiefs certainly built stone palaces, but of these only the base of the Vijayanagara throne-room, and some remains in Ceylon have survived. . . . But, though secular architecture was no doubt highly developed, it is clear that India's architects and masons devoted their greatest energies to temple buildings.'[1]

Of what remains, both in religious and secular architecture, there is little which could be dated exactly as the product of one particular time and no other, since most of what remains has been so changed and restored that it has to be regarded as the legacy of a much later time than its origins. Anuradhapura, as it has been revealed by the archaeologist, is mainly tenth century A.D. restoration of much older work. It is possible to trace the broad outlines of earlier and later work, but what is left is mostly late. The same is true of Polonnaruva which flourished for three centuries as compared with Anuradhapura's millenium.

Sigiriya, in view of this, should possess a twofold interest: its complex of buildings is mainly royal palace and fortified town, and all these belong to one short period. A few caves go back to a much earlier period—as early as the third century B.C.—when early Buddhism, still counted most of its devotees among those who meditated in cave and forest. But for these, and for some slight remains of a later period when palace became monastery, the whole of Sigiriya belongs to eighteen years at the end of the fifth century A.D., a colossal monument to the pride of a king and the skill of his architects and masons.

Historically, Sigiriya is connected with an episode frequent in the ancient records of Ceylon—the murder of the rightful king by one of his relatives, the reign of the usurper, the retribution which overtook him, as he was in his turn put out of the way either by rightful claimant or a more successful leader of rebellion. So common are such tales of murder and civil strife that the chronicler poet has had little difficulty in transforming all of it into illustration of the retributory justice which overtakes all actions devoid of the meritoriousness of supporting the religion and the priesthood. All his attention is riveted there, on the good works and donations which make a ruler an 'excellent king', and 'the best of men'. The sole test of a monarch's worth is in

[1] A. L. Basham, *The Wonder That was India*, London, 1954, pp. 363-4.

the 'several meritorious deeds' he performs for the 'great community'—the 'abundant supply of the four necessaries' which he provides. So king follows king, usurper rightful heir, it does not matter which. The queen of one king carries on an intrigue with her husband's younger brother, and stabs her husband in a lonely spot. Her lover who has in the meantime become a monk, gives up his robes and marries her. He is celebrated by the chronicler as being 'always one who rejoiced in the almsgiving and in the leading of a moral life and one who reverenced the (three sacred) objects'.[1] Apparently his later benefactions to the various communities of monks weighed much more heavily in the balance than any complicity he may have had in his brother's murder.

This may be an attitude of mind disappointing to the present-day reader of the chronicles, but as their writers had no intention either of exploring the psychology of the persons of history, or of making use of opportunities to develop human interest, or to judge situations and characters from points of view other than the formalistic religious, they are scarcely to be blamed for imperfect artistry, or of inexplicable morality. To read the *Mahavamsa* and the *Culavamsa* expecting from them the gratifications of either novel or drama, is as ill-advised as reading *Macbeth* or *King Lear* as sourcebooks of history. Whether for good or for ill the chroniclers seem to have been inattentive to most things except the maintenance of the religious community. The long roll of murders, sudden deaths and revolts which make up fair stretches of the history of Ceylon, does not differ very greatly from ancient and medieval records elsewhere in the world, and they must perhaps be accounted as much a feature of hierarchic institutions as strikes are of industrial societies in a capitalistic world.

The story of Sigiriya is one such episode in the pages of the annals of Ceylon. It tells of another palace revolt: an old king who provoked the rage of his nephew and son-in-law, the general of the forces, and paid for it with his life. For the general was able to instigate one of the king's sons to seize the throne, to order the murder of his father, and to attempt the life of his brother. Of the various subsidiary characters in the story some thousands came to an unhappy and violent end. But the general who was the prime mover in the conspiracy, died, as far as one can judge, in his bed. Like most generals he passed away full of years and honour. If he was given no state funeral, he had at any rate the satisfaction of treating himself to a state occasion of great splendour. Unlike most generals he unfortunately left no memoirs. . . .

This plain and unadorned narrative in the chronicle concerns the old King Dhatusena. In his day a great general, he had defeated the Tamils several times. He was celebrated by the chronicle as the builder of eighteen *viheras* and eighteen tanks. His great work was the Kalavapi—the Kalavava Tank—

[1] C. xxxvii, 214.

which dammed up the Kala Oya, from which a channel bore the water to the royal capital fifty miles away. In his youth Dhatusena had been for a time a *religieux*, and while he was at his meditations he was disturbed by another monk who threw some dung at his head. The young man was not disturbed, but he did not forgive the insult, for when he was king, he made no gifts to the monastery where he had been shamed. As king and builder of the Kala Vava, he himself was guilty of an act resembling the one to which he had thus taken exception. When he was building the tank, he saw a *bhikkhu* sunk in meditation whom nothing could move. In apparent exasperation that the building operations were delayed, the king had a clod of earth flung at the *bhikkhu's* head. So he laid up for himself a *karma* which was to have the most fatal consequences, in spite of all his previous warlike exploits against the Tamils, and his own good works in the name of religion.

The Chronicle mentions three children the king had—'the mighty Moggallana', apparently the heir to the throne since his mother was of 'equal caste' with the king; Kassapa, son by a mother of inferior caste; and a daughter unnamed, who was 'dear to him as his life'. The king's sister's son was commander-in-chief of the forces, Migara by name. He was married to the king's daughter. One day the king seeing his daughter with blood-stained garments, enquired what had happened, and on being told that she had been whipped on the thigh by her husband Migara for no fault of her own, in his rage had the general's mother, his own sister, stripped naked and burnt. The general schemed a meticulous revenge for the outrage committed on his mother. A palace revolt must have followed, in which the army, controlled by the general, declared for Kassapa who was instigated by him to seize the crown. Not only the army but the king's subjects, too, were apparently won over for Kassapa. The revolt was successful, Dhatusena was taken prisoner, and his son Moggallana, failing to raise a force in Ceylon, fled to India.

The general next inflamed Kassapa with stories of the treasures in the possession of the old king, which were, in his account, intended for Moggallana. Dhatusena was repeatedly questioned about these, and one day realizing what was in store for him agreed to reveal their whereabouts, if he were allowed to go to the Kalavapi. He wished to see the tank again, and to meet his uncle, the *thera* with whom he had lived when young. He was content to die thereafter.

Dhatusena was sent to the tank in a chariot with a broken axle. On the way there the charioteer shared his meal of roasted corn with the deposed king, and was given a letter to Mogallana asking him to reward the bearer for his kindness by making him a gatekeeper in the palace. Dhatusena met his old friend and relative, and 'the twain sat side by side (joyful) as if they had gained a kingdom, and their mutual converse chased their cares away. After the *thera*

20. Polonnaruva: Stucco figure—Tivanka Image-house—see p. 155

21.

Right: Polonnaruva: Detail of fresco
—Tivanka Image-house—see p. 155

Below: Polonnaruva: Detail of fresco
—Tivanka Image-house

The recently restored Kuttampokuna in the precincts of the Abhayagiri Vihara Anuradhapura— see p. 155

Polonnaruva: Siva Devale No. 2

23.
Polonnaruva:
Gal Vihara—
Two statues
of the Buddha
—see p. 156

24.

Left: Dedigama:
Bronze elephant—the
'oil tank' of the
elephant lamp—see
p. 156

Right: Polonnaruva:
Sundaramurti—bronze
now in Colombo
Museum—see p. 164

25.
Yapahuva: The
Third Stairway
—see p. 166

Yapahuva: Lion
balustrade of Th
Stairway—see p.
166

Yapahuva: Frieze—group of dancers

Yapahuva: Frieze—group of four dancers—see p. 166

27.
Left: Polonnaruva: Detail of column in Hatadage in present-day Quadrangle of the Sacred Tooth

Below: Polonnaruva: Gal Pota—a stone block 26′ 6″ long, 4′ 6″ broad and from 1′ 6″ to 2′ in height. On it is inscribed the longest epigraph in Ceylon. It celebrates the greatness of King Nissanka Malla. On the south side is the sculptured Gaja Lakshmi —see p. 167

had entertained the king, he admonished him in many ways and encouraged him to strive ceaselessly, showing him how the world is subject to the law of impermanency.' The rest of the story has been referred to already. The king, fortified by his meeting with the *thera*, 'betook himself to the tank, plunged as he liked therein, bathed and drank and spake to the king's (Kassapa's) henchmen: This here, my friends, is my whole wealth.' When this was reported to Kassapa, he was enraged and gave orders to the general that the king should be killed.

The general performed this commission with the joy of a man who has at last rid himself of a hated enemy. In his satisfaction he appeared before Dhatusena in all his regalia, and the old king knew that his death was at hand. Not willing, however, to meet it with thoughts of passion in his mind, he addressed his nephew in the gentlest of tones, and assured him that he had for him the same feelings as he had for his son Moggallana. The general laughed derisively. Shortly afterwards the king was stripped naked, and bound with chains to the wall of a building. Forcing him to observe every detail of the proceedings, the general had the king walled in and closed up in a living tomb. Dhatusena met with his death in this way, after he had reigned eighteen years.

Unsuccessful in an attempt on the life of his brother, who fled to India, Kassapa fortified the crag and environs of Sigiriya and made it his capital. On it he built 'a fine palace, worthy to behold, like another Alakmanda, and dwelt there like the god Kuvera'. This work must have occupied the greater part of his reign of eighteen years. The general, for his part, built a monastery and named it after himself, and an image house for an image of the Buddha, but was refused permission to hold a consecration festival for it greater than that performed for the famous stone image of the Buddha in Anuradhapura. This was the stone image to which Dhatusena had presented a costly pair of jewels for the eyes, 'a gleaming diadem of rays, and of dark blue gems (sapphires) a shining coil of hair,' and various other rich bequests.

Of the events of the eighteen years of the reign of Kassapa, the Chronicle makes no mention beyond listing as usual his good works, and the remorse which overtook him. The piety of his life is also referred to: 'He kept the *uposatha* festival and cultivated the *appamanna* (the four virtues), he took on himself the pious duties and had books copied. He made images, built alms-halls and the like in great numbers.' But these meritorious works did not win him the approval of the Mahavihara, who refused to receive a monastery enlarged by him, and accepted it only when it had been offered to the Buddha. Nor, according to the Chronicle, could Kassapa ever banish 'the fear of the other world and of Moggallana' from his mind.

Eighteen years after the usurpation Moggallana returned with an army from India. Kassapa, disregarding the advice of his soothsayers, went out with his

E

forces to meet him. In the battle which followed, Kassapa manoeuvred his royal elephant to avoid a swamp which lay in his way. This action was mis-interpreted by his army, who, thinking that the king was retreating, broke up in disorder. The victory lay with Moggallana. Kassappa, realizing that all was lost, rather than fall into his half-brother's hands, drew his dagger and cut his throat on the battlefield, raising the knife high in the air to call attention to his suicide. Moggallana, in the rage which distinguished the members of his family and which earned for him the nickname of *Rakkhasa* or devil, put to death more than a thousand of those prominently associated with the usurper.[1] Of Migara however, we hear no more than that 'having sent him (Moggallana) reports in a fitting manner', he was allowed to celebrate the dedication cere-mony of his Abisekha-Buddha image, this too 'in a fitting manner'. The charioteer who brought Moggallana his father's letter was made royal gate-keeper. Like his father and brother, Moggallana reigned eighteen years.

This story, it will be seen, is somewhat bald and summary. It seems to lack very notably that interest in the dramatic to which commercial film and news-paper have accustomed us, and depend for the marketing of their wares. To attempt to supply them is both hazardous and unnecessary. All we may note in passing is that the building of the palace where Kassapa is described as having lived like a god—and what is more a palace which is compared with the abode of the gods on the fabled Mount Kailasa—occupies only a short sentence. We may note, too, that whatever the reputation of Kassapa, his usurpation must have been supported by the population or the works he carried out, both at Sigiriya and in Anuradhapura, would have been difficult. If he had been a tyrant who forced his will on the mass of the people, they would have been impossible.

Moggallana transferred the seat of government to Anuradhapura and made Sigiriya over to two Buddhist sects. There are but few remains of their short stay on the rock. The site is twice mentioned in the Chronicle in the later history of Ceylon, and then it is silent about it. Twice more it played a role of a minor and accidental kind in the history of the strife between kings and generals in Ceylon. A century after the death of Kassapa, during the reign of a general who afterwards became Moggallana III when he had betrayed his king, it was the scene of the execution of King Sanghatissa, his son, and his minister. In flight from the usurper they were recognized at Minneriya, and were at his command taken to 'the secure and safe Sihagiri'.[2] All three were put to death there. Thus Moggallana paid for his crime when he was himself slain at Sigiriya by Silameghavanna who became king in his stead. This is the last reference to the rock in the Chronicle.

That it continued to be a place famed in the island for its palace and the

[1] C. xxxviii, 35–xxxix, 36.   [2] C. xliv, 32.

paintings on its rock-walls, we now know as a result of the work of the present Archaeological Commissioner of Ceylon, an *oeuvre* which resembles Kassapa's in its daring design, its arduousness and its monumental proportions.[1] The scribblings of a host of visitors from all parts of Ceylon prove that up to the tenth century it was still possible to get to the summit of the rock, and that it was among the wonders of Lanka. Disrepair, tropical rains and the fall of the Sinhalese kingdom of Rajarata sealed it off from the attention of most people and made its environs the abode of the wild animal. Of Anuradhapura within a century of its destruction by the Cholas we read that 'a mighty forest like the stronghold of Mara' had grown up round about the Thuparama and all the sacred places. Sigiriya settled down to the same fate, and even greater oblivion closed over it for nearly nine centuries, until the English rulers of the island began to interest themselves in its antiquities.

Major Forbes, of the 78th Highlanders, spent eleven years early in the nineteenth century in service in Ceylon. During that time his duties took him into parts of the ancient Rajarata which he took the opportunity of exploring. He was interested in the history of the island, and was in correspondence with George Turnour of the Ceylon Civil Service, who was just then engaged in translating the major chronicles of the island. Turnour acknowledged Forbes' interest in ancient inscriptions and archaeology, interests likely to belong to the cultivated upper-class Englishman of that time in the colonial service. Forbes published an account of his *Eleven Years in Ceylon* in two volumes in 1840, to which he added an Appendix containing an 'Epitome of Cingalese History' compiled by Turnour.

Forbes described two visits he paid to Sigiriya. The charm of his book lies in its combination of a dewy Romantic freshness with something of the good eighteenth-century classical intention of seeing man's place in the universal scheme. In his writing and in his attitudes he is the kind of Romantic Scott was, with that strong dash of serious eighteenth-century humanity. His first visit to the rock was paid in 1831, when he rode out on horseback accompanied by two others to look for its ruins. His first sight of the rock is in the best tradition of contemporary description: 'The morning mist suddenly cleared away, and we found ourselves on the verge of a piece of water, reflecting from its unruffled surface the large forest trees around, with the bare overhanging sides and brushwood-covered summit of the rock of Sigiri, which appeared to have started from the plain, and to frown defiance over the scanty fields and far-extending forests of the surrounding plain.'[2] Forbes observed that the lower part of the fortress had been constructed of massive walls of stone, supporting terraces which reached to the sides of the crag; that

[1] S. Paranavitane, *Sigiri Graffiti*, 2 Vols., Oxford, 1956.
[2] Major Forbes, *Eleven Years in Ceylon*, London, 1840, Vol. II, p. 2.

a gallery clung to the rock at some considerable height above 'connecting two elevated terraces at opposite ends', and about half the height of the main column of rock; and that this gallery had slipped from its foundations making the upper terrace (that is the present northern terrace) inaccessible. His two friends persevered, but were unable to reach the upper terrace. Forbes wrote 'I felt so giddy from the heat as to be unable to accompany my friends; and was sincerely glad to see them descend in safety, for some portions of the crumbling buildings which they displaced might be heard crashing amongst the boughs of the trees at great depth below'. He found no trace of any carving of lions which would have explained the name given to the rock, and concluded that this was a fanciful and absurd invention, like most of those given by 'the learned natives (who) derive its name from Siha or Sinha (a lion) and giri (a rock)'.

On his second visit in 1833 he traced the wall and moat fortifying the town of Sigiriya, but his investigations of the broken gallery were interrupted by a leopard disturbed by his friend's scramblings among the ruins. But he had seen sufficient to discover that the gallery was made of brick originally coated with a cement so durable that large portions of it remained; that the rock above the gallery had been painted in bright colours, fragments of which could still be perceived. Though he had been unable to get to the summit, Forbes had noted some of the main features of the site—its extensive ruins on the plain below and traces of buildings on the rock; the remains of the fortified city; the terraces; the gallery; and the paintings.

It was not to be supposed that such a challenge as the summit of an 'inaccessible' rock would long remain unanswered by a nation which prided itself on its sporting instincts and had just begun to make Alpine climbing one of the serious activities of its gentlemen. The rock was scaled by two Englishmen in 1851, and it was even climbed by a lady not long after. The scientific rediscovery of the ancient site, and its restoration was the work of H. C. P. Bell, the first Archaeological Commissioner of Ceylon. In three papers read to the Royal Asiatic Society in Colombo, the first results of Bell's work were made public. He cleared the summit of the rock and retraced the lines of the complex of buildings crowning it. He later discovered the ruins of an enormous brick and plaster lion on the north terrace, through which the ancient steps to the summit were directed. He found traces of graffiti on the polished gallery wall, made the paintings in the two pockets above it accessible, and systematically described the site of the town and its outlying defences.

To the present-day visitor to Sigiriya, its pleasant park, the tidiness of its approach, the ease with which one reaches the summit and inspects the restorations and the well-known paintings, are likely to get in the way of an appreciation of the magnitude of Bell's work and the care with which succeeding

Archaeological Commissioners continued what he began. His first three reports are a modest record of the intrepidity and devotion with which a man took up an absorbing interest. He had to contend with all manner of obstacles: wind, weather, insufficient supplies of drinking water, scanty resources, hornets, and the reluctance of his labourers to work at a place with the reputation of being the favourite haunt of demons and evil spirits. Bell's work on Sigiriya established the veracity of the main elements of the Chronicle account of the rock in Kassapa's time, that it was both fortified point and palace, with the Lion's Mouth giving it its distinctive name, and that as an engineering feat and artistic achievement it spoke volumes for the abilities of its builders and decorators. The gallery Bell described as follows: 'Along the western and northern faces of Sigiri-gala ran a gallery—one of the most extraordinary engineering feats of the ancient world—at the level where the Rock has the smallest diameter; so that while it stands upon that portion which projects below, it is at the same time protected by the part which overhangs it. The outer side of this gallery was formed by a brick wall tapering to the top. Ledges sunk in the Rock received the wall, and at a certain height transverse blocks of a quartzose stone were laid across from the wall to the Rock so as to form a pavement. The wall had a coating of hard white plaster much of which retains a high polish to the present time.'[1] On this polished wall—the Mirror Wall as it has been called by Paranavitane—Bell discovered the scribblings of later visitors to the site.

On the remains of the palace on the summit Bell permitted himself a passage which, in its lyricism, would seem scarcely to belong to a scientific report: 'Little wonder that the glory of a structure, towering to heaven on the dizzy heights of Sigiri-gala "white as snow" within and without, should call forth irresistibly the unalloyed admiration of the old chronicler, not given to spare its master-hand King Kasyapa, "that wicked ruler of men." He built there, as it is written "a lovely palace splendid to behold like unto a second Alakamanda, and lived there like (its lord) Kuvera".' How little comparatively now remains to attest the ancient beauty and grandeur of *Sigiri-nuwara,* the parricide's stronghold:

> *'Those golden pallaces, those gorgeous halls,*
> *With fourniture superfluouslie faire;*
> *Those statelie courts, those sky-encountring walls,*
> *Evanish all like vapours in the aire.'*

New light on the intention of Kassapa in his choice of Sigiriya as royal capital was thrown six years ago by Dr S. Paranavitane in his persuasive

[1] H. C. P. Bell, 'Interim Report on the operations of the Archaeological Survey of Ceylon at Sigiriya 1897' JCBRAS, Vol. XV, p. 93 ff.

thesis[1] that the usurper, as the *Culavamsa* conveyed it in a simile, was determined to build for himself a palace resembling Alaka, the Himalayan abode
of the god Kuvera. (The latter had, as has already been noted in the last
chapter, his cult in Ceylon.) Supported with a wealth of learning and illustration, the thesis claims that Kassapa's transformation of the rock was not
motivated primarily by military consideration. Nor could the inauguration
and completion of such a grand design have been possible to a man anxious
only to secure himself from probable attack. He was driven by his desire to
arrogate to himself the dignity and stature of a god-king, a conception much
closer to Brahmanical thought than to the orthodox Buddhist. This change in
the theory of kingship was not in any way an innovation on the part of Kassapa,
but his acceptance of a fairly widespread notion which must have been heretical
to the monks of the Mahavihara. This intention could, in Paranavitane's
view, be illustrated in the details of the architectural design of Sigiriya with
their resemblance to those of Kuvera's palace. What is more, the ground
plan of Kassapa's palace does not resemble that of royal palaces in either
Anuradhapura or Polonnaruva; and such features as the lake on the south of
the rock-mass, the gallery with its polished wall, the northern terrace with the
gigantic lion, and the paintings of cloud and lightning maidens, suggest their
mythical counterparts. These conceptions of a divinity of the king which
palace and precincts set out to demonstrate, would account for the hostility
of the Mahavihara towards an usurper who was, after all, neither better nor
worse, in his record as a private person, than some of the kings the Buddha
knew and some of those embalmed in the Ceylon Chronicles.

This persuasive and well-documented thesis was never satisfactorily questioned or criticized.[2] It claimed that the distinctive character of the ruins on
the rock was lent them by a directing principle neither strategic nor architecturally necessary, but politico-religious. After Kassapa's death no king
attempted to revive Sigiriya as capital city or palace, because of the bad odour
of these theories of the divinity of a king.

The mass of people, monks included, who visited the site of the palace
in the eighth, ninth and tenth centuries and left a record of their impressions
in poems scribbled on the polished wall of the western gallery, did not apparently trouble themselves with speculations which were anathema to the
Mahavihara. The main elements in the story of Kassapa must have been
known to them, but they visit the spot with neither superstitious awe nor
holy horror. What these people went to see was a royal palace magnificently

[1] S. Paranavitane, 'Sigiri, The Abode of a God-King,' 1950.

[2] Besides his store of learning—the equipment of a polymath in Orientalia—Dr Paranavitane's polemical vigour and adroitness in deploying his forces must have disconcerted his
critics. It must seem in the absence of any refutation that his case is proven.

planned and decked with its paintings, the abode of a king who came to an
unfortunate end. Most of the poems they left on the gallery wall show a
natural unconcern with the facts of history or their interpretation. They are
the more valuable therefor. To the authors of the graffiti Sigiriya was one of
the marvels of its time:

Here is an eighth-century writer turning round on a glum visitor to the
rock:

*One so despondent as you, Sir, is a person for whom heaven itself is not. When
heaven is placed in the balance and weighed, the resplendent rock (of Sigiri) is sufficient
on one side of the balance.*

To another in the second half of the ninth century it was a cure for melan-
cholia:

*Abandon these (melancholy) thoughts. What else is there to be said by me who com-
posed a verse? The splendour of heaven does not hold me. Ascend Sihigiri thyself.*

Another in the late eighth or early ninth century cannot believe the testimony
of his own eyes:

*There is a sense of deception to the mind which has been told by me, (after) having seen
a king of mountains like this, that it has been seen with (my own) eyes. I trow that it is
heaven which has arrived in this island of Lak (Lanka).*

And a ninth-century clerk, by the name of Sala Bud, rhapsodizes over what
he saw there:

*At Sihigiri, of abundant splendour, situated in the island of Siri-Lak, we saw, in
happy mood, the rock which captivates the mind of people who come (here), having longed
for this; five hundred damsels who (in their) splendour as (like unto) the crest jewels of the
king; and the resplendent mirror terrace.*[1]

Scribblings on walls, carving on trees, have long been occupations uncon-
fined to the lover and the lunatic. The mirror-wall of Sigiriya received attention of this kind from the poet, not the professional poet either, but all those
persons whose education in a literary tradition enabled them naturally to turn
a verse when the occasion demanded it. The graffiti at Sigiriya are a priceless
index both of the high educational level which seems to have been fairly
widespread at that time, and of the spontaneousness of feeling and natural-
ness of expression which mark the best of them. They are much more than
that type of casual scribbling with which the obscure seek to perpetuate their
names, the obscene their desires or the partisan his political fanaticism. All

[1] The four poems quoted are Nos. 115, 169, 433, and 560 from S. Paranavitane, *Sigiri
Graffiti*, Vol. II.

three types of scribbler are known all over the world. Since the rediscovery of Sigiriya the gallery wall has proved a strong temptation to a new generation.

These poems of one or two stanzas, written in conventional metres, resemble the Japanese *haiku* in their expression of the emotional reaction to the single incident or the single observation. They reveal how some detail of the rock or its paintings, or even another poem previously scribbled on the wall, released the writer's feelings and imposed on them the form of poetry. Their range is from the simple, or sometimes coarse, reflection to a highly wrought arabesque on a conventional theme; from the writer's emotional identification of himself with the women on the wall to a satirical anti-feminism; from pleasantries connected with the visit to serious gnomic utterances; from homely touches of realism to the finesse with which a conscious artist deliberates on the best vehicle for his reactions.

They are, besides, an invaluable record of the rock as it must have looked three or four centuries after it had been abandoned. To their writers Sigiriya was still the fabulous abode of the king who had raised for himself a monument fantastic in its beauty. For instance, the following by a writer of the eighth or ninth centuries draws attention to the way the rock was covered with paintings; the good man who wrote it was concerned that people should not deface the paintings by touching them:

When (they) go away, having come (here) and looked at this, the people, while climbing down, rubbed their hands on it, as the painting captivates their minds. Do get down without rubbing this with your hands.

Another verse, of the eighth century, shows how the paintings were exposed to the weather:

Hail! Methinks his Majesty King Kasub (Kassapa) having himself come (here) and seen those who are being washed away in torrents of water, painted them on the mountain side and went away.

A writer of the ninth century was so impressed by the lion that he was cured of his desire to see the paintings:

Having ascended Sihigiri to see what is there, I fulfilled my mind's desire and saw his Lordship the Lion. There is no desire (in me) to look at the golden-coloured one on the cliff.

Another of the eighth or ninth centuries, prefers the ladies to the lion:

Hail! When this damsel, who has taken flowers in her hand, is seen, one gets imprisoned on the rock. When His Lordship the Lion is seen by one, he (the Lion) does not become remembered.

The wonder of the gleaming pile of the palace on the rock makes a writer of the late eighth century or early ninth indulge in the mythological fancy that Sigiriya (like another Hercules obliging Atlas) comes to the help of Meru and holds up the sky for him:

Hail! The poem written by Nakka Madambi, the superintendent of slaves of the Pandyan king. When (Meru) begs (to do so), Sihigiri having gently borne up the city of the gods, (and asking) 'O king of mountains, was pain caused in this manner by this exertion?' causes the shrieks (of Meru) to cease.[1]

On the other hand, an anonymous writer of the second half of the eighth or the first half of the ninth century was disappointed, the nuisance of the thorny creepers everywhere ruining his pleasure:

Ah! having come here, how have (they) been taken in with the splendour (of this)? Wherever one sets one's foot are tibolo creepers. Pleasure (is to be had) in many places other than this.

One writer discusses the extraordinary fancy that the women in the paintings are washerwomen, another rues the thought that since he has seen them his wife at home will no longer appeal to him, on account of her unattractiveness. The writer of this stanza was the member of the household of a prince in the ninth century:

The Song of Sit, of the house of Prince Mihidale.
She of homely virtues, like (one's) wife, did not gain confidence and captivate one's mind. The golden-coloured one on the mountain side, by means of the pleasing attires that (she) has, captivates one's mind.

Others in their naïveté are flavoured with the charm that comes from innocence. The thought which troubled this eighth-century writer was echoed by the cook of Sir Edmund Gosse who wrote an affecting lyric on the backside of the moon, denied to mortal view:

I am Mana, of the house of Lord Upatis who founded Kapugama Pirivena. I wrote this.
Of the golden-coloured ones who are there on the mountain side, we saw the faces completely, but we did not see their backs at all.[2]

Some of the verses arise directly out of the occasion of a contest in verse which the wall with its harvest of inscriptions must have encouraged. One writer of the second half of the eighth century claims the victory over another, who while acknowledging defeat feels that his rival's verses were superfluous.

---

[1] The five poems quoted are Nos. 677, 153, 45, 576 and 652.
[2] The three poems quoted are Nos. 127, 53 and 275. It is only fair to add that the writer of the last poem may have been referring to the convention in painting which preferred to represent figures full face or sometimes in profile, never with the back turned to the spectator.

Or a later writer reproves an earlier one. Here is a priest in disapproval of an earlier visitor's abandonment of himself to sensuous pleasure. The earlier writer from Siripura is quoted first:

Hail! The song of (Dapul) who came from Siripura. When the loving embrace of this long-eyed one is obtained by me I shall become happy. (And) when I come to this mountain side, which is like unto heaven, I shall become rejoiced in mind, having looked at it.

To which the priest retorts:

Hail! I am Friar Sen. I wrote (this).

Having been infatuated in form, when desire comes into being, (this damsel) has been considered (by you) in this manner as an (object worthy of) embrace. When (desire) passes away, the infatuation will itself fall, as does what is cast up into the sky. By the abundance of (their) splendour, we know the store of their merit.

Which may have been good morality on the part of a churchman, but it is poor psychology. The Friar's concluding sentence shows that he too recognized the appeal of the paintings, but he deduced from the 'splendour' of the lady the moral cause of an abundance of good *karma* in the past, in previous states of existence—interesting proof again of the rigidity of the churchman's mind.

A fine rendering of the conflict in the mind of a novice—very fresh and moving—is the following:

I am the Novice who came from the monastery of Hunagiri.

That person, who has been spoken about, resides (here); (therefore) place the wakefulness of mind (in the door of) hearing and guard it thoroughly. As her broad smile spreads, having caused me (fright), my mind trembles exceedingly.[1]

The wakefulness of mind was apparently an insecure bolt when seeing was added to 'hearing'.

The best of these lyrics possess depth and sincerity with which the imagination has transcribed the evanescence of a moment of feeling. The following, written in the late eighth or early ninth centuries, in its evocation of the mood of despair which nature reflects, produces something which could well be placed beside the best of its kind in West or East:

Hail!

The wind blew. Thousands and hundreds of thousands of trees, which had put forth buds, fell down. The curlew uttered shrieks. Torrents came forth on the Malaya mountain. The night was made (to be) of the glow of tender copper-(coloured) leaves by fireflies beyond count. O long-eyed one, the message given by you—what sustenance does it afford?

[1] The three poems quoted are Nos. 536, 540 and 88.

Or this, the dissatisfaction of the eighth-century lover haunted by the memory of the beautiful lady barely glimpsed:

Hail!
Having not been able, owing to the wind on the mountain side, to look at those golden-coloured ones in a satisfactory manner, there is no happiness (for me) in my house, and the great rock appears (as a vision) in my mind.

Or the delicacy with which regret for the king and his monument speaks in these lines. The emotion here is simple:

Prosperity! The song of Kali.
With tears in (my) eyes, I saw how a king dwelt, according to his pleasure, on the mountain side so inaccessible as this, (and as lofty as the) sky.

Or this, from the eighth century, with its conventional reference to the lady's hard heart, a sentiment repeated by countless lovers all over the world:

O faithless one, wherefore did your lover of former times die (even) when you do not speak to those who are come (here)? Did he not die on account of those possessing hard hearts?

Or the lines of a man writing in the second half of the eighth century or the first half of the ninth, who found himself, like a greater poet seven hundred years later 'in sleep a king, but waking no such matter':

Hail!
She who has been obtained by you in former times is a thing not (to be) obtained for gold. Having come (here) who has been obtained by you?
The sky has been obtained in a dream.[1]

[1] The five poems quoted are Nos. 595, 117, 179, 70 and 609.

CHAPTER NINE

ROYAL CAPITAL

In the history of Ceylon A.D. 1017 is as fateful a date as 1066 is in the history of England. Both dates mark the conquest of an island kingdom by a foreign power. The Cola Rajendra I invaded Ceylon in 1017, captured the Sinhalese king, and the old kingdom of Rajarata became a province of the Cola domains. The capital of the Cola adminstration continued to be Polonnaruva, renamed Jananathapura, where a viceroy administered the annexed region in the name of his sovereign on the Indian mainland. Ceylon had had experience of South Indian invasions and South Indian rule centuries before this collapse of the Sinhalese power, but for the first time the king's country (Rajarata) became a part of a foreign empire. What might have been the result of the Cola annexation, if the old and mild policy of making little change in the way the country was administered had been followed there is no knowing, for it has been pointed out that Indian rule over parts of Ceylon, resented as it would have been, in actual fact, 'made little difference to the people as they (the Indian rulers) merely took the place of the Sinhalese kings and ruled the country more or less as the Sinhalese kings did before them.'[1] If there had been the equivalent of a Norman Conquest in Ceylon, perhaps the assimilation of two cultures not markedly different from each other would have taken place naturally and easily. As it was Cola power lacked the strength to conquer the whole of the island, and produced instead of sullen acquiescence, active hostility which would burst into flame whenever opportunity offered. To make matters worse the Cola sovereign exacted tribute from the Sinhalese peasant to maintain Hindu shrines in South India.[2] The ninth, tenth and eleventh centuries, so far as Ceylon is concerned, are marked by the threat of invasion from the mainland, disunion at home, and the repeated attention of pillaging and marauding bands when the South Indian kingdoms in the intervals of their struggles against one another had time to spare for a diversion in Ceylon. To the impartial observer it must have seemed that the security to the Sinhalese kingdom at this time depended on the maintenance of a state of war between the mutually hostile South Indian monarchies.

[1] G. C. Mendis, *The Early History of Ceylon*, Calcutta, 1935, p. 71.   [2] *Ibid.*, p. 72.

When one or other of these monarchs turned his attention to Ceylon the result was nearly always the same. The country-side was ravaged by the invading army, and the Chronicle with a repetitiousness of image records the result of these incursions from the mainland of India. In the reign of Sena I (831–851), the island was invaded by the Pandiya king who 'took away all valuables in the treasure house of the king and plundered what there was to plunder in vihara and town. In the Ratnapasada the golden image of the Master (Buddha), the two jewels which had been set up as eyes in the stone (image of the) Prince of Sages, likewise the gold plates on the cetiya in the Thuparama, and the golden images here and there in the viharas—all these he took and made the Island of Lanka deprived of her valuables leaving the splendid town in a state as if it had been plundered by yakkhas'.[1] In the reign of Mahinda V (981–1017) the Cola troops like devils despoiled Anuradhapura: 'In the three fraternities and in all Lanka (breaking open) the relic chambers, (they carried away) many costly images of gold, etc., and while they violently destroyed here and there all the monasteries, like blood-sucking yakkhas they took all the treasure of Lanka for themselves.'[2]

When the country was not suffering the shock of invasion, it often had to bear the brunt of war between rival factions, each with its bands of mercenaries. By the ninth century the mercenary regiment was a well-known feature of the Sinhalese kingdoms. We have seen how a palace revolt four centuries previously placed Kassapa I on the throne. Palace revolts, the work of generals depending on mercenary troops, become increasingly common, and these South Indian bands often made use of situations which in the politics of the time conferred power on the commander of the local Janissaries. In the reign of Sena V (972–981), the Tamil troops of the commander-in-chief 'plundered the whole country like devils and pillaging, seized the property of its inhabitants.'[3] With kings, commanders-in-chief and nobles involved in the game of trying the fortunes of war, the situation of the ordinary man can well be imagined. It may be that with a wisdom typical of the cultivated he left fighting to the mercenaries. In fact Geiger thinks that the Sinhalese, with a distaste for the discomforts of war, was not likely to have made a good fighter, and that the mercenary from the mainland took over this important duty in the medieval kingdom. The militia was hardly the core of the army any more, the agriculturist tied up with his fields and his home in the village was reluctant to set about on continual forays in the country. The presence and influence of the mercenary showed that dynastic disputes (if these internecine quarrels among princelings could be dignified with this appelation) were going to carve up the country into a number of warring principalities. The power of the mercenaries had grown so great that in the reign of Vikkama-

[1] C, L. 33–36.   [2] C, LV, 20 and 21.   [3] C, LIV, 66.

bahu II (1116–1137) they had succeeded in obtaining the right to protect the Temple of the Tooth in Polonnaruva, although they themselves were Saivites, and with it, according to the judgement of a recent historian, a claim on 'a substantial share of the rich offerings of pilgrims for their services.'[1]

The mercenary soldier helped in the process of the gradual sapping of the strength of the kingdom. It is curious that a horse-dealer, a term which is descriptive and not at all likely to have been pejorative, was credited by the Chronicle with having reported on the divided state of the Sinhalese to the Cola king, and so to have brought on the country the invasion of Rajendra I. In the same way Sena and Guttika who ruled the country in the second century B.C. were the sons of a horse-dealer. To the horse-dealer who travelled about the country as trader, its condition must have been an open book, so that if he combined with activities which need not have been dubious some little side-line of espionage, it could well be imagined that he must have been an admirable member of the secret service.

It is against such a background that the figure of Vijayabahu I (1059–1114) is projected by the *Culavamsa*, composed two centuries after the events it described by a *thera* named Dhammakitti. The figure of this king as patriot, successful warrior and unifier of the kingdom, is by way of being a rough sketch for the equally conventionally planned but much more imposing figure of the epical hero Parakkama Bahu I (1153–1186). The similarities between the *Culavamsa* account of the two kings are too obvious to be explained otherwise than by the poet's intention to adorn the character of his epic hero according to the formula, well-known in the Indian epic as well as in the Greek, and in the romances of Chivalry. Princely birth, obscure, even humble, early surroundings, impressive prophecies, and valorous deeds mark all the heroes of epic and romance. It was so with the young prince Kitti who became Vijayabahu I of Lanka. The astrologer said of him that he bore the marks of power, and that he could unite the whole of India 'under one umbrella'. How much more easily then would he unite Lanka under his rule? 'Swayed by one thought alone: how shall I become possessed of Lanka once I have rid it of the briars of the foe?' he gave himself up to a career which led him, after successes, reverses and a final victory over the Cola, to the throne of Lanka. His reign, peaceful enough, was not without its rebellious and excitements. He had to deal with recalcitrant mercenaries and with the threat of invasion. When he died, having performed during his reign the meritorious works expected of a patron of the *sangha* and the benefactor of his people, the Chronicler could write of him as a 'Ruler of men' who 'had served the Order as also the people sore vexed by the fear of the wicked Damilas'. Naturally 'he

[1] A. L. Basham, 'The Background to the Rise of Parakkama Bahu I' CHJ Vol. IV, p. 20.

ascended to the heavenly world to behold the rich reward that had sprung from his meritorious works'.[1]

As the *Mahavamsa* leads up to the celebration of the career of Dutthagamani as the religious and national hero of Lanka, so the *Culavamsa* works up to its climax in the adventures of the hero Parakkama Bahu. In both the development of the theme of the central figure is foreshadowed by subsidiary parallel themes—in the *Mahavamsa* the stories of Vijaya and Pandukhabaya, and in the *Culavamsa* the story of prince Kitti. In both cases the central figure is isolated and projected against a background which throws in sharp relief the well-recognized traits of the epical hero. Having reached the climactic point in the epical narration, the succeeding movement places besides the hero figures who recall him only to keep the more securely in the reader's or hearer's attention his grandeur as the national champion. Whether the epical scheme is Indian or European, one notices how in the simplest terms of structure repetition provides the outlines, while juxtaposition of contrasts makes up the basic colours used.

Fundamentally there are great similarities between the careers of Dutthagamani and Parakkama Bahu, but the differences between them, though they need not be thought of as contrasts, are sufficiently important to be noteworthy. To take a few similarities first Parakkama Bahu, the son of a ruling prince whose descent is as auspicious as Dutthagamani's, is destined for a career as glorious as that of his very much earlier counterpart. Like Dutthagamani he is consumed with the one desire: to unite the country and to rule it. Both permit neither ties of blood nor private considerations to turn them from the goal they set before them. Both start young as warriors, both are leaders of men, and both achieve their objectives—Dutthagamani in conquering the Tamils, and Parakkama Bahu in becoming king of the whole of Lanka, after he has defeated his uncles and their generals. Both build and adorn their royal capitals, and are distinguished by their meritorious works in the name of religion. They were both of them mighty kings with memorable achievements to their credit.

Yet in their careers and what we can, from the chronicler's account, glean of their personalities—an undertaking difficult enough for descriptions are so schematic, and character as we understand it, now, far from the poet's intention to delineate—there are differences which could be accounted for by the times in which the two heroes flourished, and which are to be reflected in the memorials of their reigns as we remember them today. Geiger, who edited and translated both the *Mahavamsa* and the *Culavamsa*, quite obviously preferred the character of the hero of the earlier Chronicle to that of the later. 'It is interesting . . . to note the fundamental difference between the narrative of

[1] *C, LX,* 91.

the *Culavamsa* and that of the older *Mahavamsa* and between the ideas of their authors as shown particularly in the comparison of the personalities of Duttha-gamani and Parakkamabahu. In the one case deeds of true heroism, culminating in the dauntless duel with Elara, in the other big, high-sounding words as prelude to an action of very doubtful courage and of still more doubtful moral justification. It is therefore significant that in Ceylon, more especially in Rohana, one meets again and again with traditions connected with Duttha-gamani. He is the real national hero of the Sinhalese and his name still lives in the popular memory. Parakkamabahu is almost forgotten though he is nearer by more than a thousand years to the present than the other.'[1]

Is it fanciful or perverse to see in the hero of the *Culavamsa*, Parakkama Bahu, the ruler and the administrator rather than the chivalrous paladin pure and simple which Dutthagamani was? And is it pursuing this fancy too far to set down the feeling that the capital of the one hero, Polonnaruva, is much more a royal city than the capital of the other, which was confirmed and continued in its chosen status of sacred city? Of both capitals, it is very clear that we can now hardly separate what was the work of one king from the work of many others. It may be easier, or less hazardous, to do this for Polonnaruva. But even so, depending on overall impression and what is associated in our minds with the monuments of both cities, we might permissibly regard one as the capital of a kingdom, while the other maintains its character as the spiritual home of a nation. Certainly it is true that both in the Chronicle and in some of his major works, the figure of Parakkama Bahu stands out as that of the prince who set out to gain a kingdom for himself, and won it through his exertions and his great skill as an administrator and planner of campaigns. The legendary which embellishes the careers of both heroes in the Chronicle, is hardly of the same kind. That round Dutthagamani is more primitive, it belongs to the earlier heroic lay, it has even something of the barbaric—the stories of his champions might be paralleled by those of the heroes Jason took with him when he set out to win the golden fleece. It is not on the personality of a king that these legends sit like the oak-leaves on the brow of a conqueror, they are there to provide the atmosphere of an age when giants trod the earth. The light they throw on the hero is not as impressive as their illumination of the stage on which the heroic deeds are performed.

In the case of Parakkama Bahu, the legendary material is of a more sophisticated king. His deeds of prowess, the signs and wonders which attest his future greatness and his doughtiness as a warrior, are all of them the focussing of the strong light of the heroic figure, as it is conceived in literature, on the central character. The person, the kind of person he is, is the more effectively spotted by that light. The personality picked out by the light of legend and

---

[1] C, Part I, p. 250.

history is that of the thorough and single-minded worker, who by rule of ancient precept sees his path to the throne, and takes it. It may be that this impression, produced by one's reading of the Chronicle and confirmed by one's recollection of the major irrigation works of Parakkama Bahu, is the result of the deliberateness with which the choncler wished to present the king as the type of ruler whom the Indian writer of a manual on statecraft would certainly have recommended as the ideal monarch. If there were any other source more reliable to which one might go to check one's impressions, there would be little doubt about the matter, but there is none.

The picture of Parakkama Bahu given in the Chronicle is of a young man who dedicated himself to the cause of his own advancement. With considerable talents which mark the born organizer he plots his course with care, and with great deliberation puts his plans into execution. As Geiger translates it 'with the help of his lightning-like intelligence he learned easily and quickly from his teachers the various accomplishments'. His reading was not only in the Suttas but 'in works of politics as in that of Kotalla and others'[1]—Kotalla being Kautilya, the minister of Chandragupta Maurya, to whom is attributed the *Arthasastra,* the grammar of politics and statecraft for a prince. There is, as a result, a slightly Machiavellian flavour given to the hero's exploits. He did succeed in uniting the characteristics of the lion and the fox, and so he himself cleared the path which led him to the throne. To question the morality of these courses is beside the point, all one can do is to see how apt a pupil of the theory that the end justifies the means Parakkama became. The killing of his uncle's general who had received him with friendliness, his institution of a system of espionage in order to acquaint himself with the state of his host's kingdom, his own assumption of the character of the young man devoted to youthful pastimes in order better to conceal his intentions, are leaves of the same branch. Here is the Chronicle on the prince at his uncle's court at Polonnaruva—it has some attractiveness, it is also sinister: 'The Prince made known his joy called forth by seeing Gajabahu and after spending some days there he in order to become acquainted with those of the King's people dwelling in the outlying districts who were for him and against him, sought out such as understood all kinds of tricks and knew the dialect of the various regions and who were distinguished by devotion to their Lord. Of these he being versed in the methods to be applied, made those who understood the mixing of poisons, adopt the garb of the snake charmer. Others skilled in telling of the lines of the hand and other marks on the body he had disguised as wandering musicians, as candalas and as brahmanas. Amongst the many Damilas and others he made such as were practised in dance and song appear as people who played with leather dolls and the like. Others again after they had laid aside

[1] *C, LXIV, 3.*

their own garb, he ordered to go round selling goods such as rings and brace-
lets of glass and the like. . . . In order to find out himself the actual conditions as these existed amongst the inhabitants of the inner district (of the
town), he by showing a great innocence founded on his youth, learned amongst
the people who came to him under the pretext of entertainment and who dwelt
on the weakness of the king, to distinguish amongst the highest officials,
officers and soldiers those who were ambitious, those who nursed a grudge,
those who were afraid and those who were avaricious.'[1]

Much more significant than all this, and that which harmonizes with both
the record of history and the survivals of his work as builder of tanks, is the
eloquent passage which describes Parakkama Bahu as the wise statesman con-
solidating his hold upon the province to which he succeeded on the death of
his uncle Kittisirimegha. He did not, as the Chronicle points out, waste his
time in empty boasting, but set about making this province his base in the
war which was going to follow—the next stage in his progress to the crown. It
was with the twofold object of providing himself with supplies and increasing
the taxable revenue of his realm, that he restored ancient tanks and built new
ones. Here one sees the mode in which a much more pragmatical hero than
the earlier Dutthagamani sets about his wars. He had no mythical champions
performing deeds of derring-do to assist him, he had therefore to depend on
his own energies as minister of public works and of finance. In order to store
grain in mass he gives order for the beginning of vast irrigation schemes. The
Chronicle on this matter is admirably clear and forthright in the words it
puts into the mouth of the prince: 'In the realm that is subject to me there are,
apart from many strips of country where the harvest flourishes mainly by rain
water, but few fields which are dependent on rivers with permanent flow or on
great reservoirs. Also by many mountains, by thick jungle, and by widespread
swamps my kingdom is much straitened. Truly in such a country not even a
little water that comes from the rain must flow into the ocean without being
useful to man. Except at the mines where there are precious stones, gold and
the like, in all other places the laying out of fields must be taken in hand.'[2]
The 'discerning prince'—to use the Chronicle's own description—the future
ruler of the country identified the building of tanks with an increased revenue:
'In the wildernesses there and at very many other places he determined everywhere what was to remain as wilderness, and assembling all the village chiefs,
he entrusted the inhabitants with the cultivation (of the remaining country).
The discerning (prince) thereby brought it about that the new fields yielded
a tax which was greater than the old taxes produced in the kingdom, and at
the same time brought it to pass that the inhabitants of the country never
more knew fear of famine.'[3]

[1] C, LXVI, 128 ff.   [2] C, LXVIII, 8 ff.   [3] Ibid., 53 ff.

He made Polonnaruva the centralized capital of his kingdom. He restored most of what was in ruin in Anuradhapura, but preferred as capital a city already selected for its strategic position both with regard to invaders from the north, and in easier control of any attempt at rebellion from the south than Anuradhapura. Actually his reign, marked by the construction of great irrigation works and the building of *stupas* and monasteries, was also marked by trouble at home and needless and grandiose forays abroad. It must have been the toughness and energy of the ruler which made the country strong enough and wealthy enough to stand the strain of these great achievements and these abortive attempts at 'universal monarchy'. In the Chronicle story of the reign we see how keenly conscious the king is of his position as king. Once again it may be that the words put into his mouth by the Chronicler are an invention, but the need in the story for such invention must have been created through traditional accounts of the kind of man the king was, and what were his main concerns. When in the course of a rebellion in the province of Ruhuna, the sacred relics of the Tooth and the Almsbowl of the Buddha were carried off by the rebels, the king's concern is both religious and political. Without the relics his own position as king is guaranteed neither by custom nor by popular acclaim, just as a king without his regalia is no king at all. One notes in the king's words grief at the state of the country desolate without the relics and also the awareness that his own kingly crown would never be the symbol it was without them: 'Shattered in combat the foe is in flight. They have seized the splendid sacred relics of the Almsbowl and the Tooth and are fain, through fear, to cross the sea. So I have heard. If this is so, then the island of Lanka will be desolate. For though here on the Sihala island various jewels and pearls and the like and costly kinds of various precious stones are found, yet of quite incomparable costliness are the two sacred relics of the Lord of Truth, the Tooth and the Alms-bowl. . . . My head adorned with a costly diadem sparkling with the splendour of various precious stones, would only be consecrated by the longed-for contact with the two sacred relics of the Great Master, the Tooth and the Alms-bowl.'[1]

One sees in his relations with the *sangha* too, the attitude of the energetic king. Parakkama Bahu brooks no opposition; in the name of efficient administration he rescues the *sangha* from the degradation into which it had fallen, prevents schism from wrecking the order, and promulgates a decree regulating the lives led by its members. One sees in this important sphere of the functions of the king—his relationship to the priesthood—the same ruthless drive in the interests of order and good administration as had marked his rule over the province from which he set out to gain his kingdom. When he came to the throne of Lanka, according to the Chronicle, there were few *bhikkhus* who kept

[1] *C, LXXIV*, 100 ff.

their vows or lived a blameless life, and there was disunity among the three 'fraternities'. Performing an almost superhuman task, like that of 'hurling the Sineru mountain', he purified the *sangha* and 'with great pains established again the community as it had been in Buddha's time'.

Unlike his heroic counterpart Dutthagamani, Parakkama Bahu suffered from no pangs of conscience at the numerous casualties of his wars, nor is the Chronicle account of his death the emotional description of the passing away of the pious being for whom, in the language of another faith, the heavens might have opened. 'Endowed with extraordinary energy and discernment, he carried on the government for thirty-three years.' After his death his sister's son who succeeded him had to release 'from their misery those dwellers in Lanka whom his uncle, the Sovereign Parakkama, had thrown into prison and tortured with stripes or with fetters. By restoring at different places to various people their village or their field he increased the joyfulness of them all.'[1] It would be fair then to see in Parakkama Bahu the efficient ruler, the prince who, determined to be king, was not content merely with enjoying the royal dignity, but was resolved to organize his kingdom according to the precepts of the political justice and the political expediency of that time. Polonnaruva was his royal capital.

It is fascinating in connection with this ruler of men, as indeed he was, to return to the conjecture already held by the peasant living near his royal capital and by more judicious critics, that the statue in the ground of the Potgul Vehera, on the southern face of the boulder not far from the bank of his greatest irrigation work, the Parakkama Samudra, is indeed that of Parakkama Bahu himself. Its difference from other examples of Indian plastic art, the known absence of portraiture in Indian sculpture until much later, made it seem unlikely, however, that here was an attempt to portray the features of a living person. Vogel, who was undoubtedly impressed by the quality of the work, was not inclined to favour the view that it could be the figure of the king: 'A work of far greater merit (than the standing Buddha in the Gal Vihara) is the colossal rock-cut image found at the Potgul Monastery, which is popularly believed to represent the great Parakkama Bahu. There exist, however, serious objections to this identification. The figure with its simple dress, imposing beard, and braided hair, shown in the act of reading a palm-leaf book, can hardly be a royal personage, but has the aspect of a Brahmanical *rishi*. Whether it represents Kapila the ascetic, as supposed by Mr Bell, or Agastya the sage revered equally in southern India and in Java, it is impossible to decide. Whatever its real meaning may be, it is certainly a masterpiece and perhaps the greatest work of art found in Ceylon. It may be questioned whether this rock-cut image which testifies to such a marvellous power of

[1] *C, LXXX*, 2 ff.

expression does not belong to a much earlier age than the reign of the king whom it is supposed to portray.'[1]

Whether inconographically a sage is represented by the statue has been questioned in recent years. Paranavitane suggests that the statue is of a king represented as holding in his hands, not a book which would have been shown with its covers and which would therefore not have sagged in the middle, but a yoke held upside down as if it were a balance, to symbolize the efficient dispensation of justice. In Sanskrit literature the image of the yoke is used for the kingly duties the monarch is called upon to perform, and the yoke of sovereignty is born by the king in token of his even-handed dealing of justice.[2] (In his play of *Richard III* Shakespeare uses the image of the 'yoke of sovereignty' to suggest just one part of the ideas conveyed by the image in Indian literature. Shakespeare thinks of the cares, the burden which weighs upon the sovereign as the yoke upon the ox.)

Besides, the proportions of the figure with its well-rounded middle—a characteristic which appears to a lesser degree in the finely moulded Naga kings of the guardstones—the fulness and benignity, as well of the features and the attitude, the richness of the garment covering the lower half of the body, do not suggest the ascetic. One receives through the dignity and gravity of the figure the suggestions of the idealization of a recognizable person. May this not be the statue of the king who took pride in his political wisdom, the sage king known to be the student of statecraft, who administered his kingdom in the character of the prince of 'extraordinary insight', 'possessed of various accomplishments'? Would it not be fitting, as Paranavitane remarks, that his statue should stand beside a *stupa* which might have marked the spot where he was cremated? That there might be something of the sage in the gravity of the expression and in its inconography, would surely not rule out the possibility that here is the king conventionally represented as the man of a power of insight usually associated with the sage, but carrying pressed close to his chest the symbolic yoke—a burden which gives the reposeful look and the half-closed eyes added meaning. If it is a 'portrait from the life' we see how the sculptor treats his figure in accordance with an idealizing convention, as in the much later south Indian bronze, reputedly of Vankatapati Raya (A.D. 1600), one notes how the figure of the person is moulded according to the iconography of the conventional Saivite devotee.[3]

Sage, or king, or the great Parakkama Bahu himself, the statue sets the standard for the distinguishing trait of Polonnaruva's monumental remains,

[1] J. Ph. Vogel, *Buddhist Art in India, Java and Ceylon*, Oxford, 1936, pp. 88 ff.
[2] S. Paranavitane, 'The Statue near Potgul-Vehara at Polonnaruva, Ceylon,' *Artibus Asiae*, 1952, Vol. XV, 3.
[3] See W. Cohn, *Indische Plastik*, Berlin, 1921, p. 45 and Plate 115.

as one sees the line which connects them with the tradition of Anuradhapura, and how that line varies in the development and modification of the older tradition. One feels in this piece of scuplture the development of a skill which might venture outside the traditional bounds because the hand of the artist has lost none of his old genius. If this were the statue of a king, then we are beginning to leave the confines of an art which tended to restrict itself to the religious. The art of Polonnaruva, however, is predominantly a religious art; its greatest manifestations, apart from the utilitarian and skillful tanks which one could regard as the industrial art of the engineer, were the *stupas*, image-houses, monasteries, with their balustrades, guardstones, and all the known devices with which the place of worship or the residence of the monk-ish community were adorned. But there is a difference which marks Polon-naruva. One is made aware of its identity as royal capital too, and in the ela-boration of some of its religious edifices one could, with some justice, see the glory of the kings who decked the city in honour of the religion they patronized as well as of themselves.

As at Anuradhapura, what is now left is the record of perhaps three or four layers of original work, restoration and amplification. But the span of time which encloses these successive traces of architectural industry is much shorter at Polonnaruva and one can with slightly more accuracy think of a specific style which belongs to the later capital. Some of the most beautiful legacies Polonnaruva has to offer could be described as the interest accumulated by one monarch upon the capital invested by another. The Lankatilaka and the Vata-dage belong to the work of more than one king, how their shares are going to be apportioned does not matter, they both belong to the art of Polonnaruva, which is at one and the same time the continuation of the art of Anuradhapura with differences which stem from the common source of both—the central Indian tradition of Buddhist art.

One is aware almost immediately of the character of Polonnaruva as royal capital in the one great difference which it obviously shows from Anuradha-pura. There is an area in the later capital, with its remains of exterior fortifica-tions, and inner citadel, exclusively reserved for the king and his court—the 'island garden', the palace, pavilions and baths. And in the special quadrangle of the Temple of the Tooth is the *mandapa* or pavilion built specially for the monarch. The island garden, its bathing pools, the Audience Hall, Council Chamber, and palace with its pavilions must have testified to the might and majesty of the king. The Chronicle which lists the buildings which the king had constructed for his pleasure provides an impression far different from that which its ruins now give. But there is in the description of this promontory which jutted into the Parakkama Samudra an exotic richness which sounds rather strange: 'There one saw the Dhavalagara (the white house) that like to the summit of the Kelasa, was made entirely of stucco, wonder exciting . . . and there too gleamed the beautiful, roomy Dolamandapa (swing pavilion) furnished with a swing hung with tiny pretty golden bells. The garden was further resplendent with the vimana called Kilamandapa (games pavilion) where the king at the head of the sport officials, connoisseurs of the merry mood, was wont to amuse himself,'[1] and so on with ivory, peacock and mirror pavilions, bath, with their paintings on the walls, and a four-storeyed palace. Of all this only the rather sombre grey granite traces of foundations, stone steps, mouldering pillars, and piles of brick remain.

Most interesting among the ruins is what is left of the old Council Chamber with its pillars indicating the positions of the king and his officials when they discussed the business of state. The lion throne on which the king Nissanka Malla sat (Sinhasanaya) is now in the museum in Colombo. One notes from the inscriptions on the pillars that the principal merchants of the realm were admitted to the council of state—an interesting piece of evidence relating to the administration of the medieval kingdom.

As for the royal pavilion with the intriguing title of the Rajavesibhujanga (the king lover of a prostitute), it must have been moved from its original position and rebuilt in the thirteenth century where it now stands. Even in its rather gaunt ruin its three friezes of elephants, lions and hilarious dwarfs running round its three basement tiers show the gusto and zest of the artist as he carved his subjects each of them in a characteristically lively attitude. Allowing for the exaggeration of the description of the palace in the Chronicle, we note again the note of baroque extravagance which creeps in. In the enclosure of the palace was 'a golden peacock which drove people out of their senses whenever screeching its peacock cry, it began its dance together with the dancing girl who danced there while they struck up a sweet rhythmic song'.[2] Here, if we may believe the poet, was some ingenious bird which the goldsmith's fantasy fashioned.

One retains the impression of the difference in character of Polonnaruva in the quadrangle now called the Quadrangle of the Sacred Tooth. (The relic must have been moved from place to place during the reign of the two sovereigns Parakkama Bahu and Nissanka Malla (1187–1196), for there was a round building in the Jetavana group which was also the repository of this palladium of the Sinhalese kings.) The Satmahal-prasada, a storeyed structure in the shape of a tower which rises to the height of seven storeys each smaller than the other, and each with niches for the stucco statue of a male figure, is unlike anything else in Ceylon, and it has been suggested that it is the counterpart of a *stupa* in Siam which goes back to an ancient Indian prototype. Brick and stucco—how often the Chronicle comments on buildings

---

[1] *C, LXXIII,* 114 ff.   [2] *Ibid.,* 81 ff.

which gleamed like Kelasa, the snowcapped mountain—tend to replace stone. Also characteristic of a later age is the Thuparama with its vaulted roof still standing, a brick built edifice with an ambulatory on the flat terrace of the roof on which the models of temples stand. This must have been the *pasada* with the 'moonlight terrace' which a courtier of Parakkama Bahu's built.

Equally distinctive is the pavilion the King Nissanka Malla built for himself when he paid his devotions to the sacred relic. This would deserve the epithet 'charming' which the chronicler lavished on the numerous buildings of Parakkama Bahu. This little pavilion entirely in stone is provided with a railing of stone with uprights carved to represent the unopened lotus flower. Its pillars are also of stone, very delightfully representing the same motif, the lotus stalk slightly bending with its delicate flower just opening. This unusual and graceful example of the sculptor's art was known as the Nissanka-Lata-Mandapa—Nissanka's flower pavilion.

This same sovereign, with a floridity which marked most of his work, left characteristic testimony to his glory in the immense monolith in the Quadrangle, recounting in seventy-two lines and to the tune of some four thousand three hundred letters his own praises, his ancestry and his good works.

The chief ornament of the Quadrangle is a type of structure known in Anuradhapura, but of which no other trace than its columns survives. The Vatadage, or Circular Relic House, in Polonnaruva is what has already been referred to as the *cetiyaghara,* the circular roofed structure erected over the *cetiya* or *stupa*. The columns standing round the Lankarama and the Thuparama at Anuradhapura indicate that they were once such shrines. The example at Polonnaruva which Nissanka Malla claimed as his own, is in reality much earlier work, but as it was restored and rebuilt it has something of the baroque excellence of the work of that vainglorious king. It is a work of art which compels admiration through the unusualness of its design and the beautiful execution of its parts. But it is, when compared with its counterpart at Mandalagiri (the present Madirigiriya) ornate and elaborate in a way that approaches *préciosité*. Of course it should be noted that the Vatadage at Polonnaruva is in ruin, but the work of conservation done in this century has preserved most things which would reveal what it must once have been. The roof, however, is missing. The difference made by this to the whole design is incalculable. One has to conclude that it would have accentuated the line of the whole structure and given it the impression of a single mass, which might have removed what seems to be the profusion of ornament in individual parts.

This circular structure on a stone-built platform with portico facing north, contains two circular terraces, the one on top of the other. From the first of the terraces at the four cardinal points rise stone flights of steps characteristically carved with the usual accompaniments of moonstones, guardstones,

balustrades, and carved figures on the vertical faces of the steps. The moonstone at the entrance to the portico is strongly and deeply carved, but it
differs from the Anuradhapura moonstones in having three concentric bands
of animals, each in a separate row, the bull being left out. As for the moonstones on the outer terrace, they all differ from each other, and leave the effect
of a rich variety. Round the inner terrace is an ornamental screen of stone with
a pleasing design of a four petalled flower which might be the jasmine. In
the centre of the inner terrace are the remains of a small brick *stupa*, and at
the four cardinal points, facing the stairways leading to it are four sedent
Buddhas in the pose of meditation. These four statues show distinctiveness
in the treatment of the hair which is not represented by the usual snail-shell
whorl, but by a line which gives the impression that the head wears a skull
cap.[1] The effect of these worn and weathered images does a great deal to give
the Vatadage a counterpoise to the richness of the structure. One might
see here how the old tradition of the simplicity of the statuary triumphs over
effects which bespeak a much more crowded and troubled age striving to get
in as much as it could in order to impress.

Quite different is the impression left by the other Vatadage which belongs
to an earlier period, but which may be taken as belonging to this—that at
Mandalagiri. Its *stupa* round which the relic house was built must have
belonged to very early times, when the slab of rock on which it was placed
was perhaps an object which attracted veneration. The circular relic house on
the rock has an astonishing dignity as it stands out of the jungle surrounding
it, the elevation given it by the flight of steps leading to the porch enhancing
the effect of its pillars standing up against the sky. The moulding of the steps,
and the simplicity both of the moonstone and guardstones at the northern entrance to the shrine are in keeping with the stately sweep of the three brick
tiers which support the circular terrace. The design on the stone screen is of
the old Buddhist railing type, and the plainness in the ornamentation of the
stone pillars and the stone flags on the floor of the shrine make a strong contrast with the richness and elaboration of its counterpart at Polonnaruva. The
ruined *stupa* in the middle of the relic house is on a limestone base, and at the
four cardinal points are four limestone statues of the sedent Buddha. Damaged
as they are, they yet preserve something in the chaste lines of the earlier work
of Anuradhapura.

In Polonnaruva's two extremely handsome image-houses will be noted again
the difference between the architecture and the execution of ornament of this
time when they are compared with those of Anuradhapura. Both these image-
houses, the Lankatilaka and the Tivanka image-house, are brick built, and
ornamented with stucco on the outside, and with paintings inside. They con-

[1] S. Paranavitane, *Art and Architecture of Ceylon*, Colombo, 1954, p. 35.

tain the ruins of colossal brick and plaster images of the Buddha, showing in
the outlines of the collapsed figures the magnificence of the artist's intention.
Both are the characteristic focal points of a group of monastic buildings—the
Lankatilaka of the Alahana Pirivena, and the Tivanka of the Jetavana, or the
monastery till recently wrongly described as the Demala Maha Seya. Their
magnificence indicates a much later stage in the development of religious
observances. Even in their ruined state one is not without some intimation of
the pride which showed itself in the soaring vertical lines of the Lankatilaka
which the Chronicle describes as 'a charming image house of five storeys for
which—as it was adorned with ornaments of flowers and creepers and with
figures and gods and Brahmas and embellished with buildings, with turrets,
grottos, apartments and halls—the name of Lankatilaka (ornament of Lanka)
was befitting. In this temple he (Parakkama Bahu) had erected a standing
image which was an elixir for the eyes which had the size of the living
Buddha'.[1] This image, which must have been some forty-one feet in height, is
led to by a narrow entrance and a still narrower passage. The effect of the
image to which the devotee was thus conducted from the spacious enclosure
of the tall building so strikingly ornamented must have been impressive. Of
what is left of the image-house, image and its exterior decoration—the
paintings have practically all disappeared—the predominant impression is of
the grandeur of the immense decapitated piers which face one, slightly aslant
and suggesting in their rich ochre tone the earth which man moulded and
raised to such heights fruitlessly.

As the eye gets accustomed to the lines of the piers and notices the richness
of the ornamentation on them, and as one walks round the image-house and
sees again the wealth of figure in stucco lavished on it—idealized gods, godlings but with very materialistic bodies, dancers, etc.—one receives another
impression, that of the profusion which gave this image-house its name. The
rich carving on balustrades and steps at its entrance supports this feeling.
The Lankatilaka is typical of Polonnaruva. It is distinctive, and it can be
thought of, in its use of its materials of brick and its stucco and its wealth
of ornament, as intrinsically the product of a later age of Sinhalese architecture and plastic art than that represented by Anuradhapura.

The Tivanka image-house—that of the Tivanka statue of the Buddha (the
standing Buddha 'with the three bends'—the posture in which Vishnu or the
Nagas are often represented)—is distinguished by its paintings more than by
anything else. What is left of the structure is the ground floor and some part
of the first storey. On the back of the wall of the shrine room which all but
frames it, is the headless ruin of the great image. 'He (Parakkama Bahu) built
the Tivanka house for the Tivanka image, shimmering with rows of figures of

[1] C, LXXVIII, 52 ff.

lions, kinnaras (mythical beings represented with human bodies and heads of horses) geese and the like, with many diversely perforated balustrades and with railings.'[1] One is struck—the Chronicler using another metaphor describes the same effect in calling the building an 'elixir for the eyes'—here again, as in the Lankatilaka, by the profusion of the decoration of the outer wall and the paintings inside.

The inner walls in vestibule, corridor and in the actual shrine-room are still rich with paintings of incidents from the stories of the Jatakas (the previous births of the Buddha) and the legends of his life. These are the most considerable survival of any from medieval or ancient times, and in their technique and style they show how strongly the great Indian tradition was still maintained in Ceylon. They are of a different kind from those at Sigiriya, there is more conscious artistry in them, and in the utilization of the ground to be covered they are strongly reminiscent of Ajanta and Bagh. Red, yellow and green have been the colours used, blue once again is missing. As in the Indian tradition, the outlines have been first drawn and then filled in with the colours, the beauty of the whole depending on the harmony of the broad lines and the nuances provided by the simple range of colour. The mellifluousness of the gods in the painting which shows them urging the *Bodhisatta* to descend from the Tusita heaven is an example of the fullness and poise of a conventional style.

In the Lotus Bath not far away one sees the key-signature of Polonnaruva again—a *tour-de-force* which can never efface the impression of deliberate and formalized ingenuity. The inverted lotus with its conventional arrangement of petals forming the range both of steps and also of the bowl of the bath, is ingenious, though at the present time the décor of musical comedy and revue could produce ingenuities which could surpass this. The carving of the granite to give the impression of the tactile quality of the petals of the flower cannot be praised too highly, but in the graciousness of the whole the Kuttampokuna or the Twin Baths of Anuradhapura, recently conserved, are chaster and lovelier.

The great *stupas* of Polonnaruva remain faithful to the old tradition of Anuradhapura—the same bubble-shaped dome, architecturally the same major features which time could hardly change since the weight of the structure could scarcely have been dealt with in any other way. The material of the spire differs from the stone which was favoured at Anuradhapura, but at the Rankot and the Kiri Viharas one might again be facing such *stupas* as had been built by kings of Ceylon centuries previously. Although the main characteristics of these structures have not changed, one notices how, in their subsidiary features, another type of material is now responsible for the old *vahalkadas*, and the numerous shrine rooms or chapels which are spaced out on the stone

[1] *Ibid.*, 39 ff.

pavement of the processional path round the *stupa*. Paranavitane has noted of these *vahalkadas* that, 'the vertical aspect which was not considered important in the earlier *vahalkadas* has been given more emphasis in the Polonnaruva examples by means of these pilasters (which replace the superimposed string courses of the earlier examples).'[1] What was lost in the lack of ornamentation here was more than compensated for by the decoration of the little shrines which dot the path. The greatest *stupa* of all which the king had planned for the city, he could not complete. Called the Damila-thupa because the labour of Tamil prisoners of war went into its construction, it shows a small dome on a disproportionately large base. It must have been too grand in its conception for a later age to execute.

In the four statues of the Buddha at the Uttararama, now called the Gal Vihara, the art of Polonnaruva seems to have reached its highest point. Using the age-old material of stone, and forcing a natural formation of rock in the park of the Northern Vihara to submit to the demands of his inspiration, the artist has created some of the most beautiful and moving examples of sculpture to be found in Buddhist art. Time has restored to these noble pieces of statuary the natural surroundings which belonged to them when the artist first worked upon his material. Gilded over as they afterwards were, and closed within the confines of a brick-walled image-house, they could not have had the same effect, however splendid the architecture and the decoration of its interior might have been, as they now have. Seen now as they must have been when first fashioned out of the grey granite cut and scooped to accomodate them, they are the more memorable. Here, as elsewhere, one admires not simply the artistic excellence of the finished work, but the extraordinary vision of the sculptor. Out of the boulder lying in the grounds of the park he produced the expressive forms he saw latent there.

The first is a sedent Buddha on a conventional lotus seat, the rock face behind decorated with all the skill and ornament which the sculptor felt due to the sedent figure. The nimbus and triumphal arch are both unusual and very finely done. As for the sedent Buddha in the cave, he is attended by the figures of Hindu deities, and two *Bodhisattas* on either side with fly-whisks in their hands. Their smaller image is much more expressive and softer than the figure on its right. The cave in which it stands bears traces of the paintings which once covered it, and in front of it are the remains of a pavilion used by devotees.

The two Buddhas on the north of the cave are perhaps the highwater mark of the sculptor's art in Ceylon. They have produced such an effect on the beholder that, quite oblivious of the fact that each once stood isolated in an image-house of its own, the brick foundations of which are still to be seen,

[1] S. Paranavitane, *op. cit.*, p. 28.

critics have imagined that the two figures represent the passing away of the
Buddha when he lay at the Sal-tree grove at Kusinara with Ananda weeping
beside him. Geiger describing the two images in his note on the Uttararama
Vihara writes: 'To the right, also hewn of the solid rock, there is a colossal
figure of a recumbent Buddha about 49 feet long, at its head the upright
figure of Ananda grieving over his dying master.'[1] It is no longer possible to
agree with this account of the two images, the result of the fancies which they
have touched off in the mind of the beholder. Sculpture in Ceylon has never
selected the narrative subject, and there are no groups or single figures which
portray the Buddha at significant points in his career.[2] The wonderful combination of the realistic with the conventional in the standing Buddha with
the unusual pose of the arms folded across the breast, may have suggested to
the sympathetic imagination lines of grief in the facial expression which may
be no more than the weathering of the granite surface. Thought of, as it must
be, as an image on the lotus pedestal, and a single figure in an image-house,
this colossal statue, like that of the Lankatilaka or Tivanka shrines, can only
be the representation of the Buddha. Current descriptions of the image as
that of Ananda must be regarded as tribute to the sculptor's greatness. It is a
moving piece of work, the position of the hands leading the attention to concentrate on the upper body, face and head which the rock-wall does not dwarf.
The eyes and the dignity of the facial expression give the figure a massive
otherworldliness.

The recumbent Buddha, in the adjacent image-house, in its sharpness of
detail and its grandeur of line, shows the loving attention of the sculptor to
the Master both venerated and loved. The depression in the rock pillow on
which the head rests, the feeling for the carving of the right hand upon which
the face is pressed, the beauty of the conventional snail-shell pattern of the
hair, and the graceful symmetry of the parallel grooves of the light robes
which drape the immense form, show how the genius behind the chisel has
been intent on glorifying and at the same time recollecting humanity. When
one considers the proportions of this image one sees how the scale could have
defeated the idealized human which the artist strove to create. It is difficult
to do justice to its harmony of god-like and the human.

One of the minor works of this period is to be found in the *stupa* Parakkama
Bahu built to mark the site of the place in which he was born—the village

[1] C, Part II, p. 111.

[2] S. Paranavitane, 'The Significance of Sinhalese Moonstones' *Artibus Asiae*, Vol. XVII, 3-4,
p. 203: 'It is important to note that apart from a few pieces of sculpture that have obviously
been imported from India, no ancient Buddha image has been found in Ceylon, either in the
round or in bas-relief, intended as a representation of an episode in his life, either before or
after the Enlightenment, as we have in such abundance in India, particularly in Gandhara and
the Andhra country.'

called Punkhagama in the Chronicle. That he so commemorated the site of his birth is in keeping with the man who felt himself destined for kingly rule. Another *stupa* which the king built at the place of his mother's cremation has not as yet been identified. That at his birthplace was never completed. Three years ago the first relic chamber of this *stupa* yielded various objects belonging to the art of this period, of which the most significant, because it recalls the charming toys which the Chronicle imagined graced the royal palace at Polonnaruva, is the bronze elephant lamp. This was suspended on a chain carved rather characteristically with three figurines of danseuse, cymbalist and drummer, and the lamp itself is an oil-receptacle in which a floating wick provided the illumination. Its oil tank was a beautifully and realistically cast elephant on which two figures are astride. The artist's ingenuity, using a hydrostatic principle which could scarcely have been common property at that time, makes the feeding of oil in the lamp automatic. The elephant is hollow and detachable, the oil being stored in its abdomen. Its right foot is both aperture for the filling of the oil and acts as a plug on the plate of the oil-receptacle to which it is attached. When the oil-level in the lamp drops, the forefoot aperture is exposed to the atmosphere, and in order to equalize the pressure, the oil from the elephant reservoir flows in through the prominent genital organ of the beast. As the oil-level rises up to seal the aperture in the fore-foot, the air supply is cut off and the flow of oil from elephant to lamp ceases.[1] This ingenious lamp on which the artist lavished his skill—for the arch on which the chain is hung, the elephant and the figures on the chain are delightfully worked—was an object which the great king enshrined in the relic chamber of the *stupa* which celebrated his birthplace. It would tend to show how the great builder of tanks and image-houses had time to spare for fancies such as these. His interest in these toys would be a reminder of that characteristic of his which led him naturally to games and to sport. The dancing troupe on the chain, the elephant through the genital organ of which the lamp was filled, must have appealed to instincts which his greatness as statesman and king could not suppress.

[1] I am indebted to Mr Abhaya Devapura, Curator of the Museum at Dedigama, where this lamp is now exhibited, for the details of this description.

EPILOGUE

THE HILLS

The energies of Parakkama Bahu I had arrested for a few years the inevitable process of decline. We have noted that when he died, there were left in the state prisons numerous captives whom his successor mercifully released. One can regard these wretched beings as the sacrifices which have to be made to the gods of efficiency and thoroughness by rulers whose personal qualities of intensive self-application to an objective will not let them rest. It has been suggested by one historian that the break-up of the Sinhalese kingdom which this ruler for a short period arrested, was in fact accelerated by the foreign adventures in which he took a hand, and the consequent strain upon his treasury and the country's financial resilience.

To leave aside the foreign wars, which the Chronicle describes in a prejudiced and totally one-sided manner as crowned with spectacular success, and to consider for a moment the great irrigational works, which financed these and the establishment and glorification of his royal capital, is to wonder at the determined drive of the sovereign, and the consuming passion of his ambitious plans. He was responsible for renovating and amplifying two schemes of irrigation so grand that he could call them on completion, without much exaggeration, 'seas'. One of these 'seas'—the damming of streams, and the linking of tanks to make vast artificial lakes—was the work of those years when he prepared the base in his principality from which he was going to wrest the crown from his uncle who ruled at Polonnaruva. It was therefore the enterprise of a young man who had nothing to fall back upon except the revenues of a single province and his own abundant energy. The first of his schemes for this province—the damming of a river—was opposed by his engineers on account of its difficulty, and even its impracticability. His reply to their objections was characteristic: 'What is there in the world that cannot be carried out by people of energy?'

The great 'sea of Parakkama' at Polonnaruva which he built by damming two rivers, and constructing a channel and aquaducts to fill the area of two tanks which he joined together, is a mighty work which compares favourably with present-day irrigation schemes into which modern planning and techniques have gone. 'The figures given in the Chronicle for the irrigation works carried out are astonishing' writes one authority. 'They are:

Anicuts constructed or restored	165
Canals constructed or restored	3,910
Major tanks constructed or restored	163
Minor tanks constructed or restored	2,376
Stone sluices constructed or restored	341
Breaches repaired	1,753'[1]

Even if one assumed that forced labour went into these works, they speak of prodigious capacities for work and a resoluteness which must have been due to the character of both ruler and people. It is difficult at the present time in Ceylon to think of endeavours and labour which could bring to realization even a small fraction of the achievements of the twelfth-century Sinhalese in this single field.

One would feel justified in concluding that something went out of the national character, if only one could feel that such entities as a national character were easily demonstrable. They certainly are tractable, because they are generally our subjective impressions secure of a position in no need of justification. How easy it is to put down these vast works to a national character which has apparently degenerated on account of one or other of the currently popular reasons—foreign exploitation, irreligion, or the lamentable practice of wearing trousers. Whatever the national character of the inhabitants of Ceylon in those days, two things are at least true now. First, that one is much more likely at the present time to secure the services of a vast army of overseers—those who in fact watch others at work rather than work themselves —than of labourers. And secondly, that already in the time of Robert Knox, who lived five hundred years later in Ceylon when the capital had moved to the Kandyan hills, it seemed to him, as an independent observer, that the Sinhalese were markedly addicted to doing nothing all day long—that agreeable state, which to most inane Western minds tired of the ceaseless agitation of life in a large industrial city, is, quite mistakenly regarded as a philosophic attitude. Knox describes the Sinhalese—of course his remarks would hold good of the king's subjects in the Kandyan country only—as 'delighting in sloth, deferring labour till urgent necessity constrain them'. The stock jest he tells of them illustrated the futility of their exaggerated modes of civility, but it is interesting to note that the same jest, repeated today, is adduced as proof of the national trait of *dolce far niente*. Knox was referring to the reluctance of a visitor to inform one of the reason for his visit, and the use of the

[1] C. W. Nicholas, 'The Irrigation Works of King Parakkama Bahu,' CHJ, Vol. IV, Nos. 1-4, April, 1955, p. 60.

28.
Gadaladeniya: The
small stupa with its
hipped Kandyan roof
—see p. 169

29. Gadaladeniya, near Kadugannawa—The Porch—see p. 169

30.
Left: Embekke, near
Kadugannawa—Wood-
carving on pillar—detail
—see p. 169

Right: Degaldoruva, near
Kandy—Detail of fresco

31. Polonnaruva—detail of colossal statue of recumbent Buddha—see p. 172

phrase *Nicamava* (I came for nothing at all) which he writes 'is their ordinary reply, though they do come for something. And upon this they have a fable.

A god came down upon earth one day, and bade all his creatures come before him and demand what they would have and it should be granted them. So all the beasts and other creatures came, and one desired strength, and another legs, and another wings, etc., etc. Then came the White men, the god asked them, what they came for. And they said they desired beauty, and valour and riches. It was granted them. At last came the Sinhalese. The god required of them what they came for. They answered, *Nicamava*, I came for nothing. Then replied he again, if you come for nothing, then go away with nothing. And so they for their compliment fared worse than all the rest.'[1]

The variability of national character is so well known, and the pastime of generalizing about it nevertheless so attractive, that it does not help much to remember that a hundred and fifty years ago, the German, in the English literature of the time, was an absurdly unpractical fellow given to philosophizing uselessly all day long and all night too. Conceptions of the Slav character a hundred years ago made one think of the Russian, by comparison with other Europeans, as a gloomy mystic with an unpredictable tendency to fits of hysterical exaltation. How much such notions have changed in our time. It is instructive to note that dabblers in national character today tend to diagnose the character of a race from the way it brings up its children. This may be a study better grounded in theory than the old, but its results are still unsatisfactory. To put down a streak of sadism discovered in the contemporary Japanese character to the weaning practices of Japanese mothers, and not to investigate how these arose, does not take us far. It leaves us where we were with one absolute instead of another.

Whatever view one takes of the character of the subjects of Parakkama Bahu I, it is undoubted that his own strength as ruler was responsible for a great part of the achievement of his reign. He may have acted against the will of the advisers and his people, but his own determination—so far as we can judge these things from the unsatisfactory poetic records of the Chronicle—was strong, and he had success crown his efforts and disprove the cautiousness of those who lacked his qualities. Some of his schemes were never completed, his foreign wars were a mistake, and he was sometimes proved wrong about his projects. His Kotthabadda causeway, as had been predicted, did not last a major flood, and the walls of the Lankatilaka were not strong enough to support the structure, and had to be rebuilt later. It could be imagined that the reign of this sovereign was a supreme effort on the part of a country and people already succumbing to forces too strong to contend against, but urged to gigantic tasks by the will of a single individual.

[1] Robert Knox, *An Historical Relation of Ceylon*, Glasgow, 1911, Ed. James Ryan, p. 169.

F

Parakkama Bahu II and Wijayabahu IV—in the thirteenth entury—may have had some temporary successes in arms, but the downward trend in the affairs of the Sinhalese kingdom continued. As disasters crowded thick and fast, kings moved from one capital to the other, and various sub-kings ruled over various provinces, the Chronicle turns from the contemplation of these reverses to set pieces of rhetorical exaggeration in honour of religious festivals. Geiger records his disappointment with the comment: 'The *Mahavamsa* has hardly anything of historical value to tell us either about the reign of Parakkama Bahu VI, except perhaps in verse 24, that his mother's name was Sunetta. It is a great pity that the compiler of the third part of the *Culavamsa* restricts himself almost entirely to stereotyped descriptions of festivals for the Tooth Relic.'[1] It is not that the sovereigns who succeeded Parakkama Bahu I were not in their own right important, or that the reigns of the best of them contributed nothing to the glory of the Sinhalese kingdom, but that the best they could show reveals nevertheless a process which one can only think of as decay. It would have been difficult for many kings from any part of the world whatsoever to have reached the stature of Parakkama Bahu I, but there is something in the kings whose roll is wearyingly unfolded in the *Culavamsa*, even in Rajasinha II, the one we know best through Knox's description of him, which speaks of a different level and a metal less strong. It might be true to conclude—if a metaphor is permissible—that the Sinhalese kingdom exhausted itself in producing its typical ruler of a state.

There is something in the Polonnaruva kingdom, as its ruins disclose its character today, to make us think of it as one of the many kingdoms in the South Indian corner of Asia destined for disintegration as a result of the wars they fought with each other. We may not be ready to think of a Sinhalese kingdom in this way, but placed in the setting of the struggles of Colas, Pandyas, Chalukyas and Hoysalas, it would seem to have been marked with the fatality which overtook all of them. Dynastic ambitions and dreams of empire set them at each other's throats and kept up a chronic state of warfare in medieval India. If it seems improper to fit the Sinhalese kingdom into this framework, as one turns to the remains of Polonnaruva and sees the *devales* (temples of the gods) to the god Siva, and the votive bronzes found among its ruins, then one feels that there is much which links all these kingdoms together. Though the hereditary enemies of the Sinhalese were the *Damilas*, its royal house in the twelfth and thirteenth centuries prided itself on its South Indian princely descent, and there had been South Indian peoples in Ceylon for centuries, and they must have been assimilated with the people of the country. They may have kept their own religion which was Hinduism, but the Sinhalese kings had their Brahman chaplains, and did honour to the shrines

[1] *C*, Part II, p. 215, n. 1.

of Hindu gods—the most famous in medieval times being that of the god Upalvan at Devundera to which we have referred already.

The Saiva shrines at Polonnaruva were, most of them, the work of the Colas in their years of rule over the city. Though they are in the South Indian style, Paranavitane notes that this style had developed from 'earlier Buddhist architecture, and therefore possesses certain features in common with that distinctive of the Sinhalese'.[1] Parakkama Bahu I himself built pavilions in the precincts of his palace for the Brahmins who were an important group in his court. By its island position and in its religion the Sinhalese kingdom was set apart from the South Indian kingdoms, but culturally it and they were not so markedly distinct from each other as to be thought of as being intrinsically different societies. The Sinhalese kingdom which went into decline in the thirteenth century was a kingdom which resembled the South Indian kingdoms in various ways. Not the special malice of Cola or Pandya destroyed the ancient Sinhalese kingdom, but with them it suffered from what might be called the occupational disease of all these kingdoms, and went the way of them all. Only the Vijayanagar emerged from the continued warfare of those times to survive the force of Islam and remain a great kingdom till the middle of the sixteenth century. By that time a new and decisive power had entered the politics of all the Indian kingdoms—the trader from the West with his soldiers and their new techniques of war.

There are no less than seven Siva *devales* and five Vishnu *devales* found in Polonnaruva. One is a beautiful example of a thirteenth-century Pandyan shrine, and lies between the royal palace and the quadrangle of the Temple of the Tooth. Another close to the *stupa* built by Rupavati, one of the queens of Parakkama Bahu I, and now called Siva Devale No. 2., is in a better state of preservation than the other. It is an eleventh-century Cola temple, reminiscent of the type of building which Rowland described as the 'nucleus of all later temple building in India, both Hindu and Buddhist'.[2] One enters it at the east, there is a little vestibule and then the shrine room with the image of the cult. The roof is flat and above the shrine is a little spire or *sikhara*. The origins of the *sikhara* Rowland describes as one of the great points of dispute in Indian archaeology: 'Some see in it a development from the *stupa*, or a translation into stone of a wooden processional car. Others have suggested an adaptation from primitive beehive huts or a figuration of the Mukhuta, the towering headdress of Vishnu.' The spire at this *devale* is dome-like in shape and resembles the miniature *stupa* found in bas-reliefs and relic chambers.

Both these *devales* are constructed of gneiss. Further away, on the path to the Rankot Vehera is another which goes back to the thirteenth century when the

[1] S. Paranavitane, *Art and Architecture of Ceylon*, Colombo, 1954, p. 22.
[2] Benjamin Rowland, 'Gupta Architecture', *Marg*, Bombay 1956, Vol. IX, No. 2.

invader Magha ruled Ceylon (1213–1234). From this period onwards one notes how the *devale* comes more and more to be associated with the Buddhist temple, until during the Kandyan period—from the late 15th century—it is common to have the *devale* situated in the same building as the *vihara*. In Ratnapura the *vihara* 'is annexed to the *devale*'.

At the *devales* in Polonnaruva were discovered bronze figures of the god and his consort, and of Saivite saints in the characteristic attitude of devotion, the hands pressed together and held at the breast, with the rapt expression of the initiate very remarkably moulded by the artist. The best known of them is the magnificent Siva Nataraja, now in the Colombo Museum. It was found near Siva Devale No. 1. It shows the god surrounded by the complete circle of flames, his braided hair streaming in the motion of the dance, at the moment when he has placed his left foot on the Titan of illusion which his enemies sent to distract him from his work of creation. The grace of the movement of the dance is symbolized by the attitude of the figure with hand and leg poised forward in the momentum of the gesture, to which the circle gives a grand sweep and completes. Another, equally beautiful in grace and the expression on the face of the figure, is that of Sundramurti at the moment in which he is summoned by the god. The young man in the rich robes of the bridegroom is enraptured by the vision, and from that moment onwards he vows himself to the god.

To leave out these bronzes and the *devales* would result in an incomplete picture of the monuments of old Ceylon. There is surely a distinctive Sinhalese style, and in this style are features which belong to the artist's re-fashioning of the great Indian heritage in which Ceylon shared. In the distinctive Sinhalese style, there are phases of styles current at one time or belonging to a particular place. There is a style which one can think of as belonging to Anuradhapura, and another which belongs to Polonnaruva. One part of this style may not have been, in the ruins we find at Polonnaruva, the work of Sinhalese craftsmen, but this seems to become more characteristic of what follows upon Polonnaruva. Whether it is better or worse than the style of Polonnaruva is for the individual to judge, but it certainly becomes, as it develops, the reflection of a cultural change. The historical period which followed upon the Cola, Magha, was a period of decadence politically, since it witnessed the gradual ruin of the kingdom which had, despite internal strife, managed to keep its control of the country. But would it be fair to stigmatize the art of this period as decadent, because something of the conqueror is taken over and shows itself in architecture and sculpture? It could justifiably be contended that, whether the Colans had devastated Ceylon or not, contacts with South India would probably have resulted in the acclimatization of Cola and Vijayanagar art in a kingdom too closely connected with

South India to be thought of as different from it, or foreign to it. Sinhalese art continued to be distinctive, but it includes in its development from this time on something taken from or given by South India, as previously it had taken over something from Central India.

The kingdom moved, relapsing under kings who had little power to control their generals and rebellious members of the royal family, from one rock fortress to another as capital city. In the process of retreat from the old Rajarata it touched states of anarchy which recall not only the disorderliness of all these Indian kingdoms in their relations with each other, but also frequent chapters in the history of the ancient kingdom of Ceylon with the rival princes of the two royal clans of Lambakanna and Moriya at war with each other. The kingdom was breaking up into the various parts which became its settled divisions at the end of this period. But before it has thus fragmented into the kingdoms of Kandy, of Kotte and of Sitavaka, a stand was made at one place or the other, and the capital of Ceylon was, for a while, Subhapabbata or Subhagiri (the present Yapahuva), Jambuddoni—'the pleasant Jambuddoni' as it was called (the modern Dambadeniya), Hatthigiripura (Kurunegala), and last of all Sitavaka and Jayawaddanakotta (the modern Kotte), where the Portuguese found the king of the lowlands, while the central region had its own king with his capital at Kandy (from Kande-uda—up on the hills). It is interesting that this trail from capital to capital did not lead through Sigiri where Kassapa had lived as a god king. It may have been easier in the thirteenth century for the commander-in-chief to build anew on the summit of Yapahuva than to try to restore the ruined fortress and palace of Sigiri.

Of the building of this fortress and palace there is a fantastic account in the *Yaphuva Vistaraya*, which is worth repeating since it refers to the main feature of what is left of this capital—its magnificent work in stone which required great labour. '. . . The building of the city of Yapahuva was begun on the rock called *Sundaragiriparvata*, after which the city was named. That same king (Parakkama Bahu II) commanded that it should be constructed of stone only, and that the following workmen should be engaged: 120 lacs of masons, 100 chief blacksmiths, 250 hangidi (foremen), 3000 painters, 400 carvers. The Adigars thereupon commanded some to cut stone pillars, some to carve, some to smooth, some to carve figures, some to paint, some to carve figures of elephants, some figures of lions, some of wolves, some figures of men, some of geese, some of birds, some *naga* figures, some figures of gods, some figures of women, some of creepers, some of parrots, some of peacocks, some figures of beaters of tom-toms, some figures of dancers engaged in the act of dancing, some of conch-blowers engaged in blowing, some of figures engaged in wrestling, some to carve representations of beds, some of stone doors, some of doorposts, and some of stone steps. These stones were then painted over by the painters.

In this style four *maligaval* of nine storeys each were built, with stairs leading up to them. Round these 500 smaller houses of inferior workmanship were also built. A store eighty cubits high, 500 houses outside the fort, 1000 double shutters for the houses, a stone wall 7 feet high, a metal rampart encircling it, 1000 golden arches, 1000 silver arches, were also constructed, and adorned with flags, and flaps and cloth-dolls appended thereto, there being 1000 elephants, 1000 horses, 24,000 mercenaries, 2 lacs and 61,000 inhabitants in all. Like Sakraya, enjoying health and happiness, and so reigning, the king built and adorned the city, the only material used being stone.'[1] For four years Yapahuva was the capital of Ceylon—from 1280–1284 —until a Pandyan army under Ariyacakkavattin sacked the city, and captured the Tooth Relic. The capital moved elsewhere and Yapahuva never recovered from its ruin.

The grandiloquent description of the preparations for the building of the town shows the one feature which remains—the profusion of carved stone-work in wing-walls of stairways and panels. It leaves such an impression of grandeur in the three stairways which lead up to the porch over the slope of the rock, that the ruins of a building beyond are a complete anticlimax. The third stairway still retains something of its ancient splendour, the tone of its style being set by the stone lions which challenge the intruder from their position on the balustrade. The totem animal of the Sinhalese, highly conventionalized, is given a formidable ferocity which reminds one both of the South Indian and the Chinese. Beyond is seen the crag of the citadel.

The porch in which the third stairway terminates is adorned with the work of the 'masons' mentioned in the *Vistaraya*, and some of the motifs listed there. Round the vestibule on its exterior face is an enchanting frieze of dancers in various positions suggesting vigorous movement, sometimes featured with the musicians who accompany their dance. These motifs of women dancing are unlike those of a similar kind found in decoration earlier. There is a greater violence in the movement depicted in the stone here, suggesting that the sculptor's intention had been concentrated on catching the abandon of the dance form. Was it his intention to give thereby the feeling of exhilaration which the approach to fortress and palace was expected to produce in the visitor? Some of the women in the friezes seem to be caught in the moment of execution of an acrobatic turn, the left leg of one touches her head. There is a group consisting of four figures, a woman on the right in a posture of dance with her hand upraised, a male 'master-of-ceremonies' also in the dance, but with staff in his right hand, seeming to draw attention to the acrobat beside

[1] A. K. Coomaraswamy, *Medieval Sinhalese Art*, Broad Campden, 1907, pp. 10–11.

him who stands on his hands and throws his legs back over his head, while the figure on the extreme left beats the drum held across his legs, as he stands in the stiff conventional position the Kandyan drummer assumes today. These panels of dancers and drummers, carved with so much animation, have nothing of the grotesque; they might be the natural development of the well-known design, giving opportunity to the sculptor to produce new evidence of his ingenuity in getting the familiar types of the community for the decoration of the royal buildings. Their accent is on rhythmical movement. There is another beautiful panel of a woman dancing between two drum beaters, the one on her right holds his hand aloft before he brings it down on the drum which straddles his legs. All in all there is such a wealth of carving here that this alone would show how the ancient skill in stone seems to divert itself in new ways.

The columns and windows of the porch were beautifully carved. The columns especially being fashioned with a richness which does not seem very characteristic of the much simpler and chaster Sinhalese style of the earlier period. Hocart felt that in Yapahuva is to be found very clear traces of Hindu influence, but he is careful to add that the Sinhalese style reflects the South Indian with a difference. 'It was always distinguished by a greater simplicity and by shallower cutting. . . . At the time Hindus were building Chola and Pandyan temples in Polonnaruva, the Sinhalese were building brick temples, which were getting nearer to Hindu art than those of earlier periods, but still remained Sinhalese.'[1] Yapahuva is therefore the Sinhalese rendering of a phase of South Indian art which, as it had previously left its mark on Ceylon, does not seem to have been an alien influence. Two ornamental arches over the windows are worth considering, with the *makara* above a central panel in which the goddess Lakshmi sits on a lotus throne, while two elephants pour water over the lotus flowers she holds in her hand—the pose known as the *Gaja Lakshmi*. This motif is the same as that on the Galpota of Nissanka Malla in the Quadrangle at Polonnaruva. In Yapahuva the treatment is somewhat different, it inclines much more to the florid, and its position above the frame of the window increases the richness of its effect.

When one part of the Sinhalese kingdom took refuge in the Kandyan hills, the legendary story of the flight of the aboriginal tribes of Lanka from the north-central region to the hills on the arrival of the Aryan settlers from India seems to have been re-enacted. Time, however, was not exacting revenge, the retreat was logical and understandable. The hills afforded protection, and the town of Kandy, which became the capital of the central region and the repository of the sacred relic of the Tooth, seemed to be trebly protected, according to the military theory of that age, by mountain, forest and river.

[1] See A. M. Hocart's reports: Ceylon Journal of Science (Section G) Vol. I, p. 148.

The kingdoms in the maritime regions, after a feeble show of independence had to give in, first to the Portuguese, and then to the Dutch whom the king of Kandy called in to oust them. Finally the English defeated the Dutch, and the days of the Kandyan kingdom too were numbered. Before the island passed into British hands the Danes and the French in the eighteenth century had also made abortive attempts to establish some foothold in it.

The Chronicle viewed the catastrophes of the ancient kingdom as the result of the 'evil done by the dwellers in Lanka' and the consequent inability of its tutelary *devas* to protect the island. In the thirteenth century when the invader Magha devastated the kingdom, the Chronicle commented: 'In consequence of the enormously accumulated, various evil deeds of the dwellers in Lanka, the devatas who were everywhere entrusted with the protection of Lanka, failed to carry out this protection.'[1] The island gods could not strive against the *karma* built up by the evil courses of the people of the country and so the kingdom was fated.

The wet hill country, largely in jungle, could not support the populations which the old Rajarata had maintained. Its trade with the rest of the world was dependent upon its good relations with the powers ruling the maritime provinces. The old kingdom had shrunk to a little measure, and the kings, in spite of some military successes against the European and the glowing accounts the Chronicle gave of their endowment to temples, were petty rulers whose revenues, according to Coomaraswamy, did not exceed £2,000 a year—which in money values would be worth about eight times as much in 1907 when he wrote. In services from their subjects they could depend for what would now have to be budgetted under the head of public works, but in reality they were princes whose court etiquette was scarcely proportionate to their power or their possessions. But it was one of the survivals of ancient grandeur, and Knox noted the pleasure taken by the old king Rajasinha II, in the seventeenth century, in the 'high and windy titles' given him. A French emissary to his court, a Monsieur de la Nerolle, paid dearly for his arrogance, according to the etiquette of the time, in daring to ride on horseback into the city (a privilege reserved to the king; in any case etiquette demanded that an ambassador had to proceed on foot), and withdrawing from the court in the early hours of the morning, tired of waiting until the king was pleased to give him audience. He was rewarded for his effrontery with chains and imprisonment. In these ways the king, as he was a man of spirit, compensated for his inability to get the better of the hated foreigner elsewhere.

Restricted and poor as the Kandyan kingdom was, a few of its temples show characteristic features of another phase of Sinhalese art. The old colossal *stupas* are no longer built and the workers in stone seem to have lost much of

[1] *C, LXXX,* 54.

their ancient skill. There is nothing to place beside the lustre of their work at Yapahuva three centuries previously. The temple at Gadaladeniya, an example of a *devale* in the South Indian style, belongs to an earlier date than the time of Rajasinha II. It was built three hundred years before. How far away these earlier times were from the people of the Kandyan kingdom of his time may be gauged from Knox's comment about the inscriptions at this temple and elsewhere: 'Here are some ancient writings engraven upon rocks which pose all that see them. There are divers great rocks in divers parts in Kande Uda and in the Northern parts. These rocks are cut deep with great letters for the space of some yards, so deep that they may last to the world's end. Nobody can read them or make anything of them. . . . They are probably in memorial of something, but of what we must leave to learned men to spend their conjectures.'[1]

This temple, built entirely of stone, resembles in its windows the style of Vijayanagar, but its columns are simpler, showing here a Sinhalese characteristic. The small *stupa* near by with its hipped Kandyan roof is certainly later. So the direction taken by the religious art of the country, from the elegant Sinhalese transformation of the South Indian shrine with porch, shrine room and spire directly overhead, to the typically Kandyan building in miniature, could be seen in these two structures on a Kandyan knoll.

If the skill in stone was no longer of the epical kind, but confined itself to smaller arabesques on columns and friezes, the Kandyan period provides evidence of other skills of which time has not spared the ancient originals. There still exists carving in wood of the Kandyan period, on the capitals of wooden pillars, or on that part of the stone pillar where pillar met roof, and in the cube which interrupted the bevel in the middle of the pillar, which enabled the artist to exhibit his cunning in ancient and newer motifs. At Embekke, the Skanda *devale* has a number of typically Kandyan carvings on the cubes of the pillars. These are of various dates, but they all belong to the period, and show the good taste and the sureness of the craftsman's sense of composition. The decorative tradition of the times secured him from the dangers of launching out on his own, and, within its limits, to produce admirable arabesques. The man on horseback, the woman with her child, and the two wrestlers are graceful, if not very remarkable, compositions.

In its painting too the Kandyan style is distinctive. It follows the traditional techniques and is bound by the rules which governed the mixing of colours and the preparation of the ground on which the painter worked. In its results, which have been overpraised today perhaps, one notices much more strongly the high-water mark of the work of able craftsmen than the traces of genius among them, as one might feel of the work at Sigiriya, or in the Tivanka

[1] Knox, *op. cit.*, p. 180.

shrine at Polonnaruva. The name of one of the painters responsible for the wall-paintings at the Degaldoruva rock temple near Kandy is known, and the scenes from the Vessantara Jataka have been attributed to him. In this style of painting the absence of perspective and the depiction of a narrative sequence from left to right produces a good test of the artist's skill in decoration and his eye for possibilities of grouping, so he unfolds the story he paints. Without in any way being remarkable, these cave paintings in their simple and strong colours prove the existence of a tradition which could prevent a lamentable lapse of good sense and taste, even it could not produce more than a good level of competence in execution.

The work of Kandyan artists and craftsmen includes much else besides what has been referred to above in the spheres of temple architecture and painting, the subject of the distinctive Kandyan style in what is left of original work and lingering tradition in the crafts still awaiting systematic and serious investigation. Ananda Coomaraswamy's work in 1907 on *Medieval Sinhalese Art*, exclusively concerned with the art of the Kandyan period, was important in its time and much more significant as a protest, like that of William Morris, against the ugliness of contemporary art and decoration than as a reliable study of its subject. As we are concerned with the Kandyan here, in the restricted field of our approach, it is possible to see in it little more than a pale reflection of a great tradition, so pale that its gleam might well be the uncertain light of fires kindled at quite other sources. We could regard the great tradition in art and architecture as one part of the characteristic Sinhalese development of its Indian heritage. This great tradition was co-eval with the ancient kingdom, and the effective pressure of that kingdom's economy and its political and social life on it have yet to be studied. Much has been achieved in archaeology, both in the field and descriptively and critically. But with so much still in the grip of the jungle—about one half of the island—it must be concluded that much remains to be done. It is possible that future work in excavation and in epigraphy will throw such new light on ancient Ceylon and its great artistic tradition, that some of our contemporary insights will have to be reoriented.

How should one value this great tradition, and how should one regard the ancient monuments of Ceylon? There must naturally be a difference in valuation as the beholder is different. To the Sinhalese Buddhist it must mean something more than it could mean to anyone else. But there is nearly a millenium between the ancient tradition and the present. Besides, there is the rift which some five hundred years and more of foreign rule have made in ways of life and of thought. Just as the Indian settlers came to an island in which primitive cults were replaced by Buddhism, so it might seem that the West came to Ceylon in the sixteenth century, and has since then been responsible for a 'spiritual' and material conquest of the island. But in both these cases what truly belonged to it was never lost, it persisted, ready to issue forth again. Recent events show how strongly it has flowed underground, and how intensely it can gush out.

Whether in the altered social and economic structure of Ceylon, where 'all's changed now', these waters can be a healing source or a bitter potion, only the collective wisdom of all the present-day inhabitants of Lanka, and not of the Sinhalese alone, must decide. But this would be the subject of another study.

Whatever the future may bring, to all those who come to the ancient monuments of Ceylon, they must possess a value and a character. They may chasten our pride, amaze our intellects, or move our feelings, but it is well to remember that even their computations are values of limited currency. The sensibilities of the majority of men are so hardened today that if any one single priceless possession of the world's art were to disappear, it would apparently make little difference to the sum of things. The scale of what we are now asked to comprehend is so vast, that it would be prudent to be unmoved if Chartres were to be destroyed, and a bomb obliterated Athens. It may be that only little of the ancient art of Ceylon could be placed beside the wealth of ancient Egypt, or Rome or India; but such things as the *vahalkada* at Mihintale, the moonstones at Anuradhapura, the statue of the king at Polonnaruva, and Sigiriya, stand in their own right of excellence as records of artistic achievement, in no need of support from comparative judgement or prejudice.

The aesthetic emotion has been variously described in various cultures, but one might, in general, understand by it that state of feeling—of pleasure or joy—removed for the time being from practicality, and created by the contemplation of an artistic object which continues to stimulate our reactions. There is in the feeling created a species of growth which, as our senses return to the object, receives new impulses through our delighted attention to it. The Indian conception is thus put by Melle Auboyer in connection with the paintings of Ajanta: 'The aim of the painter . . . is to produce in the spectator a psychic state called sentiment (*rasa*) or more properly savour. This is the science of the hidden significance of external appearances, of the formation of a traditional mental image to be projected to the sensibility of the spectator, arousing in him a subjective sentiment. . . . The painter . . . determines the form and produces artificially in the spectator certain sentiments equally artificial but also beneficial in kind.[1]

The ground common to these descriptions is an area of feeling which the transformation of reality produces in the sensitive spectator. No such spectator confronting the best of the art of the ancient tradition of Ceylon

[1] Quoted by S. Paranavitane, *op. cit.*, p. 38.

could fail to respond aesthetically. There is, in ancient Buddhist thought, an emotion described as a state of serene joy derived from the contemplation of a Buddha image—assuredly its strongest components may be religious, but in its essence this, too, is an aesthetic emotion. So whether one is a Buddhist or not, there could be aroused in one the emotion of *Buddhalambapiti* as one stands before the sedent Buddha at Anuradhapura, or sees the statues in the Gal Vihara at Polonnaruva.

GLOSSARY OF TERMS USED IN THE BOOK

ADIGAR: A Kandyan chieftain.

AHIMSA: The practice of doing no injury to any living thing.

ANICUT: A dam built across a river.

ARAHATSHIP, ARAHAT: The state of being an AHARAT, a person no longer subject to re-birth.

ASALHI: The Indian lunar month of May-June or June-July.

BHIKKHU: generally translated by 'priest' or 'monk', but T. W. Rhys Davids notes that 'a *bhikkhu* claims no such priestly powers as are implied by the former term, and would yield no such obedience as is implied by the other.' A mendicant, a member of the Buddhist order.

BODHISATTA: A being destined to be re-born ultimately as a Buddha, and therefore destined to attain perfect Enlightenment.

BRAHMA SAHAMPATI: The Brahma who is lord of all.

CANDALA: An outcast, a person who performs the most menial tasks.

CETIYA, DAGOBA, STUPA, THUPA: An edifice built over a relic, generally a domical monument crowned with *tee* and spire.

DAGOBA: See Cetiya.

DAMILA: Tamil. This term is generally used in the Ceylon Chronicle to designate the South Indian.

DEVA: A heavenly being.

DEVATA: A divine being, a deity.

DHAMMA, (DHARMA): Doctrine. 'In pre-Buddhist use *Dhamma* is conceived as a prescribed course of action for anything in nature which may follow a natural or normal process. It may thus be translated "law".'

DONA: A measure of weight.

IDDHI: Supernatural and magical powers.

JHANA (DHYANA): A state of ecstatic mental absorption, often rendered by the word 'trance'.

KARMA, KAMMA: 'Action' or 'deed' in its general meaning. The results of action which, as it produces merit or the opposite, determines the kind of future re-births. Kamma brings as its consequence our present birth and our actions together with past Kamma will bring as their consequence our future re-birth.

KARISA: A unit of linear measure, about 4 acres.

LAC, LAKH: Common expression for 100,000 in India and Ceylon.

MAHA BRAHMA: The great Brahma.

MAHAVIHARA: See VIHARA. The great vihara at Anuradhapura, the home of the community of the Theravadins (see THERAVADA).

MAHAYANIST: A follower of that development of Buddhist thought known as Maha-yana, or the Great Vehicle. In the metaphor used Maha-yana was compared to a bullock chariot, while the others were likened to goat and deer-chariots. The Mahayanist would lay stress on the *Bodhisatta,* and the ideal of devotion (*bhakti*), holding that each man was potentially a Buddha.

MAKARA: A mythical animal, of a saurian type. A decorative motif used for the balustrades of stairways.

MALIGAVAL: The plural of MALIGAVA, Sinhalese for 'palace'.

173

MARA: Literally Death. The personification of passions and objects of desire which tend to overpower human beings.

MITHUNA: An amorous couple.

NAGA: Snake. Also supernatural beings represented in human form with a snake hood.

NIRVANA (NIBBANA): The state of the individual who is free from being born again—the goal of the Buddhist. Literally the word signifies 'extinction', as of a flame which is extinguished for lack of fuel.

PAGODA: A general term for temple.

PASADA, (PRASADA): A large building of several stories.

PHUSSA: The Indian lunar month of November-December or December-January.

PIRIVENA (PARIVENA): A collection of cells where monks lived, a building in the monastery precincts intended for the instruction of the bhikkhus.

RISHI: Sage.

SAKKA, SAKRA, SAKRAYA: The king of the gods.

SAMANA, SRAMANA: An ascetic—generally used in Buddhist literature of the yellow-robed ascetic.

SAMANERA: A novice.

SAMSARA: The chain of re-births, the perpetual flux of being.

SANGHA: The Buddhist order—the community of bhikkhus.

SANGHARAMA: A dwelling place for the sangha.

SASANA: The religion.

SRAMANA: See Samana.

STUPA: See Cetiya.

SUTTA, SUTTANTA: A text of which it is claimed that it was spoken by the Buddha himself.

TATHAGATA: 'He who has thus gone' or 'thus come'.—an epithet used by the Buddha when speaking of himself or of other Buddhas.

THERA: A term of respect used of a monk—Elder. THERI—feminine, used of a nun.

THERAVADA: One of the great Buddhist schools which claimed to preserve the original teaching of the Buddha as handed by the great Theras.

THUPA: See Cetiya.

TIPITAKA, TRIPITAKA: Literally the 'Three Baskets' of the Buddhist Canon.

UPOSATHA: The ceremony in the life of the Buddhist order which imposed fasting, the recitation of the Patimokkha (the collection of rules), and the confession of transgressions of the rule on four days of the month —new moon, full moon and the eighth day following these.

UTTARASALHA: The Indian lunar month of June-July.

VESAKHA, VESAKH: The Indian lunar month of April-May. Vesakh in Ceylon commemorates the birth of Gotama Buddha.

VIHARA,—VEHERA: Temple.

VIMANA: Palace.

VINAYA: The monastic rule, one of the 'three baskets' of the Buddhist Canon.

YAKKHA, f. YAKKHINI: Devil or demon. In the Mahavamsa the indigenous inhabitants of Ceylon when Vijaya landed in the island.

YOGI: An ascetic devoted to the ideal of yoga—union with the divine being—and an adept in the practice of the physical and psychic exercises leading thereto.

YOJANA: A measure of length, originally the distance which could be travelled by a yoke of oxen in a day. Has been taken to be about 12 kms.

LIST OF ABBREVIATIONS USED

A: *Anguttara Nikaya* (Pali Text Society Ed.) 1888–1910.
ASCAR: Archaeological Survey of Ceylon, Annual Report.
C: *Culavamsa*, Translated by W. Geiger and Mrs Mabel Bode,
              2 Vols. (Pali Text Society Ed.) 1929–1930.
CHJ: Ceylon Historical Journal.
D: *Digha Nikkaya* (Pali Text Society Ed.) 1889–1910.
Dh: *Dhammapada*, translated by Max Müller, 1898.
Dha: *Dhammapadattakatha* (Pali Text Society Ed.) 1906.
Jat: *Jataka*, ed. Fausböll.
JRAS (CB):   Journal of the Royal Asiatic Society—Ceylon Branch.
M: *Majjhima Nikaya* (Pali Text Society Ed.) 1935.
Mhv: *Mahavamsa*, Translated by W. Geiger (Pali Text Society) 1912.
S: Samyutta Nikaya (Pali Text Society Ed.) 1884–1904.
Thig A: *Therigatha* Commentary (Pali Text Society Ed.).
UCR: University of Ceylon Review.
Vin: *Vinaya Pitakam*, Williams and Norgate, London, 1881.

41

INDEX

GEORGE ALLEN & UNWIN LTD
London: 40 Museum Street, W.C.1

Auckland: 24 Wyndham Street
Bombay: 15 Graham Road, Ballard Estate, Bombay 1
Calcutta: 17 Chittaranjan Avenue, Calcutta 13
Cape Town: 109 Long Street
Karachi: 254 Ingle Road
New Delhi: 13–14 Ajmeri Gate Extension, New Delhi 1
São Paulo: Avenida 9 de Julho 1138–Ap. 51
Sydney, N.S.W.: Bradbury House, 55 York Street
Toronto: 91 Wellington Street West

THE CULTURE AND ART OF INDIA
by Radhakamal Mukerjee

Indian culture fashioned a unity of Asian civilization across the millennia just as Christianity did for Europe and a merely political history is inadequate for a people who have a dominantly metaphysical outlook on life. Professor Mukerjee describes the broad philosophical and religious movements from age to age and reveals their permanent contributions to the rich Indian heritage. The three phases of Asian unification, represented by the march of Mahayanan Buddhism across the Himalayas to China and the Mediterranean, the Golden age of Gupta culture with the rise of Hindu colonies, and the Tantrika renaissance responsible for fresh Hinduisation in Nepal, Tibet, further India and Indonesia, are for the first time sociologically delineated.

Indian art was the chief vehicle of Indian cultural expansion abroad. The grandeur and symbolism of the four great temple cities of Asia—Pagan, Borobodur, Prambanam and Angkor Thom—as well as the influence of Buddhism, Saivism and Saktism and of the Epics and the Dharmasastras on the entire culture and humanism of South East Asia amply testify to this. The art of India through its varying images and motifs is in this volume refreshingly treated as recording the soul and tempo of particular ages and renaissances. No country has had more renaissances and reformations than India. Nowhere else are *Patria* and *Dharma* or culture identified so closely. Professor Mukerjee has integrated the extremely complex Indian cultural history into a harmonious whole. His admirable book contains a wealth of information, imaginatively presented in a lucid and absorbing style.

Small Royal 8vo   *About 42s. net*

THE DOCTRINE OF THE BUDDHA
by George Grimm

Over two thousand years ago Buddha claimed to have solved the great religious problem of mankind in such a manner that everyone by his own direct perception might convince himself of the truth of this solution. His teachings circulated at first by word of mouth and even after they were codified they were still handled down orally in accordance with the traditional method of transmitting the Vedas. The written form of the Pali Canon was made some 400 years after Buddha's death and by then the characteristic Indian practice of using an author's words to explain a later development of his philosophy rather than using them to expound the original thought had obscured and altered the master's teachings.

George Grimm in his book makes a successful effort to return to the original doctrine of Buddha. Taking only those passages which have the mark of authenticity he reconstructs, like an architect restoring the blocks of a fallen temple, a complete exposition of Buddhist thought. He builds exclusively upon the sayings of Buddha and of those disciples who lived contemporaneously with him. The four parts of his book deal with The Four Most Excellent Truths; The Most Excellent Truth of Suffering; of the Arising of Suffering; of the Annihilation of Suffering; and of the Path Leading to the Annihilation of Suffering.

The Doctrine of the Buddha was first published in 1926. It has been out-of-print for some time but nothing has been published to replace this excellently and carefully prepared work. It has played its part in preparing the ground for the great interest in Buddhism in the western world and still offers one of the best guides to Buddhist thought.

Small Royal 8vo   *42s. net*

GEORGE ALLEN & UNWIN LTD